CHRISTIAN GNOSIS

From St. Paul to Meister Eckhart

Wolfgang Smith

CHRISTIAN GNOSIS

From Saint Paul to Meister Eckhart

*"The Lord, then, into whom we have been
transplanted, is the Light and the True Gnosis."*

—Clement of Alexandria, *Stromata* VI.1

ANGELICO PRESS
SOPHIA PERENNIS

First published in the USA
by Sophia Perennis
© Wolfgang Smith 2008
Angelico Press / Sophia Perennis edition 2011
All rights reserved

Series editor, James R. Wetmore

For information, address:
Angelico Press
4709 Briar Knoll Dr.
Kettering, OH 45429
angelicopress.com

Library of Congress Cataloging-in-Publication Data

Smith, Wolfgang, 1930–
Christian gnosis: from St. Paul
to Meister Eckhart / Wolfgang Smith.

p. cm.

Includes bibliographical references and index.
ISBN 978-1-59731-092-5 (pbk: alk. paper)
ISBN 978-1-59731-093-2 (hardback: alk. paper)
1. Gnosticism. I. Title
BT1390.S553   2008
230—dc22   2008048173

Cover image: 'The Holy Trinity',
icon painted by Andrei Rublev (c. 1411),
Moscow Tretyakov Gallery

An die Seligste Jungfrau Maria,
Mutter vom grossem Sieg

CONTENTS

PREFACE

To be sure, "gnosis" means *knowledge*: but what *kind* of knowledge? That is the question. And what is it, precisely, that is thus to be known? Is it the cosmos, the "creation"? Or is it God? Or is it, perhaps, "both at once"? Above all: does the idea of gnosis have a basis in the legacy of Christ? And if so, what exactly is its place or role in the Christian life, be it here or hereafter?

It appears that contemporary theology has little to say on these issues. The word "gnosis" itself has been virtually abandoned as a theological term, due presumably to its long-standing association with so-called Gnosticism; and along with the word, it seems, the idea of gnosis has been all but lost as well. The notion of a "higher knowing"—a knowing that "pierces the veil" and penetrates to the very heart of things—is not topical these days: theologians and philosophers alike appear to have their eye on other things. This may largely be due to the oracles of science, which are in fact based, according to the prevailing wisdom, on a knowing that does "pierce the veil." On the other hand, the contemporary deposal of gnosis may also be due, more profoundly, to an unprecedented estrangement, on the part of modern and post-modern man, from all that renders us receptive to the idea of a higher knowing that is to be attained, not by way of telescopes or cyclotrons, but simply through "purity of heart."

Not only, however, has the idea of gnosis fallen into disrepute and oblivion: it has been virtually replaced in theological discourse by the hybrid notion of "mysticism." This is unfortunate, I say; for apart from the fact that there are apparently many kinds or "grades" of mystical vision, it is not at all clear what, precisely, the adjective "mystical" actually signifies. One cannot, of course, fault those who would characterize gnosis as "mystical vision," so long as the sense of that nebulous term is specified accordingly. Admittedly, the idea of gnosis is vague to us, somewhat as the flavor of a mango is "vague" to those who have never tasted one; or to change the metaphor: as a theorem of mathematics is "vague" to the layman. What I wish to say is that gnosis is in fact specific to the point of being *sui generis* or "one of a kind": it is the transcendent nature of that specificity, I contend, that renders the idea of gnosis hard to comprehend, and has led in time to its *de facto* replacement by the protean notion of "the mystical," which actually has little if anything to do with gnosis, properly so called.

I wish to make it clear from the start that the tenets regarding gnosis, expounded in the sequel, are most assuredly not my own: I present no "theory," no doctrine that is new, but adhere, closely and rigorously, to authoritative sources of the first rank, literally "from Saint Paul to Meister Eckhart." The orientation of the book is not, however, "historical": what dictates its structure, rather, is the idea of gnosis itself, which we propose to unfold, not in terms of some stipulated historical development, but by way of what might broadly be characterized as a philosophic or "dialectical" approach. And as the reader may have come to surmise, it will be in the last two chapters—namely, in the exposition of Meister Eckhart's doctrine—that the idea of gnosis shall attain its fullest expression.

Actually, however, the subject of our discourse is not simply "gnosis," but "*Christian* gnosis"—which is not quite the same thing. Unquestionably, the generic concept of gnosis is to be found in every major religion, from Hinduism to Islam, and most certainly in every sapiential tradition worthy of the name; yet I contend that the gnosis offered by Christ stands alone in its conceptual parameters by virtue of the fact that it is distinctly—and irreducibly!— *Trinitarian*. It is this "Trinitarian signature" that distinguishes Christian gnosis categorically from that of the Vedantist or the Tibetan Buddhist, or of a Sufi master, let us say. Beyond this attestation of conceptual or "doctrinal" uniqueness, however, we shall not venture to proceed; as promised, we go where authentic Christian sources take us, and not a step further into the unknown.

I would like to emphasize that this book is not an academic exercise, but has in fact an eminently practical aim. The very concept of gnosis, to the extent that it is understood, affects our perception of everything else. Gnosis may be likened to the "point at infinity" which—though inaccessible—defines a perspective. Virtually every

scriptural text (from either Testament), as well as every basic conception of theology, reveals a hidden and often "startling" sense
when viewed "in the face of gnosis." Now, such a shift is bound to
have an impact on one's spiritual life, which can be for better or for
worse, depending upon the qualifications and propensities of the
individual; it is with doctrine as it is with food: what agrees with one
and conduces to his well-being may be harmful to another. It needs
thus to be noted that the content of this book — the "unexpurgated"
idea of gnosis, if you will — is not for everyone, that in fact it is
"strong meat" in precisely the biblical sense. On the other hand, it
might also be argued that the times are hard for the Christian
believer, and that "strong meat" is precisely what we need. Whatever
the case may be, it is the author's ardent hope that this treatise will
find its way into the hands of readers who shall profit from what it
contains, and that a kindly providence will keep it from those who
might incur harm; as Clement of Alexandria has put it, one does not
"reach a sword to a child."

It should be mentioned that Chapters 2–6 derive from articles
previously published in *Sophia* and *Sacred Web*. To anyone who may
have read one or more of these, I would point out that the text has
now been quite thoroughly revised, and that in any case the deeper
sense and implication of these essays comes to light precisely as a
result of being thus united into a coherent treatise or monograph,
which comprises in essence a single train of thought. It was in fact
the recognition of that underlying thread that sparked the idea of
the book and presided over its execution; to which I should add that
only in the last phase of the process — namely, during my engage-
ment with the writings of Meister Eckhart — did the pieces of the
puzzle finally fall into place. It is thus in the last two chapters that the
argument, begun in Chapter 1, reaches its term. As many before me
have likewise believed, the most explicit account of Christian gnosis
ever given — the last word, one is tempted to say — is to be found in
the teachings of the controversial Dominican, "from whom God hid
nothing" as someone has wisely remarked.

Camarillo, Feast of the Transfiguration

1

GNOSIS AND NASCENT CHRISTIANITY

The truth is, O men of Athens, that God alone is wise.

PLATO

*And if any man think that he knoweth anything,
he knoweth nothing yet as he should.*

SAINT PAUL

WHEN Jean Borella published his ground-breaking studies on the subject of "gnosis" some three decades ago,[1] he unleashed what he later described as a storm of protest "from the extreme theological left to the extreme theological right, for once united."[2] It seems that the word was tolerated only in the context of so-called Gnosticism, that is to say, in the sense of a false or pseudo-gnosis. Professor Borella must have been surprised: after all, only once, out of the 29 times the Greek word "*gnosis*" occurs in the New Testament, is it used in a pejorative sense.[3] The word occurs twice in the Gospels: first, in Luke 1:77, where Zacharias, "filled with the Holy Ghost," prophesies the coming of Christ, the Messiah who would "give the *gnosis* of salvation unto his people by the remission of sin"; and a second time from the lips of the Savior himself: "Woe unto you,

---

1. Beginning with *La Charité Profanée* (Paris: Éditions du Cèdre, 1979).
2. See Jean Borella, *The Secret of the Christian Way* (State University of New York Press, 2001), Prologue.
3. In the phrase "gnosis puffeth up," 1 Cor. 8:1.

lawyers! for ye have taken away the key of *gnosis*: ye entered not in yourselves, and them that were entering in ye hindered."[4] It is needless to point out that the "gnosis" referred to in either verse is *not* what the contemporary heresiologists have in mind. One may wonder, in fact, whether the stricture of Christ, directed against the Pharisees of old, might not apply also to those who, in our day, would "take away the key of gnosis" by hijacking the word.

It has long been Jean Borella's thesis that "there exists a way of gnosis [properly so called] within the bosom of Christianity";[5] and this, too, is the central claim of the present book. Given that Christ—who is himself the Way—is indeed "the Gnosis of the Father," one may go so far as to contend that Christianity *is* in fact, by its very essence, "a way of gnosis." It is only that this truth does not commend itself readily, nor to all, and certainly not at the level of catechisms.

Getting back to "Gnosticism," one finds (strange as it may seem) that, *strictly speaking*, there *is* no such thing! As Borella explains:

The idea hardly goes back beyond the seventeenth century. That there was a *single* possibly complex movement, with enough unanimity, however, to be subsumed under a single concept, a movement brought together under a single label ("Gnosticism")—this was something totally unknown to medieval doctors and theologians. What is more, and despite appearances, it was in fact unheard of in Christian antiquity: "In early Christianity, there is no trace of 'Gnosticism' in the sense of a broad historical category, and the modern use of 'gnostic' and 'Gnosticism' to designate a religious movement, at once broad and ill-defined, is completely unknown in the first period."[6] To which I will add—for the sake of the most implacable foes of gnosis—that there is no written trace, in the official texts of the Church's magisterium, of the condemnation of a heresy named "Gnosis" or "Gnosticism."[7]

4. Luke 11:52.
5. *The Secret of the Christian Way*, op. cit., p5.
6. Casey, "The Study of Gnosticism," *Journal of Theological Studies*, vol. 36, p55.
7. *The Secret of the Christian Way*, op. cit., p9.

To be sure, since the time of the Apostles there have been attacks, in behalf of the Church, directed against heretical teachers and heretical sects now classified as "Gnostic"; but it turns out that these condemnations were aimed precisely at those who claim to transmit a *gnosis* which in truth they do not possess. It was a question of distinguishing between authentic gnosis and its counterfeit, and thus of protecting the Church against the profanation of a teaching considered to be sacred (and perhaps secret as well). In time, some of the heresiarchs and heretical sects did co-opt the term "Gnostic"; it was a matter of usurping a designation which in the early Church commanded high esteem. Yet, even so, the appellation was never employed, in the unqualified sense of modern heresiology, as encompassing all the so-called "Gnostic" sects of antiquity; as Borella avers, such usage was unknown prior to about the seventeenth century.

I find it amazing that there could be theologians who look upon gnosis askance, as if it were some pagan aberration, failing to recognize that the idea—and even the word itself—stands at the very heart of the Christ-given teaching. That the term "gnosis" has been employed by Greek philosophers—for example, by Plato—in a related but distinctly pre-Christian sense, and again, that it was co-opted in early Christian times by certain sects, does nothing to demote the idea of gnosis, but only underscores its centrality. The theologian, of all people, should be cognizant of this: even a cursory glance at the Gospels, and at the Epistles of St. Paul, suffices (as we shall presently see) to make this clear. Yet, as we have said, the very word "gnosis" has become for many a "red flag" provoking instant attack. One dotes on the Pauline dictum that "gnosis puffeth up, but charity edifieth," as if this were the last word the Apostle spoke on the subject, and turns a blind eye to the rest. We will leave it to others to ascertain what, precisely, may have brought about this "anti-gnostic" bent, this deep-rooted bias, which has long obscured the message of Christ. What will concern us, rather, is to understand, as clearly as we can, what gnosis is, and what role it plays in the perfection of Christian life.

⊕

We begin our treatise on the subject of "gnosis" with the single Christic logion containing that word:

> Woe unto you, lawyers! for ye have taken away the key of gnosis: ye entered not in yourselves, and them that were entering in ye hindered.

There are two possible ways of interpreting this verse: one may take it to mean that gnosis itself is the key — the means of "entering in" — or, alternatively, that gnosis is that into which one enters by way of the key; and as a matter of fact, both readings prove to be admissible. For as we shall presently see, St. Paul distinguishes between two kinds of gnosis: a gnosis *in via*, which constitutes the means, and an ultimate gnosis, which constitutes indeed the end to be attained. Meanwhile it is to be noted that a parallel verse occurs in the Gospel according to St. Matthew, where the logion assumes the following form:

> Woe unto you, scribes and Pharisees, hypocrites! For ye shut up *the kingdom of heaven* against men: for ye neither go in yourselves, neither suffer ye them that are entering to go in.[8]

What is to be "entered" is here declared to be in fact "the kingdom of heaven" itself. It thus becomes apparent that the term "gnosis"—so far from designating simply an ancient heresy—refers, in fact, either to the means or to the consummation itself of the Christian life, depending upon which *kind* of gnosis one is speaking of.

It is further to be noted that in Luke the term "lawyer"[9] is used to designate those who have "taken away the key of gnosis," an epithet which, in the given context, evidently signifies someone who is overly "legalistic," or perhaps a pedantic rationalist, reminiscent of those who, once upon a time, are said to have disputed "how many angels can dance on the point of a pin." Both traits, moreover, are clearly "pharisaical," and indeed "perennial."

---

8. Matt. 23:13.
9. "*Nomikos*" in Greek, from "*nomos*," meaning "law."

Turning now to the Pauline Epistles, I would note, first of all, that Saint Paul ranks among the Apostles as the "expositor of gnosis" par excellence: the very frequency with which he employs the word already testifies to this fact.[10] We begin our study of the Pauline teaching on the subject of gnosis with a crucial passage which distinguishes *true* gnosis from false, taken from the discourse on "idolatry" in the First Epistle to the Corinthians:[11]

> .... we know that we all have gnosis. Gnosis puffeth up, but charity edifieth. And if any man think that he knoweth anything, he knoweth nothing yet as he ought to know.[12]

There is a "gnosis" which "puffeth up"; but there is also another kind, which is a knowing "as we should know." And there is a criterion that distinguishes the two: for "if any man *think that he knoweth anything*," he knows not "as he should." These words carry an immense implication, a hidden sense which we shall endeavor to expose in the course of the following chapters. Suffice it to say, for the present, that when it comes to true (or "supreme") knowing, the subject or "knower" is no longer the creature—no longer what Ananda Coomaraswamy likes to call "this-man-so-and-so"—but is actually God himself. So long as a man thinks that "he" knows something, the knowledge in question is not true gnosis. Now, St. Paul begins by saying "we know that we all have gnosis": what does this mean? Could it mean that "we all" presently know "as we should"? To be sure, the Epistle is addressed to the disciples at Corinth, and thus to initiates of the Christian faith; yet it obviously cannot be supposed that each has already attained to the perfection of knowing: that all presently know "as they should." The point, I take it, is that every human being has some kind of knowledge, a "gnosis" of some sort. There is a scale of human "knowing," extending from the more perfect to the less, all the way to the illusory and

---

10. Out of the 29 times the word *"gnosis"* occurs in the New Testament, 24 pertain to the Epistles of St. Paul.

11. This Epistle contains 10 of the 22 verses of the Pauline opus in which the word *"gnosis"* occurs.

12. 1 Cor. 8:1, 2.

the absurd, a gradation to which the Apostle alludes by contrasting the two extremes: the gnosis of those who "know as they should," and the kind that "puffeth up," which in fact is not a knowing or gnosis at all, but a counterfeit, a mere pretense to know when in fact we do not.

It is of interest to note that the passage occurs in a discourse concerning "things offered unto idols." Now, it is certainly true that St. Paul was actively involved in the debate on whether Christians are permitted to eat "things" thus offered, and there can be no doubt that the given chapter in First Corinthians, taken according to its literal sense, deals precisely with this question. Yet there is also, of course, a higher sense, a more profound interpretation, which in fact will concern us greatly in this book. Suffice it to suggest—by way of pointing out what stands at issue—that whatsoever we know, or think we know, by the kind of "gnosis" that "puffeth up," proves ultimately to be indeed an "idol," by virtue of the fact that the intentional object of this knowing is not in truth what we take it to be. What is more, that "knowing" itself is a kind of idolatry, which is to say that, so far from being "objective" or "disinterested," it constitutes invariably an ego-centered quest. What is it, then, that gives the Christian who "knows as he should" the liberty (proclaimed by St. Paul) to "eat" or abstain from "eating," without, in either case, incurring harm?[13] It is the ability, I say, to enter into imperfect modes of knowing without detriment, or to abstain therefrom, again without loss. The man of gnosis—the true Gnostic—is comparable, thus, to someone able to converse with children—to enter into their world, so to speak—without forfeiting the superior knowledge that is his own.

Getting back to the distinction between true gnosis and false, it is to be noted that, in the First Epistle to Timothy, St. Paul again opposes the two, this time by differentiating between gnosis and what he terms "*pseudonymou gnoseos*" or "gnosis falsely so named," which, I take it, can be properly assimilated to the kind that "puffeth up."[14] There is also, however, a distinction to be made between two

13. 1 Cor. 8:4–13.
14. 1 Tim. 6:20.

kinds of (true) gnosis, and St. Paul refers to it in his celebrated discourse on Love:

> Charity never faileth: but whether there be prophesies, they shall fail; whether there be tongues, they shall cease; *whether there be gnosis, it shall vanish away.* For we know in part and we prophesy in part. But when that which is perfect is come, that which is in part shall be done away.[15]

St. Paul is speaking, basically, of what theology knows as "gifts of the Holy Spirit," of which "knowledge" is one. And this already makes it clear that the "gnosis" referred to in this passage is not "falsely so named." Yet, even so, it is sharply distinguished from the final or perfect gnosis, which in this passage is not in fact mentioned: its place is here taken, as it were, by Love (*"agape"* in the Greek, *"caritas"* in the Vulgate translation). Why this preference? After all, the *caritas* possessed here below is likewise imperfect, likewise as yet incomplete: why, then, does it not "vanish away" as well "when that which is perfect is come"? The reason can only be this: Love is indeed the force that drives us on—*"zieht uns hinan"* as the final Chorus in Goethe's *Faust* proclaims. It is the "more than human" force that takes us *all the way.* To transition from gnosis *ex parte* to the final consummation, it is needful to "pass through" an *immolation*: everything that we know, everything that we possess, everything that we presently *are* (or take ourselves to be) must be offered in sacrifice; and this is something only Love—only the highest Love!—can do. It is this *agape*, then, whose praises the Apostle sings: the *agape* which, *Deo volente*, will "see us through" to the End. And that *agape*—as the Mother of supreme gnosis—does *not* "vanish away," but remains eternally united with her Child (as we behold in icons of the Virgin).

It has become clear by now that gnosis in the ultimate sense, if attainable in this life at all, will be the lot, here below, of exceedingly few.[16] Even in point of doctrinal expression, or on a doctrinal plane, that gnosis is not for everyone; as St. Paul writes to the Corinthians: "And I, brethren, could not speak unto you as unto spiritual, but as

---

15. 1 Cor. 13:8–10.

unto carnal, even as unto babes in Christ. I have fed you with milk, and not with meat: for hitherto you were not able to bear it, neither yet now are you able."[17] The Apostle thus echoes, and in a way elucidates, the words of Christ, spoken on the eve of his Passion: "I have as yet many things to say unto you, but ye cannot bear them now."[18] We are told, first by Christ himself and then by St. Paul, that there is "more" to be said, "but ye cannot bear it now."

Yet, even so, what Christ imparts to us by the Holy Spirit— "incomplete" or *ex parte* though it may be—constitutes gnosis, and needs, as such, to be distinguished from the "*pseudonymou gnoseos,*" the "gnosis falsely so named" of the heretics and the profane.

It needs also, however, to be differentiated categorically from the plenary gnosis of the final consummation, which exceeds that "preliminary" gnosis immeasurably: for "eye hath not seen, nor ear heard, neither have entered into the heart of men, the things which God hath prepared for them that love him."[19]

As regards the lesser gnosis, the gnosis *ex parte*, we are given to understand that there is here a gradation and an unfolding, in accordance with the Pauline formula "*ex fide in fidem,*" or his "*a claritate in claritatem.*"[20] All that is given by the Holy Spirit—even to the "babes in Christ"—is indeed "glorious": for whether we know it or not, what the Spirit gives is itself divine, is in fact "the light of the gnosis of the glory of God in the face of Jesus Christ."[21] But "we

16. The possibility of gnosis in this life (understood as knowing "the essence of God") has indeed been recognized by the Church. St. Thomas Aquinas, for example, has this to say: "As God works miracles in corporeal things, so also he does supernatural wonders above the natural order, raising the minds of some living in the flesh beyond the use of sense, even up to the vision of his own essence; as Augustine says of Moses, the teacher of the Jews, and of St. Paul, the teacher of the Gentiles." (ST I.12.11) And again, referring to the same exalted state of gnosis: "It is not incredible that this sublime revelation is vouchsafed certain saints without their departing this life so completely as to leave nothing but a corpse for burial." (ST II.II.175.5)

17. 1 Cor. 3:1–2.

18. John 16:20.

19. 1 Cor. 2:9 (St. Paul is quoting Isaiah 64:4).

20. These expressions—"from faith to faith" and "from glory to glory"—occur in Rom. 1:17 and 2 Cor. 3:18, respectively.

21. 2 Cor. 4:6.

have this treasure in earthen vessels"; it is this circumstance that defines the curious ambivalence of the Christian *in via*, which in fact the Apostle proceeds to describe:

> We are troubled on every side, yet not distressed; we are perplexed, but not in despair. Persecuted, but not forsaken; cast down, but not destroyed. Always bearing in the body the dying of the Lord Jesus, that the life also of Jesus might be made manifest in our body.[22]

As the Church has always taught, our "life in Christ" begins at the moment of baptism, "weak" and fragile though that life may be. Here below, already, the light of Christ shines in us: "shines in the darkness," even though the darkness "comprehends it not."

When the Apostle speaks of gnosis, it is, for the most part, the lesser or "preliminary" gnosis to which he refers. When he does speak of plenary gnosis, he is wont to employ the term *"epignosis"* to indicate that what now stands at issue is indeed "supreme": the very gnosis that comprises the Eschaton of the Christian life.[23] In the Epistle to the Ephesians, for example, he enunciates that Eschaton in the following words:

> That the God of our Lord Jesus Christ, the Father of glory, may give unto you the spirit of wisdom and revelation in the [plenary] knowledge of him: The eyes of your understanding being enlightened, that ye may know what is the hope of his calling, and what the riches of the glory of his inheritance in the saints.[24]

Let us focus upon the phrase "in the knowledge of him" (*"en epignosei autou"*), and note that the pronoun refers to God the Father: it is he that is to be known. What stands at issue, clearly, is "life eternal" as Christ himself has defined it: "And this is life eternal, that they might know thee the only true God, and Jesus Christ whom

---

22. 2 Cor. 4:7–10.

23. It is to be noted that St. Paul does not always use the term in that sense: thus, in Rom. 3:20, he speaks of an *"epignosis* of sin."

24. Eph. 1:17–18.

thou hast sent."[25] We shall have more to say (in a later chapter) regarding the reference to "Jesus Christ whom thou hast sent"; what concerns us presently is the fact that "eternal life"—the Christian Eschaton, namely—consists in a "knowing of the Father," and thus in a supreme gnosis: an *epignosis* as the Apostle affirms. What St. Paul implies—the point he is making—is that, "the eyes of your understanding being enlightened," one forthwith attains to that ultimate consummation: to the Eschaton of the Christian Way. There is nothing more to be added, nothing more to be done; all has now been accomplished: "*Consummatum est.*"

After Saint Paul comes Clement of Alexandria (153–217) as the expositor par excellence of gnosis. A man of vast erudition, Clement embodies the wisdom of the Greeks, crowned however with the gnosis bestowed by Christ. It appears that in his youth Clement roamed the Mediterranean world in search of enlightened teachers, gathering such bits of knowledge and wisdom as he could find,[26] till at last he met his master in Pantaeus, head of the famous Catecheti-cal School at Alexandria, through whom, apparently, he obtained in full what he had been searching for. "He, the true Sicilian bee," writes the disciple (in the prefatory chapter of the *Stromata*),[27] "gathering the spoil of the flowers of the prophetic and apostolic meadows, engendered in the souls of his hearers a deathless element of gnosis."[28] It is thus, clearly, from the Judeo-Christian transmis-sion that Clement derived the gnosis of which he subsequently

25. John 17:3.
26. There is reason to believe that Clement received initiation into the Eleusin-ian mysteries.
27. The title of Clement's extant *magnum opus* (which literally means "the mis-cellanies"), a massive work comprising eight "books," each divided into so many chapters. We shall follow (with occasional deviation) the translation as given in *The Ante-Nicene Fathers*, Vol. II (Edinburgh: T&T Clark, 1989). References will be by Book and chapter.
28. I.1.

speaks, and it is this "deathless element of gnosis" which in turn speaks to us, as it were, from his *magnum opus.*

It is moreover of prime significance that he refers (again in the prefatory chapter of the *Stromata*) to a "tradition of the blessed doctrine derived directly from the holy Apostles, Peter, James, John, and Paul, the sons receiving it from the father," and states that this transmission "came by God's will to us also to deposit those ancestral and apostolic seeds." What stands at issue, as Clement goes on to tell, is an *oral* teaching as distinguished from the written:

> He [Jesus] did not, certainly, disclose to the many what did not belong to the many; but to the few to whom, he knew, that they [the teachings in question] belonged, who were capable of receiving and being molded according to them. But secret things are entrusted to speech, not to writing, as is the case with God [i.e., with Christ when he taught the disciples].

It has often been said that Christianity, breaking with the religious traditions of the past, has no "secret" or "esoteric" doctrine: that Christ has made the truth accessible to all. In support of this view one quotes various texts, beginning with Matthew 10.2: "What I tell you in darkness, that speak ye in light; and what ye hear in the ear, that preach ye upon the house-tops." Clement, however, understands these words differently: in commanding the disciples to proclaim "upon the house-tops" what has been "spoken in the ear," Christ does *not* mean that this teaching is to be made public in written form (why, in that case, speak it "in the ear"?); rather, says Clement, the Master thus bids the disciples to "receive the secret traditions of true gnosis, and expound them aloft and conspicuously ... but does not enjoin us to communicate to all without distinction what is said to them in parables."[29] So too, in response to those who would cite Luke 8:17 in support of their "democratic" conception of Christianity, Clement replies:

---

29. I.12. It is to be noted that the injunction "to proclaim from the house-tops" what is "spoken in the ear" has itself a "secret" sense, as becomes clear from Matt. 24:17 and Mark 13:15, which evidently carry an esoteric connotation, as also from Acts 10:9, which is in fact suggestive of a spiritual interpretation.

And if some say that it is written, "There is nothing secret which shall not be revealed, nor hidden which shall not be disclosed," let him also hear from us, that to him who hears secretly, even what is secret shall be manifested. This is what was foretold by this oracle. And to him who is able secretly to observe what is delivered to him, that which is veiled shall be disclosed as truth; and what is hidden to the many shall appear manifest to the few.[30]

Not only, however, does Clement answer those who deny the existence of an oral and indeed "esoteric" transmission going back to the Apostles, but he offers scriptural proofs of his own, based not just upon such obviously relevant texts as the injunction not to "cast pearls before swine," or on the Pauline distinction between "milk" and "strong meat," but often citing, to that effect, passages proclaiming the same in a way which itself is "secret" (as do, for example, the familiar words "Day unto day uttereth speech, and night unto night sheweth knowledge," in which the first phrase is said to refer to "what is clearly written," and the second to "what is hidden behind a mystic veil"[31]).

Clement leaves us in no doubt that he too abides by the aforesaid "rule of secrecy":

Some things I purposely omit, in the exercise of a wise selection, afraid to write what I guarded against speaking: not grudging—for that were wrong—but fearing for my readers, lest they should stumble by taking them in a wrong sense.... Some things my treatise will hint; on some it will linger; some it will merely mention.[32]

Even so, it is his intention, in the *Stromata*, to reveal—to those who have "ears to hear"—as much of the teaching as he can: "It [his treatise] will try to speak inaudibly, to exhibit secretly, and to demonstrate silently." Later, in the preface to Book VI, he goes so far as to

30. I.1.
31. V.10. The verse is from Psalm 19.
32. I.1.

refer to his *magnum opus* as "a compendious exhibition of the Gnostic's form of religion, as far as it is possible, without danger, to commit such to writing in a book of reference." And that is precisely what the *Stromata* proves to be: a treatise on Christian gnosis, the first—and as it happens, also the last—of its kind, a work unequaled in authority as well as in scope.

Among the inestimable benefits to be derived from this book, I will mention—in passing—the light it throws on Greek philosophy, and especially on the Pythagorean and Platonist schools, which Clement knew, so to speak, "from within," and which, unlike other converts to Christianity, he never ceased to hold in high esteem. As he tells us in the very first chapter, he perceived Greek philosophy to be "in a sense the work of Divine Providence," that is to say: a divinely ordained preparation, both theoretical and moral, for the reception of Christianity. Like certain other savants of old, more-over, Clement was persuaded that Greek philosophy derived its highest teachings from the Jews, that is, from the Mosaic transmis-sion. In keeping with this belief—which he documents at length[33]— he perceives the Platonist teaching, in particular, as a means of pre-paring the soul for the attainment of gnosis: the very gnosis, namely, given in Christ. Time and again he quotes from the Pla-tonic dialogues to exhibit their kinship to the teaching of Christ (for example, when he contends that the Socratic profession of igno-rance "is, then, the first lesson in walking according to the Word"). The student of Greek philosophy, and of Plato especially, will dis-cover in the *Stromata* a wealth of precious insights not to be found anywhere else.

More than to any other literary source, apart from the Gospels, Clement is indebted to the Pauline Epistles, from which he quotes incessantly. He too distinguishes categorically between "prepara-tory" and "supreme" gnosis; yet, unlike the Apostle, he prefers to designate the former by the word "faith," thus reserving the term "gnosis" for use according to its highest connotation. So too Clem-ent speaks habitually of "the Gnostic" as a person endowed with the perfection of gnosis, someone who is no longer *in via*, but has

33. I.15, 22, 29; II.5; V.14; VI.3.

attained to the end of the Way: "The real Gnostic," he tells us, "is he that knows Christ, and his Father by him."[34] Gnosis, as thus conceived, is not a means to an end—no longer a "key"—but is clearly the End itself; and Clement takes pains to dispel all doubt on that score:

> To desire knowledge of God for any practical purpose, that this may be done, or that may not be done, is not proper to the Gnostic; but the knowledge itself suffices as the reason for contemplation. For I will dare aver that it is not because he wishes to be saved that he, who devotes himself to knowledge for the divine science itself, chooses knowledge. For the exertion of the intellect by exercise is prolonged to a perpetual exertion. And the perpetual exertion of the intellect is the essence of an intelligent being, which results from an uninterrupted process and remains in eternal contemplation as a living substance. Could we, then, suppose any one proposing to the Gnostic whether he would choose the knowledge of God [i.e., gnosis] or everlasting salvation; and if these, which are entirely identical, were separable, he would without the least hesitation choose the knowledge of God, deeming that property of faith, which from love ascends to knowledge, desirable for its own sake.[35]

The passage is of course difficult, perhaps intentionally so; yet it does, clearly, make the point that gnosis is itself the supreme End to be attained. Admittedly, the idea that "exertion of the intellect by exercise is prolonged to a perpetual exercise" resulting in "eternal contemplation as a living substance" is not to be taken literally; yet, from the standpoint of the *viator*, such appears indeed to be the case. On the other hand, if there be continuity, thus, between the means and the End, Clement reminds us that there is radical discontinuity as well: a requisite Death, in fact. What must die, to be precise, is the "old man," the Pauline *psychikos anthropos*, who "receiveth not the things of the Spirit of God,"[36] that is to say: is

34. II.11.
35. IV.22.
36. 1 Cor. 2:14.

incapable of gnosis. "To him [the true Gnostic]," Clement goes on, "the flesh is dead; but he himself lives alone, having consecrated the sepulchre into a holy temple to the Lord...." The body—or more precisely, the psycho-physical organism—if it survives, has become a sepulchre: the abode of one who has "died in Christ," in keeping with the words of the Apostle: "I live; yet not I, but Christ liveth in me."[37]

It must not be supposed, therefore, that the Gnostic is simply a man: that he is "this-man-so-and-so" as we tend to think; for indeed, the man, as thus conceived, has been put to death. As Clement observes: "Our gnosis, and our spiritual garden, is the Savior himself, into whom we are planted, being transferred and transplanted, from our old life, into the good land... The Lord, then, into whom we have been transplanted, is the Light and the true gnosis."[38] Authentic gnosis, then, is something divine, something that belongs, not to a man, but to God himself. So, also, it is not the result of action or discipline—is not in fact generated by "exertion of the intellect"—but is freely bestowed by God: first "obscurely," as in faith, and ultimately, in full. As Clement explains: "The gnosis itself is that which has descended by transmission to the few, having been imparted unwritten[39] by the Apostles."[40] It is as if the "flame of gnosis," once kindled from above within the depth of the human soul, is subsequently fanned (but not produced!) by "the perpetual exertion of the intellect," until it has consumed all that is foreign to itself—all that is mortal and imperfect—that "mortality might be swallowed up of life."[41] And it is at this point that "the exertion of the intellect by exercise," to which Clement refers, "remains in eternal contemplation as a living substance."

37. Gal. 2:20.
38. VI.1.
39. We can understand why this transmission is to be enacted by "speech": what is transmitted, after all, is not a matter of concepts, or even of "ideas," but of life itself—"life eternal" no less! Now, it is by "speech," let us recall, that the Father "begets" the Son, and by "speech" that he creates the world: is it any wonder, then, that "life eternal" is transmitted, again, "by speech"?
40. VI.7.
41. 2 Cor. 5:4.

Strictly speaking, every conception—no matter how lofty or "spiritual" it may be—needs in the end to be left behind; as Clement points out: "It is not therefore possible to share in the gnostic contemplation unless we empty ourselves of our previous notions."[42] And this is the reason, let us note, why the Socratic profession of ignorance—the "knowledge" that we do not know—is indeed "the first lesson" to be learned: the prime condition, that is, upon which "the following of Christ" is based in the case of those called to the path of gnosis. Clement gives us to understand that this "following" takes us eventually out of the created order: "the Gnostic," he tells us, "ought to rise out of the sphere of creation." One is vividly reminded, at this point, of Meister Eckhart's claim that it is needful—again, in the pursuit of gnosis—"to annihilate all created things," a thesis concerning which we shall have much to say in the final chapters of this book. Suffice it to note, at this point, that having once "emptied ourselves of our previous notions," the universe—as we know it—will have disappeared.

Meanwhile—and again, from *our* point of view—the Gnostic may remain here below, in this world, if such be the will of God, as was the case, certainly, with Saint Paul. It is not a question, however, of forfeiting the fullness of gnosis: that attainment, like death itself, is irreversible. Speaking, in particular, of the Incarnate Son of God, Clement paints for us a picture of "the perfect man" unrivaled in Christian literature: "He was entirely impassible (*apathes*)," he declares, "inaccessible to any movement of feeling, either pleasure or pain," in seeming contradiction to the common teaching. Even the highest affections, though good, "are nevertheless inadmissible in the case of the perfect man." Take "courage," for example: the perfect man—the true Gnostic!—Clement insists, "is incapable of exercising courage; for neither does he meet what inspires fear, as he regards none of the things that occur in life as to be dreaded; nor can aught dislodge him from this, the love that he has toward God."[43] And so it is, Clement goes on, with all other human emotions and acts of will, which have now been forever transcended.

42. VI.17.
43. VI.9.

Yet, as the Apostle apprises us, *love remains*. It is however a love void of desire, a love no longer in quest; as Clement explains:

> But he who by love is already in the midst of that in which he is destined to be, and has anticipated hope by gnosis, does not desire anything, having, as far as possible, the very thing desired.

And thus "he continues in the exercise of gnostic love, in the unvarying state." It is a state, let us note, in which time is no more; as Clement has it: "through love, the future is for him already present, . . . and he has already received the knowledge of all things."[44]

Elsewhere, having discoursed on the degrees of perfection pertaining to the various orders in the angelic hierarchy, Clement speaks of the Gnostic as one who towers above all these ranks and grades:

> But I affirm that gnostic souls, that surpass in the grandeur of contemplation the mode of life of each of the holy ranks ... embracing the divine vision not in mirrors, but in the transcendently clear and absolutely pure and insatiable vision which is the privilege of intensely loving souls, holding festival through endless ages, remain honored with the identity of all excellence. Such is the vision attainable by the "pure in heart."[45]

The allusion to "mirrors" refers evidently to the celebrated words of the Apostle: "now we see as in a glass, darkly,"[46] the implication being that even the angelic orders are yet comprehended under this Pauline "now." Only Christ himself—and those who have been "transferred and transplanted" into him—is exempt from this otherwise universal condition of nescience; for as the Savior declares: no one has seen the Father, "but he which is of God, he hath seen the Father."[47]

44. Ibid.
45. VII.3. The reference to "the pure in heart" pertains of course to Matt. 5:8.
46. 1 Cor. 13:12.
47. John 6:46.

⊕

What then can be said regarding the "vision" at issue here: what does he see who *sees*? The question is of course unanswerable in human terms; yet Clement addresses it indirectly in speaking of Christ:

> From his own point of view the Son of God is never displaced; not being divided, not severed, not passing from place to place; being always everywhere, and being contained nowhere; complete mind, the complete paternal light; all eyes, seeing all things, by his power scrutinizing all powers.[48]

"From his own point of view": here lies for us the problem, and also the key. To pass from the "creaturely" to the *divine* "point of view," it is necessary to abandon the "non-divine" ways of knowing; and this is to be accomplished at one stroke—"in a moment, in the twinkling of an eye" as the Apostle declares[49]—through a *metanoia* that is inconceivable (virtually by definition) from the human standpoint. On a doctrinal plane, moreover, the transition—the discontinuity—is to be understood in strictly negative terms: as a denial, namely, of what constitutes the defining characteristic of creaturely knowing. And what is that characteristic? It is division, or better said, *duality*. It is this that defines "cosmic" existence: "*Omnia duplicia*" ("All things are double") as we read in Ecclesiasticus.[50] Divine vision or gnosis, then, is characterized precisely by its transcendence or "negation" of duality: and this is why the Son of God—"from his own point of view"—is "always everywhere," that is to say, unaffected by the divisions of space and time. For him there is no duality of "here" and "not-here," or of "now" and "not-now." It is not that the cosmos has shrunk, as it were, to a single point: the divine vision is not "monist" but "nondualist," which is something else entirely. To behold "a single point" to the exclusion of all others would be a mark of deficiency, whereas the divine vision, on

48. VII.2.
49. 1 Cor. 15:52.
50. Eccl. 42:25.

the contrary, is characterized precisely by its infinite capacity, its unlimited power: "all eyes, seeing all things, by his power scrutinizing all powers" as Clement declares.

It is by virtue of his divine omniscience, moreover, that the Son of God is God; as Clement explains:

> Wherefore also all men are his; some through gnosis, and others not yet so; and some as friends, some as faithful servants, some as servants merely. This is the Teacher who trains the Gnostic by mysteries, and the believer by good hopes, and the hard of heart by corrective discipline through sensible operation. Thence his providence is in private, in public, and everywhere.

"Wherefore also all men are his": let us ponder these words. How does it follow, from what has been said regarding "his own point of view," that "all men are his"? The short answer can only be: by virtue of *nonduality.* As Meister Eckhart tells us, God knows no *aliud,* no "other." All men, therefore, "are his," because—"from his point of view"—they are not "other," not *aliud.* But that "non-otherness" is not to be conceived as "identity" or "oneness" in *our* sense: again, God is not a "monist."

All men "are his"; and yet there are grades. The Gnostic—the man who belongs to Christ "through gnosis"—"is his" in the highest degree: to the point, in fact, where "I live; yet not I, but Christ liveth in me."[51] Next come his "friends": those, I take it, who have attained to a degree of gnostic contemplation. Then come his "faithful servants": those who love Christ with a selfless love, but have "not yet" embarked upon the gnostic way. In fourth place Clement mentions the "servants only": those, namely, who worship God for the sake of recompense, be it health, or worldly goods, or even "salvation," as they conceive of it. Even "the hard of heart" who reject God "are his." "Thence his providence": Christ, "being always everywhere"—"all eyes, seeing all things"—is present to all beings and extends his providential care to all.

---

51. Gal. 2:20.

Not only, however, does Christ *know* all things—and "extend his providential care to all"—but also, in a most profound sense, he *is* all things. As Clement expresses it:

> And the Son is neither simply one thing, nor many things as parts, but one thing as all things; whence also he is all things.[52]

The Son is not "simply one thing," by virtue of the aforesaid "non-otherness"; and by the same token, he is not "many things as parts." He is thus indeed "one thing as all things" ("one thing" by virtue of the fact that he is "not many," and "all" since he is "not simply one thing"). And thus he "is all things."

But this metaphysical fact, obviously, has consequences relating to human life, which Clement proceeds to summarize:

> Wherefore also to believe in him, and by him, is to become "one," being indissolubly united in him; and to disbelieve is to be separated, disjoined, divided.

Everything depends upon our knowing, which—as St. Paul and Clement both declare—*begins in faith*. It is not, however, a question simply of faith "in him," but equally of faith "by him," which is to say that there is—there must be—something supra-human and indeed divine even in the simplest act of faith, failing which it is *not* faith, nor can be of any use in the spiritual life. Gnosis, even in the least of its "degrees," is ever a *gift*; and this is where the mystery of baptism, and of the other sacraments, and indeed of the entire "transmission," comes into play. What, then, is the result of faith, of "believing in him and by him"? It is "union," precisely: a union which has in fact two aspects; for as Clement states, it is both "to become 'one'" and to become "indissolubly united in him." The point is that these are not two different accomplishments, but complementary aspects of one and the same "unification." To "become 'one'"—and thus "to be"—is quite the same as to be "indissolubly united in him." Clement's thesis, taken in full, has however two parts: for whereas "belief" conduces to union, "disbelief" leads to separation, which again can be understood in two ways: namely, as

52. IV.25.

separation from God, or as division within ourselves: a separation or estrangement, if you will, from what in truth we are.

The Gnostic, then, is the perfect man. And it is this, precisely, that Clement sets out to establish; as he tells us in the preface to Book VII: "It is, then, our purpose to prove that only the Gnostic is holy and pious." In the entire throng of the Christian faithful, the Gnostic alone measures up to the commandment of Christ: "Be ye therefore perfect, *even as your Father in heaven is perfect.*"[53]

Let us take stock of what has thus far been stated. There are, basically, *three* kinds of knowing or "gnosis" in the widest sense: the kind that "puffeth up," which is a "gnosis falsely so called"; a true gnosis that admits of degrees and "passeth away"; and finally, a gnosis that is perfect and eternal. True gnosis, moreover, *begins* in faith, and is received by means of a sacred transmission. That gnosis, thus, is in a way "carried" by language, and may consequently be termed "doctrinal." One might add, however, that it does not, on that account, "reduce" to language, say, in a post-modernist sense. Rather, it pertains to the essence of language in general, and of sacred language especially, *to point beyond itself,* and thereby to serve as the carrier of a gnosis, precisely. And a gnosis, thus carried, may be termed "doctrinal," as we have said. My point, then, is that *true gnosis of the "preliminary" kind* and *doctrinal gnosis* are essentially one and the same.

Given that there are two modes of sacred transmission—a written, as we have seen, and an oral—there is, moreover, a distinction to be made between two kinds or "levels" of *doctrinal* gnosis. Since Jesus generally taught in parables—"All these things spoke Jesus unto the multitude in parables, and without a parable spake he not unto them"[54]—and it is these parables that have come down to us in writing, one may conclude that the first kind of doctrinal gnosis is thus "parabolic" in a corresponding sense. On the other hand, it

53. Matt. 5:48.
54. Matt. 13:34.

was to the disciples, and thus "in the ear," that Jesus unfolded the deeper—or "hidden"—sense of these parables; and this, presumably, is the teaching, or doctrine, which was passed on to succeeding generations by way of an oral transmission. One may, of course, object to this hypothesis on the ground that the Gospels record these "oral explanations" as well; one needs to bear in mind, however, that what is thus recorded may not be the full oral teaching of Jesus, and that, even if it were, it may not be possible to penetrate the inner sense of what has thus been recorded without the "power" originally conveyed by the spoken word (a power which is presumably passed on, from one generation of disciples to the next, again, by way of an oral transmission).

There are then, we say, two kinds or "levels" of doctrinal gnosis, corresponding to these respective modes of transmission. However, the difference, as we have seen, does not reside necessarily in the "words," but in the level, rather, on which these words are understood or interpreted. A given scriptural verse, for example, may convey either kind of doctrinal gnosis, depending upon how it is received. Nonetheless, the difference between the two kinds of doctrinal gnosis is radical: too drastic, in fact, to be conceived as a difference of "degree." It is as if the direction of the intellective gaze had changed, had in fact reversed. What separates the two kinds of doctrinal gnosis, thus, is not simply an "increase" as of a continuous magnitude, but a break: an abyss as deep and as hard to cross as that which separates the living from the dead. It is, in fact, as if the Death that awaits us at the threshold of eternity had its counterpart or foretoken on the plane of doctrinal gnosis: here too, on the level of beliefs and values, a kind of sacrificial immolation takes place. All "former notions," as Clement says, are here to be abandoned, in what amounts to a total Socratic profession of ignorance; and rare indeed is the man who can honestly say: "I know that I know nothing at all." Let us add, moreover, to obviate an obvious objection, that this statement is not in fact contradictory, since the word "know" is used in two very different senses, the point being that "I know" (according to sense A) that I do not know (according to sense B). The Socratic profession signifies, thus, a radical shift from one way of knowing to another: from a lower (or false) knowing to one that is higher, which is affirmed to be true (on pain of having said nothing at all). At this stage, however, that higher knowing is realized precisely in an act of negation: in the very recognition, namely, that "I do not know." To proceed further, a "gift"—a kind of infusion from above, or from within—is required: and this is precisely where the *oral* transmission comes into play. It is the "spoken word" that engenders, in the soul of the disciple, "a deathless element of gnosis," as Clement relates in reference to his own Master. It is however the Socratic recognition that renders the soul receptive to that "spoken word," that "deathless element of gnosis": only in ground thus cleared and harrowed can "those ancestral and apostolic seeds" take root and germinate.

It is to be noted, moreover, that the category of the "unreceptive" includes, among others, the ordinary believer, the person brought up "on milk"—that is to say, formed by the customary catechetical instruction—who accepts all this teaching at face value, and moreover remains satisfied, so to speak, with the ontological status quo of this world. To be sure, it is not a question simply of philosophical training or "erudition"—even though Clement avers that "the Gnostic must be erudite"[55]—but primarily of inner makeup, that is, of vocation. One does not, out of the blue, decide to enter upon the gnostic way; and here below, at least, that way is not for everyone. The question arises, of course, whether all are called to gnosis in the end—whether "gnosis" and "salvation" are indeed synonymous—and it appears that one could mount an argument on either side: affirmatively, based on the premise that life eternal is "to know the one true God," and against, based on Matthew 13:8, for example, a text which seems to distinguish three "degrees" in the "kingdom of heaven." The question proves thus to be difficult, to the point of being seemingly unanswerable in human terms. It is an issue, however, with which we shall not be concerned. This book is about gnosis, properly so called; and regardless of whether there be "grades" in the kingdom of heaven—answering to the parable of the seed that "fell into good ground and brought forth fruit, some a hundredfold, some sixtyfold, and some thirtyfold"—it is clear that the

55. VI.8.

gnosis, "perfect and eternal," of which Clement speaks constitutes, most assuredly, the *non plus ultra*, since it is indeed *the gnosis of Christ himself*.[56]

There are then, as we have seen, two kinds or levels of *preparatory* gnosis, corresponding to the respective means of transmission: written and oral. Moreover, despite the confusion surrounding the epithet "esoteric" and the adverse reactions it tends to provoke in some quarters, the latter mode *is* in fact *esoteric* in two respects: first, insofar as it is restricted to an inner circle or subclass of the faithful, and secondly, because that gnosis is itself "interior" in relation to the first kind. I would further point out that it is not a question simply of "faith versus knowledge," since both kinds of "preparatory gnosis" constitute a mode of gnosis, and both, moreover, entail belief in a reality not yet directly perceived (failing which these modes of gnosis could not be characterized as "preparatory"). The aspirant following the "esoteric" path—or "the way of gnosis" as one can say—still sees "as through a glass, darkly"; and although that "glass" may be "thinner," so to speak, there is in fact no common measure between "doctrinal" enlightenment of whatever kind and gnosis, perfect and eternal.

St. Paul, as we know, distinguishes the aforesaid modes of "preparatory gnosis" metaphorically in terms of *age* ("childhood" versus "maturity") and *nourishment* ("milk" versus "meat"), which refer to the recipient and to what is received, respectively; as Clement explains:

56. This is none other than the gnosis theology knows as the Beatific Vision, which however it conceives from its own (inherently "dualist") point of view. Regarded theologically as a gnosis of the "essence of God," it is yet subject to degrees. The phrase *"totum sed non totalite"* ("whole but not wholly"), commonly applied to this gnosis, strikes me as an attempt to have it both ways: to transcend theological dualism without actually doing so. The point of difference between the theological and the "gnostic" or "nondualist" perspective will be progressively clarified in the course of this treatise.

If, then, the "milk" is said by the Apostle to belong to the babes, and "meat" to be the food of the full-grown, milk will be understood to be catechetical instruction—the first food, as it were, of the soul. And "meat" is the mystic contemplation; for this is the flesh and the blood of the Word, that is, the comprehension of the divine power and essence.[57]

It needs to be understood that the "mystic contemplation" to which Clement alludes refers yet to the level of the seeker: that of the "advanced" aspirant, which is to say, of someone who, having been initiated into the mysteries of the gnostic way, engages in the practice of "mystic contemplation": it is thus that he partakes of "meat," and is nourished as by the Eucharistic "flesh and blood." It is of interest that Clement refers, in this context, to "the truth-loving Plato" as one who speaks of contemplation as "nourishment of the soul," and goes on to say:

This, then, is the import of the silence of five years prescribed by Pythagoras, which he enjoined on his disciples: that, abstracting themselves from the objects of sense, they might, with mind alone contemplate the Deity.[58]

Clement is here speaking of the philosophic life as practiced in the Pythagorean and Platonist schools, that is to say, as a distinctly esoteric discipline: he is not speaking, obviously enough, of "philosophy" as pursued in our universities! Yet, advanced and indeed "esoteric" as the "mystic contemplations" to which Clement refers may be, they must not be confused with full and everlasting gnosis. What stands at issue is an inherently yogic discipline, in which "abstraction from the objects of sense" and "contemplation of the Deity" go hand in hand, and constitute in fact complementary aspects of a single gnostic act. That act, however, is yet preparatory, and subject to degrees: the greater the "abstraction from the objects of sense" (which begins with the outer senses and proceeds to the

57. V.10.
58. To which Clement adds: "It was from Moses that the chief of the Greeks drew these philosophical tenets." See V. 11.

inner), the deeper and more perfect will be the associated "contemplation of the Deity." Clement completes the picture with a final comment; in words worthy of a true Gnostic, he declares:

> Now the sacrifice that is acceptable to God is unswerving abstraction from the body and its passions. This is the really true piety. And is not, on this account, philosophy rightly called by Socrates "the practice of Death"?

Whether the simple believer—or the rank and file theologian— knows it or not, there *is* another level of comprehension and another way, which may indeed be characterized as "esoteric," and can be said to constitute the direct path or "final ascent" to gnosis, perfect and eternal. Moreover, it must be this esoteric teaching, and this gnostic path, to which Christ refers in alluding to "the key of gnosis": for it is truly by means of this "key" that one does "enter in." So too, it is this "key," precisely, that is "taken away" by those to whom Christ refers as "lawyers." Who are they, these lawyers? Clearly, they are those who interpret the doctrinal teaching, as given in written form, "according to the letter," that is to say, according to its external sense, while they prohibit the higher or esoteric reading thereof: for in so doing, they do indeed "take away the key of gnosis"—literally so. It is exactly as Christ has declared it to be: not having "entered in themselves," they "hinder those" who would. These pedantic and tyrannical men would impose the narrow limits of their own understanding—their own ignorance!—upon all. Like the fox in Aesop's fable, having "lost their tail," they would that all other foxes share in their mutilation by cutting off their own. That tendency, or temptation, is however something perennial: the Pharisees will be with us till the end of time; and truth to tell, there may be a bit of "Pharisee" in us all.

"The letter killeth, but the spirit giveth life"[59]: these words should be engraved over the entrance of every theological seminary. Note the consummate precision: the "letter" ("*gramma*" in the original) refers exactly to the *written* transmission. It is the "written word"

---

59. 2 Cor. 3:6.

that has a tendency "to kill"; on the other hand, it is the *spirit* that "giveth life." Now "spirit," as one knows, is associated with "breath," and it is by means of "breath" that the *spoken* word is produced: what does this signify? It means that the spoken word is instinct with spirit; as Christ declares: "the words that I *speak* unto you, they are spirit and life."[60] And these "words" the Apostles, in turn, spoke to their disciples, and so forth down the initiatic line of oral transmission, thereby passing on the words of the Savior, replete with "spirit and life." When it comes to the written transmission—to "the letter"—on the other hand, the words, originally spoken, have become detached, as it were, from the breath of the speaker, and thereby deprived of their spiritual freight. What then remains are marks on paper, or letters inscribed in stone. But this dichotomy itself must not be taken *literally*, that is to say, "according to the letter"! If that were so, the Good Book would carry no force, no power to enlighten, or to console. Yet, even so, the dichotomy "written versus oral" is real and indeed binding—whether we understand what it means, or do not.

One more point. Getting back to the admonition of St. Paul, it will be of interest to recall the full verse in which these words occur:

> Who also hath made us able ministers of the new testament: not of the letter, but of the spirit: for the letter killeth, but the spirit giveth life.

We need to ask ourselves what, in this instance, is the "old" testament as opposed to the "new." Now, the reference to Moses and to what is "written and engraven in stones"[61] leaves no doubt on this issue: the former can be none other than the Mosaic Law. It is that Law which St. Paul likens to "the letter that killeth." The contrast, thus, between "letter" and "spirit," becomes exemplified in the opposition between the "bondage" of those who are "under the law" and the "glorious liberty of the children of God."[62] And this brings us back to the "lawyers": here they are again, imposing the law

60. John 6:63.
61. 2 Cor. 3:8.
62. Rom. 8:21.

according to its "literal" sense, thereby depriving "the children of God" of their "glorious liberty"! But what *is* that liberty? It is none other than the total emancipation of gnosis: "Ye shall know the truth, and the truth shall make you free."[63]

Enough has now been said on the subject of Christian gnosis to serve as a foundation for the chapters to come. There are, however, three other "traditions of gnosis" to which reference will be made in the sequel: Kabbalah, Tantrism, and Vedanta, namely. As to the first, this should come as no surprise, given that the Kabbalah (from the Hebrew *qabbālāh*, meaning "tradition") embodies precisely the oral transmission pertaining to the Mosaic Revelation, which as such gives access to the higher or "esoteric" sense of the Torah. And since the latter—what we term the Old Testament— "speaks secretly of Christ," it is only to be expected that Kabbalah should be "not foreign, but domestic" as Cardinal Egidio di Viterbo[64] has observed.

The case is different when it comes to Tantrism and Vedanta, which are evidently *not* "domestic," and in no wise pertain to the Judeo-Christian transmission. They will be, for us, "foreign" also in the sense that such Tantric and Vedantic conceptions as shall be referred to, here and there (by way of their Sanskrit designations), will be mentioned parenthetically, and without adequate explanation. Why, then, refer to these "foreign" conceptions at all? As to the Tantric, these will enter the picture (quite naturally) in Chapter 2, for reasons which will become apparent at the time. But why speak of Vedanta? I would point out, first of all, that the Vedanta constitutes the oldest *living* tradition of gnosis known to man. No one can put a date on the Vedas, or on the earliest Upanishads, which appear to fade into the mist of prehistory. Yet we can read their Sanskrit,

63. John 8:32.
64. One of the most eminent representatives of Christian Kabbalah, a movement extending roughly from Pico de la Mirandola (1463–1492) to Franz von Baader (1765–1841). See chapter 4.

and allow these venerable books to speak to us. And if we care to travel to India—to "ancient" India, which, though shrinking rapidly, still survives—we will see men and women observing, to this day, the ancient rites, and may encounter *sadhus*, clad in the flame-colored garb of the world-renouncing mendicant, devoting themselves still to "the practice of Death." Nowhere else, it seems, has the ideal of *gnosis* exerted so great a fascination for so long, and inspired so many to dedicate their life to that all-transcending and all-encompassing goal.

It is to be noted as well that we find ourselves in a world where, at last, Christianity and Hinduism have met. There is no more excuse, in this day and age, for uninformed and prejudiced opinions concerning foreign or so-called "pagan" religions. The belief has by now become widespread that there is a need for mutual understanding, and as is often said, for "dialogue." The Christian world seems presently to be searching for a new sense of self-identity, based upon a deeper understanding of religious traditions foreign to Christianity, which can no longer be ignored or marginalized, and yes, offended and defamed with impunity. There are, of course, many such "other traditions"; what I find special, however, in the case of Vedanta, and what motivates me to touch upon the subject, is that the latter presents itself, among all these "other traditions," as the "religion of gnosis" par excellence. It is here, moreover, that we seem to encounter the quintessential formulation of gnosis in non-Christian mode. It may not in fact be too gross an oversimplification to suggest that there are, basically, two options on the plane of doctrinal gnosis: the Christian, namely, and the Vedantic. The encounter of Christianity with the non-Christian traditions may thus be viewed—so far as gnosis is concerned—as an encounter, essentially, with the Vedanta.

Yet, even so, why bring up the subject in a treatise on *Christian* gnosis? The primary reason is to show that there *is* in fact a "Christian gnosis" as distinguished from the Vedantic. I am here speaking, of course, of *doctrinal* gnosis: the only kind one *can* speak of. Moreover, in making the point that there *is* a Christian gnosis, I am taking issue with the notion, held by many, that the Vedantic conception of gnosis—as formulated principally by Shankara—

covers the entire ground, a view, I say, which strikes at the very heart of Christianity. For if that were the case, it would mean, basically, that when it comes to its deepest teaching, the Christian doctrine can be nothing more than a disguised or "mythologized" form of the Vedantic, adapted presumably to the needs and capacity of the Occidental mind: remove the veil—"demythologize" as the expression goes—and what remains is Vedanta! It would seem that among those who have some conception of the esoteric at all, this has now become perhaps the dominant view.

I should make it clear that in controverting this position, I am not taking issue with the so-called "transcendent unity of religions," but am in fact affirming the *transcendence* of that stipulated "unity" by declaring that the Vedanta is not in truth a "super-doctrine" encompassing the Christian. What distinguishes the latter is the fact that it is fundamentally *Trinitarian*, a question which we shall treat at length in this book. Meanwhile it needs to be understood that the Christian teaching—when interpreted on an esoteric plane—is likewise "nondualist";[65] as Clement expresses it:

> And the Son is neither simply one thing, nor many things as parts, but one thing as all things; whence also he *is* all things.

Yet the Christian and the Vedantic notions of nondualism or *advaita* turn out not to be identical, due to the fact, once again, that the Christian is *irreducibly* Trinitarian, as I propose to show in the final chapter.

So much regarding my primary reason for broaching the subject of "Vedanta." A second motivation stems from the life-experience of the author, who, as it happens, was "returned to his Father's house" through the living touch of "ancient" India. Briefly stated, it is my belief that "India" may have a role to play in the spiritual revitalization of contemporary Christianity: that the "East-West dialogue,"

65. The term "nondualism" (or its cognates in other European languages) is the Occidental equivalent of the Sanskrit term "*advaita*," first used as such by Rudolf Otto (*West-Östliche Mystik*, 1926), and later, in a corresponding sense, by Vladimir Lossky, with reference specifically to the doctrine of Meister Eckhart (*Théologie Négative et Connaissance de Dieu chez Maître Eckhart*, 1960).

about which we have heard so much, may indeed be providential.[66] Given that the very idea of gnosis has been all but forgotten in the West, such an exchange with the oldest living tradition of gnosis may help to remind us what actually stands at issue. It is not a question, certainly, of a need, on the part of Christianity, to "borrow" from Eastern sources; it is rather a matter of "anamnesis." The Christian seeker of our time—more, perhaps, than ever before—has need to "recollect," to take possession of what in a way is already his by virtue of bequest. The treasure he seeks is "hid in a field"[67] as the Savior declares; but sometimes it takes a "stranger" to lead us there.

66. The case of the French Benedictine Henri Le Saux, who traveled to India and took initiation to become Swami Abhishiktananda, strikes me as highly significant. This is not "New Age," much less is it "apostasy," but something far deeper, which needs to be approached with due reverence. An excellent presentation of Abhishiktananda's life and teachings, along with complete bibliographical references, can be found in Harry Oldmeadow, *A Christian Pilgrim in India* (Bloomington, IN: World Wisdom, 2008).

67. Matt. 13:44.

2

COSMOLOGY IN
THE FACE OF GNOSIS

God knows creatures, not according to the
creature's knowledge, but according to his own.
Dionysius the Areopagite

None of the things which are comprehended by the senses
or contemplated by the mind really subsist; nothing
except the transcendent essence and cause of all.
St. Gregory of Nyssa

There is then—according to the teachings of Saint Paul and the oral tradition delineated by Clement of Alexandria—a categorical distinction between gnosis, perfect and eternal, and a knowing "in part," which admits of innumerable degrees and includes all human modes knowing. What is more: by the standard of ultimate gnosis— which is indeed the Knowing of God himself—all these modes and degrees are not only imperfect, but in fact "miss the target" if one may put it so. Why? Because they see "otherness," see *duality*, where there *is no* "otherness," there *is no* duality. The point is simple (yet also beyond human comprehension): only he sees true, who sees "with the Eye of God."

This recognition proves to be fundamental, not only in Christianity, but in every major sapiential tradition of mankind, beginning with the Vedic. As we read in the Mundaka Upanishad: "*Dve vidye veditavye: parā ca, aparā ca*" ("Two kinds of knowledge are to be known: the supreme and the non-supreme").[1] The supreme knowing—the *paravidyā*—is indeed *brahmavidyā*, the "Knowledge of God," and it is so in two senses: a knowing *of* God, and *by* God, namely. That *brahmavidyā* constitutes thus in a way a "self-knowing," and in fact, *the* self-knowing: the only *true* self-knowing there can be.[2] All other knowing—all knowing, in other words, in which the object constitutes an *aliud*, something "other than" the knower—is thus subsumed under the *aparavidyā*, the lower or "non-supreme" knowing. These, then, are the two kinds of "*vidyā*" that "are to be known" ("*veditavye*"): what does this mean? It means, in the first place, that the dichotomy is all-inclusive: these are the two categories of knowing within which *all* knowing is comprised. However, there is a second meaning as well: the *aparavidyā*, though "non-supreme," is yet "to be known." For indeed, as we read in another Upanishad: those who relinquish the lower knowing prematurely—namely, before having attained the supreme—"enter into a greater darkness" (a "darkness" more total than that of ordinary human existence). Yet in order to attain the *paravidyā*, the *aparavidyā* needs ultimately to be relinquished, cast off; as Shankara states in his gloss on Mundaka I.1.4: "*aparavidyā* constitutes ignorance ("*avidyā*") and must be eradicated inasmuch as nothing in reality is known by knowing the objects of ignorance."

Such indeed is the fundamental premise upon which all major sapiential traditions—inclusive of the Christian—concur. One might think that this tenet simply denies the cosmos and proclaims the absolute invalidity of all human knowing—which of course would be absurd! Yet nothing could be further from the truth; as Peter Kingsley has brilliantly observed: "To dismiss the illusion as just an illusion is itself just an illusion."[3] It is not in fact a question of "denying" the cosmos, but of knowing what it really is; and he alone knows it in truth, who in gnosis has transcended that cosmos.

1. I.1.4.
2. Hence the profundity of the Delphic oracle: "Know thyself!"
3. An authority on ancient Greece, Kingsley has distinguished himself by his ground-breaking studies of the Presocratic sapiential tradition, beginning with Parmenides. See *Ancient Philosophy, Mystery and Magic* (Oxford University Press, 1990) and *Reality* (Inverness, CA: Sufi Center Publishing, 2003).

How, then, are we to conceive of this, our world, which we perceive with our senses and investigate in a thousand ways by the venues of science? An illusion it is in a way; yet not "just an illusion": what does this mean? The key to the resolution of this conundrum proves to be simple in the extreme: *What we take to be the universe exists "for us" as an object of intentionality.* Not "in us," most assuredly, but *for us*, precisely. Here, in this absolutely basic recognition, is to be found the true "principle of relativity" which all cosmology is obligated to respect; to violate this principle is to absolutize the universe, and to do so is to err.

Philosophically speaking, the position we have staked may be characterized as a "realism" inasmuch as it does not reduce intentional objects, be they "particulars" or "universals," to human subjectivity: "anthropic realism," we shall call it. To be sure, the position itself is as old as the hills, since it is in truth implicit in every (authentic) sapiential tradition, and constitutes in fact *the only* realist position that *can* be upheld "in the face of gnosis." On the other hand—and by the same token—it differs fundamentally not only from what has sometimes been called "naïve realism," but from the prevailing forms of "academic" realism as well, beginning with the Cartesian variety. It is most closely allied to phenomenology as originally conceived by Edmund Husserl; one might go so far as to surmise that Husserl was in fact an "anthropic realist" at heart, that is to say, in his primary intuition. What apparently impeded his quest is the fact that he stood alone, unassisted by the life-giving touch of an initiatic transmission; as the aged Husserl confided sadly to Edith Stein, his former disciple, who by then had become a Carmelite nun on her way to sainthood: "I tried to find God without God!"

Anthropic realism, on the other hand, to the extent that it is conceived "in the face of gnosis," pertains by that very fact to sapiential tradition. Yet, like Husserl's phenomenology, it too can be said to stand squarely "upon the bedrock of unmediated apperception": for in its "principle of relativity" it simply acknowledges a truth that is verified the moment one reflects, without prejudice and with a modicum of inner calm, upon our conception of "the world." One then sees that this "world," though conceived as something external or objectively real, is by no means unknown: that if we did *not* know it, it would *ipso facto* not be what we term "the world." One can of course play with words and speak of "worlds" in the abstract; but when it comes to "*the* world," we naturally mean *our* world, the one that exists "for us." And to be sure, it does so precisely because we do have a certain knowledge of that world. Not a complete knowledge, of course; and as a matter of fact, by that very knowledge we realize that the cosmos exceeds immeasurably what we do know. The world exists, if you will, as a white circle surrounded by a black field: both the white and the black are needed to make a world. For indeed, "now we know in part": that is precisely how we know, and the world is precisely the intentional object of that knowing.

Moreover, in its very constitution the world bears witness to the limitations of our knowing.[4] As we *know* "in part," so too the world *exists* "in part": as a mixture, one can say, of being and non-being, of light and darkness, of act and potency. "But when that which is perfect is come," proclaims St. Paul, "then that which is in part shall be done away."[5] If we were to know "in full"—as God himself knows—the world would instantly vanish, even as pictures projected on a screen disappear in the fullness of light. The analogy proves in fact to be exceedingly apt, since it is not the preceding light that disappears, but only the darkness. So too, what is negated in the supreme gnosis are precisely "negations," as Meister Eckhart affirms. Nothing is actually destroyed, because nothing that disappears actually existed: "I am not come to destroy, but to fulfill" Christ declares. This "fulfillment" will be consummated at the Second Coming of Christ, which however constitutes a future event only from *our* point of view. Meanwhile "the world" exists "for us": it is what we know, and what we *can* know in our present state of knowing. This is what anthropic realism affirms.

4. Whether the physicist has grasped it or not, this is what quantum theory has in fact brought to light.
5. 1 Cor. 13:10.

⊕

It hardly needs pointing out that the contemporary Weltanschau-ung stands in stark contradiction to that perennial realism. Strangely enough, in what is otherwise an age passionately devoted to relativism, one has absolutized the universe. That assumption, however, proves to be false, not only in light of gnosis, but even from a philosophical point of view, as I now propose to make clear. The decisive problem with our cosmology—the deficiency which invalidates its absolutist claim—is that this realism has no place for man, the human witness, and that it becomes impossible, within the confines of that world-view, to account for the fact of human knowing. It turns out that even the humblest act of perception has become unthinkable.[6] In that cosmology man has been reduced to the status of a cosmic entity, a mere *part* of the cosmic whole. It matters not whether that "part" be viewed Darwinistically, as con-stituting in effect a "molecular accident," or whether one brings into play a concept of "intelligent design": in either case one has implic-itly denied the very essence of man, which is the Intellect, the fac-ulty by which he *knows*. If there were not within man something that transcends the cosmos in its entirety, something literally "not of this world," he would not be the witness in relation to whom the cosmos exists as an object of intentionality. That role—as witness of the universe—can indeed be forgotten, but it cannot be exorcised: man is perforce present as the knower, even when he pleads his ignorance. No one denies the vastness of the galactic realm, the existence of cosmic immensities unknown to man; but neither can it be denied that the very conception of the "galactic universe" is indeed a construct of the astrophysicist, what Einstein himself termed "a free creation of the human spirit."

The reason why one is unable to account for the act of knowing on the basis of contemporary cosmology resides in the fact that *knowing* does not reduce to *being*, does not reduce, thus, to a cosmic

6. See my articles, "The Enigma of Visual Perception" (*Sophia*, vol. 10, no. 1, 2004) and "Neurons and Mind" (*Sophia*, vol. 10, no. 2, 2004), republished in *Science and Myth* (Tacoma, WA: Angelico Press/Sophia Perennis, 2012).

process of any kind; as Whitehead once put it: "Knowledge is ultimate."[7] The quest for the knower, hotly pursued nowadays by the
neuroscientist, is therefore doomed to fail: the knower has been for-
feited by the very premises upon which our world-view is based.
The only way to make room for him is to conceive of the cosmos in
relative terms, that is to say, as the intentional object which in fact it
is. To absolutize the cosmos—to conceive of it simply as "the real"—
is to exclude the knower; and once excluded, he cannot be brought
back. It follows that what we have termed anthropic realism is not
just the only realism compatible with gnosis, but proves to be, in the
final count, the only philosophically tenable realism as well.

It emerges that the cosmos does not stand alone, but is complemented by man: the anthropos is not in reality a part or constituent
of the cosmos, but constitutes, so to speak, one full half of a complementarity. It is true, of course, that man has a presence in the
cosmos by virtue of his body; but even so, it is only the body as
something unconscious—a cadaver, if you will—that reduces to a
cosmic entity. Man and cosmos "overlap," which is to say that man
shares "the outer shell" of his being with the universe; and it is
clearly by way of this "shell" that he knows the cosmos and acts
upon the world. It could not be otherwise: if man and cosmos were
sharply separated, there could be no question of a complementarity.
In truth the two belong together; even as man cannot exist—*qua*
man!—apart from the cosmos, so too the cosmos does not exist
apart from man: the world exists "for us," to say it again. The microcosm and the macrocosm belong together like the faces of a coin.

One sees that the idea of anthropic realism has consequences,
that in fact it entails the rudiments of what might be termed a complete cosmology, one in which man, the human microcosm, is perforce comprehended. However, it should also be apparent that this
cosmology can in truth be none other than the *cosmologia perennis*
which has come down to us in countless forms and guises, ranging
from folklore and mythology to the technical treatises of esoteric
schools. One sees, moreover, why the ancient cosmology generally

---

7. *The Concept of Nature* (Cambridge University Press, 1964), p32.

presents itself to the contemporary mind as something quite absurd: it is in fact the absurdity of *our* cosmology that gives rise to that impression.

The primary means by which we know the world is of course sense perception: we see and we touch corporeal objects, hear sound, and employ our olfactory and gustatory faculties to access two additional dimensions of the perceptible universe. The paramount faculty of sensory knowing, however, is doubtless the visual, which is why one speaks of a "world-view" rather than of a "world-hearing" or a "world-touch," and why the term "perception" is frequently used to refer specifically to sight. The world, then, exists in the first place as something to be *seen*, something to be perceived visually.

We have noted that knowing "is ultimate," which is to say that it cannot be reduced to the category of "being": no cosmic process can explain or account for even the simplest such act. Yet physical processes do, obviously, play a necessary role in every mode of human knowing, and we are all aware of the fact that cognitive neurophysiology, in particular, has made impressive strides. In the case of visual perception, for instance, the anatomy of the so-called primary visual system has been meticulously investigated, with the result that one now disposes over a "wiring diagram," extending from the retinal ganglion cells (of which there are more than 100 million in each eye) to the hippocampus, a network which dwarfs in its Gargantuan complexity anything the electrical engineer has ever conceived. But while it is certainly true that this research has enabled us to give at least partial answers to numerous questions relating to visual perception, when it comes to the central issue it has so far only confirmed our ignorance; as Sir Francis Crick has put it: "We can see how the brain takes the picture apart, but we do not yet see how it puts it together."[8] There are however compelling reasons why in fact the brain *cannot* "put it together," a question with which I have dealt elsewhere.[9] What is more: not only is the

8. *The Astonishing Hypothesis* (New York: Simon & Schuster, 1995), p159.

brain incapable of "putting the picture together," but it has been shown, on the basis of conclusive empirical evidence, that contrary to what had long been assumed, visual perception is not in reality a matter of seeing a picture or a visual image at all.[10] What one sees, in *bona fide* acts of visual perception, are not "pictures," but corporeal objects, precisely: one sees a mountain or a tree, for example, and not just an image of a mountain or a tree. One can also, of course, see pictures, as happens, for instance, in an art gallery.

We need to understand that perception, like every other act of knowing, is consummated in a certain union or contact between the subject who knows and the object that is known; as Aristotle has observed, "in a certain manner" the two become one. It needs further to be noted that "knowledge is ultimate" precisely because this union is unlike any other: it is a union *sui generis* by which the act of knowing is defined. It follows that neither neurophysiology, nor any other natural science, can comprehend that union, or explain how it comes about. Though human knowing, in any of its modes, does most assuredly involve the physical body—what we have characterized as the intersection of man and cosmos, their common locus—it is perforce consummated in the Intellect, which exists neither in space nor in time. All that the contemporary cognitive sciences have brought to light—not as conjectures, but as fact—stands in full agreement with this conclusion.

Yet, since the waning of the Middle Ages, this fundamental metaphysical truth has become progressively obscured; and by the time of the so-called Enlightenment, man had come to be perceived as a creature confined within the natural world. This radical change in the prevailing anthropology was moreover accompanied by an equally radical shift in our conception of the universe: from a world

9. "Neurons and Mind," op. cit., pp 29–31.

10. This decisive recognition was achieved by James J. Gibson after decades of research in the field of visual perception. For a summary of Gibson's work I refer to "The Enigma of Visual Perception," op. cit.

replete with colors, sounds, and fragrances, a cosmos filled with qualities manifesting transcendent essences, the cosmos was transformed, within a century or two, into the Cartesian universe of *res extensae*, entities void of all qualitative content, a world, in fact, which no eye could ever behold. This is not to say that René Descartes himself was a materialist, or that he denied the transcendence of the Intellect; the harm derives mainly from an erroneous theory of perception, which had the effect of cutting the universe off from man, the human observer. The scission was motivated by the prevailing penchant for a mechanistic physics, the predilection of the age for a *mathematical* understanding of the universe. By eliminating the qualities and postulating a world comprised exclusively of "extended things"—the kind of entity which can presumably be described in mathematical terms—Descartes was laying the foundation for a new science, the very science which had already been envisaged by Galileo and was soon to attain fruition in the monumental discoveries of Newton. The veritably titanic force of this "transformation" can be recognized in retrospect: looking back over the intervening centuries, one discerns the uncanny power of these founders, who with their thought have "moved the world" (a feat which itself attests to the truth of anthropic realism).

Yet that thought proves to be erroneous, and indeed contradictory. According to the new epistemology, the perceptual act terminates, not in an exterior object, but in a subjective representation of some kind, a phantasm pertaining to the *res cogitans* or "thinking entity." All qualitative elements, which hitherto had been attributed to the external object, were now assigned to the sphere of the *res cogitans*, and thus reduced to the status of a subjective apparition. What remains is a putative world cut off from the human subject: a so-called universe which is obviously not "our" world. Yet, strange as it may seem, this is precisely the world modern science claims to investigate and gain knowledge of: ever since the new philosophy came into vogue, this has been the prevailing belief not only of the scientific community, but of the educated public at large. But the question remains: how can a Cartesian universe be investigated? How can it be—not just conceived philosophically and speculated upon—but *known*? Thus put, the question can be readily answered:

the Cartesian universe *cannot* in fact be known, and by that very token, *does not exist*. The physicist may of course *think* that he has knowledge of a universe made up of *res extensae*—that is, even today, the dominant position—but in this philosophical belief he errs.

What is it, then, that he *does* know? It is clear that the physicist deals with two kinds of intentional objects: as a theoretician he is concerned with mathematical structures, and as an experimentalist he deals—not with *res extensae* which no one perceives—but indeed with corporeal entities: the kind of things that can be seen, touched, heard, tasted, and sniffed. Physics is basically the science of mensuration: the experimentalist measures, and the theoretician theorizes, based upon the results. What matters is the relationship between mathematical structure and experimental data: *res extensae* have nothing at all to do with the case. Yet, despite this rather obvious fact, the Newtonian physicist was apparently convinced that he is in truth dealing with "extended things" in a Cartesian universe. Whether it be solids, liquids, gases, or so-called fields, everything was conceived in basically Cartesian terms. The underlying scientific conception was in fact "mechanical" in a rather crude sense, and as late as the latter half of the nineteenth century the ill-fated "ether" theory was invoked in an effort to extend that conception even to the newly-discovered electromagnetic field. It appears that the idea of universal mechanism, for the sake of which Descartes had postulated his fateful scission, was accepted without qualms till the beginning of the twentieth century.

I will mention, in passing, that it was by no means Albert Einstein who dethroned that prestigious notion. It is of course true that his revolutionary and exceedingly brilliant papers, published between 1905 and 1917, have shaken the foundations of the preceding physics; yet Einstein never opposed the idea of mechanism: he refined it, rather, and gave it its consummate expression.

What led to the downfall of mechanism was not the theory of relativity, but its rival, that is to say, quantum mechanics, which in fact is not a "mechanics" at all. The new physics has broken with the mechanistic paradigm, which is precisely the reason why Albert Einstein opposed it to the end. To be sure, Einstein acknowledged its marvelous accuracy, the fact that in a thousand experiments it had never yet been proved wrong; what he disputed, rather, is the notion that quantum theory is fundamental. Staunch mechanist that he was, it seemed to him that "beneath" the level to which quantum theory refers, there must yet be a mechanism which in principle explains everything pertaining to the physical universe.

Be that as it may, the fact remains that the new physics, by virtue of not reducing to a mechanics, can no longer be conceived in Cartesian terms. Prior to the advent of quantum theory, the notion of *res extensae* could play at least a heuristic role in the economy of scientific thought. Granting that this Cartesian concept is void of scientific content, it could nonetheless serve as a kind of "ontological peg" to which measurable quantities could be formally attached: in his imagination the physicist could populate the universe with *res extensae* clothed, as it were, with the scalar and tensor magnitudes classical physics had defined. But this is precisely what quantum physics forbids us to do: the mathematics no longer permits such an identification. On the strength of quantum theory it has thus become clear that the physical universe *cannot* in fact be conceived in Cartesian terms; physics itself, it appears, has finally proclaimed the Cartesian ontology defunct.

But whereas that ontology has thus become untenable, quantum physicists continue staunchly to uphold the corresponding epistemology: one continues to believe, without question, that human perception terminates, not in a real object, but in a mental phantasm, and as Whitehead has pointed out, back in 1934, "any doctrine which does not implicitly presuppose this point of view is assailed as unintelligible."[11] Yet it happens that this very "point of view," no less than the notion of *res extensae*, has likewise been disavowed by quantum physics itself: this is what I have brought to light in a monograph devoted to that subject,[12] and what I propose now to explain in brief terms. It turns out that what has sometimes been termed "quantum paradox" is simply Nature's way of repudiating a spurious philosophy.

11. *Nature and Life* (New York: Greenwood Press), p 6.
12. *The Quantum Enigma* (San Rafael, CA: Sophia Perennis, 2005).

⊕

It is to be noted, in the first place, that the long and arduous investi-
gations in quest of "atoms" came finally to fruition near the beginning of the twentieth century; what turned up, however, was by no
means an "indivisible *res extensa*," but the so-called quantum particle, which proves not to be a particle at all. Yet it is an existent entity
of sorts, something that is to be distinguished, on the one hand,
from a "mere" mathematical structure, and on the other, from a
corporeal object. As Werner Heisenberg has put it, the quantum
particle constitutes "a strange kind of physical entity just in the
middle between possibility and reality."[13] One knows today that the
world of the physicist—the physical universe, properly so called—is
indeed composed of these "strange" physical entities and their
aggregates.

It is needless to say that quantum particles cannot be perceived:
this much, at least, they have in common with the ill-fated Cartesian *res extensae*. But then, how are they detected? If the corporeal
world exists "for us" by way of sense perception, does the physical
universe exists "for us" as well? It does indeed; it is only that the corresponding way of knowing is radically different: the physical universe is known, not directly, through perception, but indirectly, by
way of a complex *modus operandi* based upon mensuration. The
fundamental idea is simple enough: a physical entity is made to
interact with a corporeal instrument, which registers the effect of
this interaction in a perceptible state. It is by way of such interactions that physical objects, which as such are imperceptible, can be
detected, measured, and experimented upon. These interactions
constitute the "bridge" between the "two worlds" upon which all of
modern physics is finally based.

The problem, however, is that the physicist recognizes only one
world: the physical, namely. Misled by a spurious epistemology, he
imagines that such things as *green* grass or *red* apples exist only as a
phantasm in some *res cogitans*, while "the real world" consists precisely of quantum particles and their aggregates. The question

13. *Physics and Reality* (New York: Harper & Row, 1958), p 41.

before us, then, is this: how does quantum theory "disavow" that philosophy? How does it militate against the "one-world" premise of the physicist? To answer this question, it needs to be noted that every corporeal object X is associated with a corresponding physical object SX, which is precisely what X "is" in the eyes of the physicist. If X is a lump of salt, for instance, SX is a certain collection of sodium-chloride molecules. Let us now consider the act of measurement: the "bridge" between the two worlds to which we have referred. It is found that when a physical object O interacts with a measuring instrument I, its mathematical description or so-called state vector exhibits an inexplicable discontinuity, a phenomenon known as state vector collapse. Normally the state vector of a physical system evolves in accordance with the so-called Schrödinger equation; but in the act of measurement this Schrödinger evolution is suddenly interrupted, or as the physicist likes to say, the Schrödinger equation is "re-initialized." Now, at first glance this may not seem strange: after all, measurement entails an interaction with an instrument, a fact which might very well account for the discontinuity. From the physicist's point of view, however, the instrument I reduces to a physical object SI, and O combines with SI to constitute a physical object O + SI, whose state vector should itself evolve according to the Schrödinger law. But in fact it does not! Again one encounters a discontinuity, and again the resultant state vector—not only of O + SI, but of O as well—experiences a "collapse." Why should that be? Nothing of the kind happens in the case of composite systems in which no term is the SX of a corporeal object X: the phenomenon, it turns out, is endemic to the act of measurement. What does this imply? In light of the preceding considerations, the answer is clear: it implies that Nature itself distinguishes between what we have termed "the two worlds"! The fact that an instrument I is *corporeal* turns out to have quantum-mechanical implications: where the physicist recognizes only SI, Nature apparently is cognizant of I as well. The enigma of state vector collapse—which has mystified physicists since 1927—proves thus to be indicative of a "two-world" ontology corresponding to a realist view of perception.

⊕

One sees that the Cartesian premises are now defunct: its misbegotten epistemology no less than its putative universe of *res extensae*. This is not to say, of course, that physicists have renounced these premises: as we have noted before, this is by no means the case. The Cartesian Weltanschauung still claims, by and large, the unquestioned allegiance of the scientific community, and continues to be taught in colleges and universities, not indeed as a philosophical theory, but as the unspoken foundation of scientific thought. But this is another matter, one with which I have dealt at length in various articles and books.[14] What presently concerns us, rather, is the two-world scenario to which modern physics has led. We are left with two worlds—the physical and the corporeal—which are as different as night and day, and yet seemingly coexist in the same terrestrial space, the same empirical *hic et nunc*: how can this be? The answer should by now be clear: the two worlds can coexist precisely because, so far from being absolute, each exists "for us" as the intentional object of a corresponding way of knowing. The nature of the object depends upon the cognitive means: *what* we know is a function of *how* we know it. The seeming contradiction of "two worlds" disappears thus in light of what we have termed anthropic realism.

It is needful, however, to distinguish between a "world," properly so called, and an ontological domain within a given world: we have thus far spoken of "worlds" rather loosely. Let us now say that a "world," properly so called, is defined by a *primary* way of knowing, whereas a secondary mode, based upon the primary, determines, not a "world," but an *ontological domain* within a given world. In particular, it is a primary way of knowing which in fact defines our common humanity and its corresponding world.

It needs now to be noted that this primary mode of cognition, definitive of our humanity and its world, is indeed sense perception, which is presumably what St. Thomas Aquinas affirmed when he

14. See, for instance, *Cosmos and Transcendence* (San Rafael, CA: Sophia Perennis, 2008), especially chapters 1 and 2.

stated that "there is nothing in the [human] intellect which is not first in the senses." This is not to say, of course, that we cannot conceive of anything beyond the sensible order: that would be absurd; what is meant, rather, is that human knowing originates in sense perception, a principle clearly exemplified in the mental development of a child, which begins in the simplest acts of perception, and progresses to more and more abstract modes of knowing, aided by the acquisition of linguistic means. But whereas the sensible order is indeed transcended, it remains even in maturity as the basis of human knowing, as is evidenced by the fact that we cannot think without the use of sensible images, what Scholastics called phantasmata; even the expert mathematician, in his cogitations, say, concerning infinite-dimensional spaces, is yet subject to this constraint.

In light of these considerations we can now refine and clarify what we have previously affirmed, in exceedingly broad terms, regarding the physicist's way of knowing. A profound asymmetry between that cognitive means and sense perception has now come into view, which implies that the physical, so far from constituting a world or universe, can be no more than a particular domain *within* the corporeal world: for whereas the corporeal stands, epistemologically speaking, on its own, the physical, by its very definition, bears reference to the corporeal. It can in fact be said that the physical stands to the corporeal as potency to act.[15] One finds, in the end, that Heisenberg's "strange kind of physical entities, just in the middle between possibility and reality" are indeed *potentiae*, as the great physicist himself had surmised.

But although the so-called physical universe is not in fact a universe, is not in truth a "world" at all, it has nonetheless its own reality, which is to say that it exists in relation to the corporeal order, as is in fact the case with numerous other domains of reality within the sphere of human interest. Take the case of what may be termed "the financial world": this too—as everyone knows full well—is a domain with its own reality, which reduces neither to quantum particles nor to perceptible entities, and yet clearly belongs to what we

15. *The Quantum Enigma*, op. cit., chapter 3.

have referred to as "our world." One can say that this world, though based upon the corporeal order, comprises manifold non-corporeal domains, none of which is reducible to another.[16]

We have spoken of a primary way of knowing which defines our common humanity and determines "our" world; one needs also, however, to take account of the fact that there are higher degrees of knowing which are in a sense "more primary" still. There exists, in fact, a hierarchy of such "primary" ways of knowing, and a corresponding hierarchy of worlds. It appears, moreover, that our present primary means—that is to say, our sense perception—constitutes a degree of *aparavidyā* near the bottom of the scale, by virtue of what Christianity terms the Fall; yet that degree of knowing can in principle be transcended, which is of course what all sapiential traditions maintain, and all forms of yoga are intended to effect. It is to be noted, furthermore, that the resultant "worlds" present themselves as discrete—like so many energy states, say, of an atom—and can be represented iconographically by a system of concentric circles or spheres. A distinction is therefore to be made between "worlds" or *lokas* (as they are termed in Vedic tradition) and the integral cosmos, conceived as the totality of these worlds; and let it be noted that traditional cosmology understands the term "cosmos" in precisely this integral sense.

It thus appears that what some have termed *cosmologia perennis* does indeed constitute an anthropic realism, which is to say that the various cosmic levels are traditionally conceived in relation to the corresponding degrees of knowing. That cosmology is consequently associated perforce with an anthropology, and ultimately with a system of yoga which provides the operative means whereby the higher degrees of knowing can be actualized. We should not fail to point

16. This fact has of course implications in virtually every domain of scientific inquiry. I refer the interested reader to *Ancient Wisdom and Modern Misconceptions* (Kettering, OH: Angelico Press/Sophia Perennis, 2015), where I have dealt with a number of such issues.

out, moreover, that this is precisely what causes insuperable difficulties to the contemporary reader who would make sense out of the ancient texts: having left out of consideration the "anthropic pole," not to speak of authentic yoga, he lacks the key—the Rosetta stone— by means of which these texts can be deciphered.

Let us then consider, however briefly, the principal degrees of knowing, together with the corresponding levels of the integral cosmos, as these have been variously described in the sacred literature of mankind. The simplest and most basic division is threefold, and is given in the Vedic doctrine of the *tribhuvana* or triple world. According to the Mandukya Upanishad, the three "worlds" of the *tribhuvana* correspond, in ascending order, to the waking state, to the dream state, and to *sushupti*, the state of dreamless sleep, which we normally do not associate with any way of knowing at all. And yet it is precisely in a state comparable or analogous to that of dreamless sleep that the *spiritual* world, properly so called, is to be known; as we read in the Bhagavad Gita: "In that which is night to all beings, the in-gathered man is awake; and where all beings are awake, there is night for the *muni* who sees."[17] One may note, parenthetically, that the modern West, by the very fact that it has based its cosmology upon ways of knowing corresponding to the waking state, has limited its purview to the lowest division of the *tribhuvana*, which, even so, far exceeds what falls within the scope of our scientific means of inquiry. Even our contemporary theological schools, moreover, appear no longer to be cognizant of the *tribhuvana*, which is to say that, early on, the intermediary domain— the Vedic *bhuvar*—seems to have dropped out of view, leaving what amounts to a two-tier cosmology. It is true that the original trichotomy has survived in our theological anthropology in the form of the *corpus-anima-spiritus* ternary; but here too there has been a tendency to collapse the ternary into a duad, resulting in the *corpus-anima* conception of man. One thus retains precisely the intermediary component, the very stratum jettisoned in the corresponding cosmology. It is hard to avoid the conclusion that these

---

17. II.69. The term "*muni*" designates an ascetic given to the practice of yogic contemplation.

respective truncations have not been conducive to theological enlightenment.

Yet, even though both our science and our theology have lost sight of what sapiential tradition knows as the intermediary or "subtle" world, it is worth noting that there have always been individuals who, by one means or another, have found access to at least the lower reaches of what occultists term the "astral" plane. In the nineteenth century it was mainly psychics or so-called media who entered into that realm, while in the twentieth, with the advent of hippiedom and the New Age, young people in droves did likewise with the aid of psychedelic drugs. One must remember that not only is there a subtle world, but there is perforce in us a corresponding faculty of knowing, latent though it may be in our present state. I will mention, in passing, that this capacity should not be activated prematurely, nor without the protection of sacramental grace, a danger with which our ecclesiastic guardians are ill-equipped to cope so long as they remain unaware of the fact that there *is* indeed a "subtle" world. The situation seems to be somewhat better in the Orthodox Church, where the astral plane is recognized as the so-called "aerial" world, said to be the abode of demons, and where the faithful are alerted to the fact that they shall be obliged, after death, to pass through that uncanny realm: it appears that what, in the Catholic tradition, is termed Purgatory and conceived as a post mortem state, is viewed by the Orthodox as an ordeal to be suffered *in via*.

The sharpest boundary, however, is the one that separates the intermediary world from the third and highest domain of the *tribhuvana* (named *svar*), which constitutes the celestial or angelic realm: it is the transition from *bhuvar* to *svar* that entails a radical discontinuity, which in fact constitutes an inversion.[18] So too the major break on the side of knowing is situated between the second and the third of the corresponding degrees, as the analogies given in the Mandukya Upanishad in fact make clear: nothing could indeed be more radical than the transition from the dream-state to

18. I have dealt with this question in *Ancient Wisdom and Modern Misconceptions*, op. cit., chapter 4.

sushupti, the state of dreamless sleep, which for this very reason is generally viewed as a state in which there is no knowing at all. It hardly needs saying, moreover, that no amount of psychedelic drugs can take us across that divide, and that even the techniques of yoga cannot effect that transition in the absence of initiatic grace. One might add that it is the failure to distinguish between the psychic and the authentically celestial world that invalidates much of what contemporary authorities have to say concerning the so-called "spiritual" life.

We have so far referred to the threefold division of the *tribhuvana*, which constitutes the basis of traditional cosmology; it needs however to be understood that each of the three principal domains admits of further subdivisions, which are likewise designated as *lokas* or "worlds." One knows from the Tantric tradition that every such *loka* has a corresponding center in the human microcosm, called *cakra* or *padma*, which is normally dormant in us, and that the adept, by activating a given *cakra*, gains access to the corresponding *loka*.[19] There are six primary *cakras*, of which the first four (taken in ascending order) correspond to successive domains within the Vedic *bhurloka* (the lowest division of the *tribhuvana*), the fifth (named *vishuddha*) corresponds to *bhuvar*,[20] and the sixth

19. I do not wish to imply that the science of *cakras* is restricted to the Tantric tradition, or has been discovered only on Indian soil. Granted that the development of this science, especially in Kashmiri Tantrism, seems to exceed considerably what is to be encountered elsewhere in that regard, it is nonetheless to be noted that a certain knowledge of these matters is to be found in other sapiential traditions. It appears, for example, that Johann Gichtel, a disciple of Jacob Boehme, had knowledge of the six principal *cakras*, along with their planetary correspondences. See Oscar Marcel Hinze, *Tantra Vidyā* (Delhi: Motilal Banarsidas, 2002).

20. It is to be noted that the first four *cakras*, taken in ascending order, correspond respectively to the four classical elements, namely earth, water, fire and air, whereas the fifth *cakra* corresponds to *ākāsha*, the aether or *quinta essentia* of the Occidental tradition. It is hardly needful to point out that this fact alone places the subject of the "elements" in a radically new perspective, and should suffice to dispel the notion that what stands at issue is a primitive or "pre-scientific" chemistry, which we have long outgrown.

(named *ājñā*) corresponds to *svar*.[21] Since the first four of these *cakras* are located in the torso, the fifth in the throat, and the sixth in the head, one sees that these three principal divisions of the human body reflect the trichotomy of the *tribhuvana*, and that the neck, in particular, does indeed represent the connecting link or isthmus between the celestial and the earthly realm. I will mention in passing that there are sound reasons to suppose that these six centers and their associated *lokas* correspond in fact to our Six Days of creation.[22] It is further to be noted that there also exist, according to the *tantra vidyā*, an indefinite number of secondary *cakras*, corresponding to ever finer subdivisions of the *tribhuvana*.

It is essential to realize that all this is not mere "speculation"—a matter simply of faith or of culture-driven belief—but is based upon human experience, actualized by the techniques of Kundalini Yoga. What confronts us here is in fact *science*: not in the contemporary sense, to be sure, but *traditional* or *sacred science*, properly so called. Suffice it to say that the science of which we speak exceeds immeasurably in its scope what we nowadays designate by that term: where our physics, in particular, has discovered a "sub-corporeal" plane, which corresponds to no *cakra* and can only be known indirectly through mensuration, the Tantric masters have laid the foundations of an integral cosmology, based upon superior modes of direct perception.

It has thus been discovered that the cosmos consists of "many worlds," and indeed of "worlds within worlds," in which however each *loka* within the cosmic hierarchy contains preeminently all that is comprised in the lower domains. I would like to emphasize that the

21. The *ājñā cakra* is the center corresponding to the spiritual domain, that is to say, the celestial world. Note the root *jñā*, as in *jñāna* (the Sanskrit form of the Greek "*gnosis*"), and the prefix *ā* (long *ā*!), which does not negate, but indeed "amplifies."

22. One should add that whereas there are six primary *cakras*, there is a seventh *padma*, the so-called *sahāsrara* or "thousand-petalled lotus" near the crown of the head. This corresponds to the *paravidyā*, and is therefore not associated with a corresponding *loka*. Attaining to this level of cognition, the Yogi enters *nirvikalpa samādhi*; transcending the integral cosmos, he is said to attain *purna jñāna*, "full" or supreme gnosis.

vastness of the integral cosmos is matched by a corresponding immensity of the anthropos: the immensity of man himself. The human individual, on the other hand, lives generally on the surface; even what contemporary psychology knows as the "unconscious" is something comparatively superficial. We are "normally" in a state of dormancy, in which the vital force—what Tantrism knows as *kundalini*—remains "coiled up," like a sleeping serpent, in the *mūlādhāra*, the lowest *cakra* of the human microcosm. Modern man has scarcely begun to know himself, and so has hardly begun to know the cosmos as well; and strange to say, it is by virtue of this profound ignorance that he fancies himself to be, in a way, all-knowing.

It is no wonder that the *cosmologia perennis*, as it presents itself in countless formulations scattered throughout the sacred and initiatic literature of mankind, generally strikes the contemporary reader as a fantastic jumble of "primitive" speculation, which he is sorely tempted to dismiss as nonsensical, or feels called upon to interpret in contemporary terms and thus to "demythologize." Not everyone, of course, is similarly uncomprehending; yet it may be safe to surmise that only those who have had some living contact with the East, or with what remains of sapiential tradition in the West, are likely to find authentic access to the vistas of ancient cosmology. The very genre is no longer recognized: the wisdom of which we speak is not a question of "philosophy," nor of "religion," much less is it a question of "science" as we understand the term. It is "science" in a long-forgotten sense: a kind based upon self-conquest, a journeying "within," such as is still practiced, here and there, in remote regions of the globe. Perhaps one of the last recognizable traces, in our hemisphere, of such a *scientia* is to be found in Goethe's scientific opus, beginning with his *Farbenlehre*, which, needless to say, was met with total incomprehension by his Newtonian peers.[23] What we know as civilization and prize as "progressive" is not congenial to such a quest, and tends in fact to extinguish it as water douses a flame.

---

23. It appears that Goethe's scientific legacy has generated considerable interest in recent times, particularly among biologists. Even a few physicists, including

We know the cosmos to the extent that we know ourselves; we are able, indeed, to know the outer world precisely because it corresponds to the inner. There exists, in fact, an isomorphism between the microcosm and the macrocosm, stupendous both in its scope and its accuracy. As Oscar Marcel Hinze has demonstrated, the *cakra* anatomy, as described in the texts of Kashmiri Tantrism, is mirrored—down to its finest details!—in the phenomenology of planetary motions,[24] a recognition which evidently opens vistas not even "dreamed of in our philosophy." It emerges that the microcosm and the macrocosm go together, that they constitute indeed two sides or complementary aspects of a single Reality, as we have noted before.

But then, what *is* that "single Reality"? The answer, clearly, is to be found nowhere but in *gnosis*, in the *paravidyā*: the *aparavidyā*, quite obviously, does not reach that far. For it pertains to the very nature of the lower knowing thus to polarize, to split the Real into subject and object, an "inner" and an "outer" world. In true gnosis or authentic *jñāna*, on the other hand, there is no such cleavage, no such duality: if we could know as God himself knows, the world as such would disappear, as we have said, and so would the microcosm. That is why sages speak of "*māyā*," and why Shankara refers to the lower knowing as *avidyā* or ignorance. Meanwhile the cosmos—in all its immensity—exists "for us," and we ourselves exist, be it as erring mortals or as pilgrims in quest of God.

Werner Heisenberg, have evinced respect and sympathy for Goethe's scientific views. One of them, a student of David Bohm by the name of Henri Bortoft, has in fact written a marvelous book on the subject. See W. Heisenberg, "Die Goethesche und die Newtonische Farbenlehre im Lichte der modernen Physik," in *Wandlungen in den Grundlagen der Naturwissenschaft* (Zürich: Hirzel Verlag, 1949); and H. Bortoft, *The Wholeness of Nature* (New York: Lindisfarne Press, 1996).

24. See O.M. Hinze, op. cit. See also my review of Hinze's book in *Sophia*, vol. 12, no. 1 (2006), reprinted in *Science and Myth*, op. cit.

3

TRANSCENDING THE *CREATIO EX NIHILO*:
The Kabbalistic Exegesis

There is no new thing under the Sun.
ECCLESIASTES

THEOLOGY CONCEIVES the creation as consisting of existent things "other than God." Whatever is not divine, whatever is not God, pertains to creation; as St. Thomas Aquinas states: "Everything that is not the divine essence is a creature."[1] The cosmos in its entirety comes thus to be viewed theologically as something created or "made" by God. But whereas this notion may seem incontestable, it proves nonetheless to be open to question: for it absolutizes the cosmos, forgetting that this cosmos exists "for us" as an object of intentionality. In a word, the theological concept of creation violates the "principle of relativity" to which—as we contend—cosmology is obliged to submit "in the face of gnosis." Certainly God is the ultimate cause of all that exists; the question, however, is whether the cosmos, as we conceive of it, does in truth exist: for as a discerning few have always realized, it answers to an imperfect mode of knowing, a knowing "in part," or "through a glass, darkly."[2] The problem

1. *Summa Theologiae* I.18.2
2. 1 Cor. 13:12.

is not that the cosmos is imperfectly known, but that it constitutes the intentional object of an imperfect knowing, which is something else entirely. As noted before: if we did know in full—as God himself knows—there would *be* no cosmos; in the supernal light of plenary gnosis it disappears like the Vedantic "snake in the rope."[3] And this is precisely what the theological notion of a *creatio ex nihilo* fails to comprehend: in affirming the cosmos to be "created," it assumes that cosmos to be real; for it is manifestly inconceivable that something "made by God" should prove not to exist.

Similar considerations apply evidently to the theological conception of man as the *viator* in quest of God: how can there be a voyager if in truth there is no world to traverse? Man and cosmos—microcosm and macrocosm—prove to be complementary notions, as we have come to see; and therefore, if either goes, so does the other. When, *Deo volente*, we shall know "as also I am known,"[4] man—as creationist theology conceives of him—shall be no more; indeed "It doth not yet appear what we shall be."[5] It is finally to be conceded that the creationist view, both of man and cosmos, pertains incurably to a "non-supreme" mode of knowing, an *aparavidyā* that falls short of the absolute truth: the Truth that shall "make you free."

We must not forget, on the other hand, that the theological conception of a *creatio ex nihilo* has nonetheless its place and its justification, given that theology is obligated to address, not just enlightened saints and Vedantic sages, but men and women who find themselves confined—as we all do!—within a terrestrial ambience which they can neither transcend nor transfigure: our world is far too real, its bonds far too strong and sharp to our flesh to permit such an emancipation. What Meister Eckhart terms "the breaking through" comes at the very end, and transcends in fact the domain of religion, properly so called, which by its very nature must speak

3. Someone, walking in semi-darkness, mistakes a rope on the ground for a snake: such is the metaphor.
4. 1 Cor. 13:12.
5. 1 John 3:2.

to us all; as Christ said to the Pharisees: "They that are whole have
no need of the physician, but they that are sick: I came not to call
the righteous, but sinners to repentance."[6] It is imperative, for the
serious seeker of truth, to understand these words, not just in a
moral sense, as is customary, but metaphysically, if one may put it
so: the disease which afflicts us all is finally a nescience, an *avidyā*.
Our affliction may thus be termed a disease of the eye, a condition
which causes us to see a world made up of *dvandvas*, of "pairs of
opposites" such as future and past, pleasure and pain, birth and
death, and so forth without end. And that is why the divine Physician exhorts us to conquer the *dvandvas*, to root them out, which
is a matter of doing violence to ourselves: "Let thine eye be single"
he commands.[7] From "the standpoint of gnosis" the injunctions
of Christ assume a significance not even dreamed of by the moralistic theologian. Why should we love our enemies, why should we
"turn the other cheek," responses which hardly seem equitable,
hardly in accord with the rudimentary principles of justice. The

6. Mark 2:17.
7. The logion (Matt. 6:22) actually reads: "The light of the body is the eye; if
therefore thine eye be single, thy whole body shall be full of light." It appears that
this verse has rarely been understood in depth. Cornelius A. Lapide, in his *Great
Commentary*, quotes only a single interpretation: "Those who have bad eyes, says
St. Jerome, see many lamps instead of one. A single and clear eye beholds things
simply and purely as they are" (*The Great Commentary*, vol. I, Edinburgh, 1908,
p279). This leaves us none the wiser. Students of Hindu wisdom are likely to suggest that the "single eye" to which Christ alludes refers indeed to the *ājñā cakra* (the
highest of the six principal *cakras*, corresponding to the celestial world), which is
indeed "single" not only in its iconographic representation (as a "third eye" at the
center of the forehead), but in its mode of vision as well. According to Tantric doctrine, at this level all *dvandvas* are transcended; even the opposition of "past" and
"future" is said to exist no more. Having attained to this plane of vision, the adept
is reputedly able to perceive the *trikāla* or "triple time" under the aspect of simulta-
neity. Considering the fact that access to the *ājñā* plane is by way of the fifth *cakra*
(situated in the throat), which in Tantric tradition is known as "the Gate of the
Great Liberation," one is likely to conclude as well that the latter must be indeed
"the narrow gate" to which Christ alludes in Matt. 7:14. But whereas these parallels
may have their validity, what actually stands at issue transcends the cosmos in its
entirety, as by now we have come to see.

theologians and ministers have of course their answers to such questions, which we need to respect; yet the Christian nondualist has answers of his own, which cast everything in a new light. And I would add, in passing, that there are today among the faithful not a few who could profit greatly from an advaitic approach; one senses, in fact, that the customary (and predominantly moralistic) interpretations have lost much of their former persuasive force for the contemporary seeker. It is not, however, a matter of rejecting the accustomed teaching, of branding it "erroneous"; it is a question, rather, of gaining access to a higher point of vantage, while acknowledging the validity of dualistic theology on the level to which it applies.

Unlikely as it may seem, it *is* possible to conceive of creation in non-dualist terms—even though, on the face of it, the notion of a non-dualist creation appears to be self-contradictory. It seems that a created entity must be—by definition, as it were—something "in addition to God," and thus an *aliud* or "other," as in fact theology has always affirmed: how is it possible, then, to conceive of creation in advaitic terms?

The answer is to be sought in the familiar and perennial notion of *theophany*. Let us consider, first of all, what the term means in the context of creationist theology. It is affirmed that created things exemplify ideas or archetypes "in the Mind of God," which reduce ultimately to the divine essence; and as St Thomas Aquinas, among others, has explained, these ideas, though many in their participations, are one in God, one in his essence. The creation, thus, exemplifies in its multiplicity what in God is "one," or better said, what in God is nondual. Yet, even so, the fundamental duality of God and creation, the Uncreated and the *creatura*, is in no wise transcended, and is in fact presupposed. The nondualist interpretation of the archetypes, which traces back to St. Augustine, does nothing to mitigate the fundamental dualism which in fact underlies all Patristic and Thomistic theology. The very notion of theophany, or of exemplarism, as conceived in theology, proves to be dualistic: for the archetype or exemplar is one thing, and its exemplification another.

To arrive at a nondualist conception of theophany, it is needful, therefore, to understand the notion in a radically unfamiliar way. Simply put: what confronts us in creation, according to the non-dualist view, are not *manifested* archetypes—not created things exemplifying divine realities—but *manifesting* archetypes. It is now the archetypes that manifest themselves; we have passed, if you will, from a static to a dynamic conception of the "divine exemplars."[8] To the extent, therefore, that the manifestation deviates from its arche-type, it has no being at all. We are back to the Pauline notion of see-ing "as through a glass, darkly": what we see is indeed the archetype, but we see it as if "through a veil."

I would like to emphasize that the theophanic view of creation which we have staked is indeed nondualist, since it admits no sec-ond being or reality in addition to the self-manifested archetype. According to this view, God does not create in the sense of "mak-ing," be it *ex nihilo* or from some pre-existent substrate. In place of a "making," the creative act is now conceived as a "manifesting," a making visible of something which already exists. According to this doctrine, there *is no* created order in the dualistic sense, nothing that exists "in addition to God"; there is only God revealing himself: in a word, creation *is* theophany.

Thus conceived, creation is the manifesting of what may indeed be termed the infinite riches of God, which is not a numerical multi-plicity of beings, but an infinite diversity-in-unity. What does this mean? One wonders whether there is life, whether there is move-ment in that "creation." Yes, indeed there is, most assuredly: but not in our temporal sense. For the life "created by God" is in fact eternal: "ever resting in its movement and ever moving in its rest" as Franz von Baader has beautifully said. All that ever was or ever shall be is in

---

8. There is an evident kinship here with the Palamite notion of "uncreated ener-gies," a correspondence which however is only partial; for it is clear that St. Gregory Palamas does retain the theological notion of "created being," as does every "ortho-dox" theologian. We shall have occasion to return to this question in chapter 6, when we consider Meister Eckhart's views on the subject of "creation."

truth *there*, in that eternal creation. But then, if such be the case, where does this leave this temporal universe, which is indeed "our" world? One sees that there are yet, in effect, two realms, and that we find ourselves still on the "wrong" side of an Abyss; but it is no longer a question of two ontological realms: of the temporal versus the eternal, the cosmic versus the divine. Instead, there are now two kinds of *knowing*, corresponding precisely to the Vedantic distinction between *para* and *aparavidyā*: that is the crux of the matter. What we take to be the cosmos *is* the eternal creation, but seen "as through a glass, darkly." The theophanic concept of creation entails the notion of a partial knowing, whose intentional object is a world or cosmos "outside of God," and whose subject is the *viator* or transmigrant.

This does not, however, imply that the Christian position, as here conceived, reduces to the Vedantic: for the former is yet affirmative of creation, on pain of not in fact being Christian. What has been called into question is not the belief that "God created the heaven and the earth," but a particular stand regarding the *kind* of "heaven and earth" God did create: whether it be eternal and divine, or temporal and cosmic in the accepted sense. According to the theophanic view, *nothing* that God creates is temporal or "other-than" divine. The theological conception of a *creatio ex nihilo* has thus been replaced by a *creatio ex Deo et in Deo*; and let us note that it is the *creatio ex nihilo* that is comparable to the proverbial "snake in the rope." But this Vedantic metaphor—let it be clearly understood!—does *not* apply to the *creatio ex Deo et in Deo* of which we speak; for indeed, given that this divine and eternal creation is perforce conceived in *Trinitarian* terms (as we shall come to see), and that the Christian conception of the Trinity transcends what may be termed the "Vedantic universe of discourse" (as we contend), it follows that Vedanta neither affirms nor denies that divine creation: for clearly, what cannot be named can be neither affirmed nor denied as well.

"In the beginning God created the heaven and the earth": this *must be* our starting point. The question, then, is whether this biblical verse—the first, upon which everything is based—admits a *theophanic* interpretation of the aforesaid kind. Given that Christianity does not possess a formal or "institutional" esoterism,[9] and that Judaism does comprise a tradition of that kind, charged precisely with the task of eliciting the higher ranges of meaning contained in the sacred text, it will be fitting to turn now to that esoteric tradition—namely, the Kabbalah—to resolve the issue at hand. I will divide the ensuing exposition into four parts: the first will present a brief general introduction to the Kabbalah; the second will pertain to the *Zohar*, its single most important book; the third has to do with the Lurianic Kabbalah, a major school; and the fourth will deal, finally, with the question we have raised. To be precise, I propose to demonstrate that the theophanic view of creation—the conception, namely, of a *creatio ex Deo et in Deo* in place of the theological *creatio ex nihilo*—conforms indeed to the Kabbalistic reading of Genesis 1:1.

I. THE KABBALAH: AN INTRODUCTION

It is to be noted, in the first place, that the Kabbalistic doctrine constitutes, not a theology, but a theosophy: a teaching, that is, whose primary subject of discourse is the Self-Revelation of God. It needs further to be understood that in Kabbalah, "doctrine" has been supplemented from the start by operative means, comprising mystical methods of prayer and contemplation, which can rightly be termed yogic, and which, as a matter of fact, closely resemble certain forms of Indian yoga. Apart from techniques of breath control and yogic postures, the Kabbalist operates principally with mantric words and sounds, in keeping with the fundamental belief that speech, in the sense of "*Ursprache*," constitutes the formative principle of all

9. The notion of "formal esoterism" has been sharply defined by Jean Borella. He distinguishes between two kinds: one "of a religious order, directly apportioned to a spiritual hermeneutic of the *revelatum*," the other pertaining to the cosmological order. With regard to the former he concludes: "In the Christian religion there is no formal esoterism of the first [religious] order, at least in the sense of a general, permanent, and recognized structure. There is none, there has never been, and the whole of this book is devoted to proving this." *Guénonian Esoterism and Christian Mystery* (San Rafael, CA: Sophia Perennis, 2004), p75.

things, cosmic and divine. In its own distinctive way, the Kabbalah is premised upon the proposition "*in principio erat Verbum.*" To the Kabbalists, moreover, Hebrew *is* in effect the *Ursprache*, the sacred and divinely revealed language, of which even the 22 letters of its alphabet are endowed with a mystical significance. In conformity with this fundamental tenet, they view the Torah as a Self-Revelation of God, a Book in which all the mysteries of God, man and cosmos are encrypted; as Gershom Scholem has expressed it: "The Torah is to them a living organism animated by a sacred life which streams and pulsates below the crust of its literal sense."[10] In this regard, Kabbalism differs sharply from the rabbinical schools, which by comparison may be characterized as fundamentalist and distinctly "exoteric" in their outlook, and which tend to dwell predominantly upon questions of morality, that is to say, upon the Halakhah or Mosaic law. The Kabbalist is of course also concerned with Halakhah; but he perceives in sacred law, in addition to the moral sense, a symbolic significance which elevates the moral act to the status of a mystical rite. Even though, for a period of several centuries, some of its more exterior teachings became widely disseminated in the Judaic world, the core doctrine and operative means of the Kabbalistic transmission have remained hidden from public view. The Kabbalah constitutes thus a formal esoterism, which apparently has survived centuries of hardship and persecution and remains alive to this day. Gershom Scholem reports that among the approximately 80,000 Jews living in Jerusalem in the early 40's, he has had occasion to meet "men who to this day adhere to the practice of mystical meditation and prayer" in accordance with the Kabbalistic teachings, and that "there are still thirty or forty masters of mystical prayer who practice it after years of spiritual training." And he adds significantly: "I am bound to say that in the majority of cases a glance is sufficient to recognize the mystical character of their devotion."[11]

10. *Major Trends in Jewish Mysticism* (New York: Schocken, 1954), p14. In the sequel I shall draw heavily upon this now classic treatise.
    11. Op. cit., p278.

Historians inform us that the Kabbalistic schools emerged from an earlier phase of Jewish mysticism known as Merkabah or "throne" mysticism, whose prototype is to be found in the celestial visions of Ezekiel. What stands at issue in Merkabah mysticism—as its literature makes clear—is not Midrash or commentary, but visionary experience of a mystical kind, whose primary object was the God who reveals himself to angelic gaze upon the celestial Throne. It is to be noted that the dualism of this conception was already mitigated by the notion of the *pargod*, a curtain or veil before the Throne of God, which served to obscure the light of his glory—a concept that would re-emerge in Kabbalah. One has here the germ of an idea that could in principle be expanded into a non-dualist conception of God, man and cosmos; but it was, apparently, left to sages of a later era to take this step. The Merkabah mystics, no less than their Kabbalistic successors, were keenly interested in the *Maaseh Bereshith*, the "work of creation" as described in the first two chapters of Genesis, but were apparently satisfied with the idea of the "throne-world" as the prototype of the cosmic hierarchy. The Kabbalists, on the other hand, wished to penetrate beyond the God revealed in that throne-world: they wished to understand, in other words, how *En-Sof*, the *Deus absconditus*, gives rise to the Personal God of the Merkabah mystic. In a word, the Kabbalists were in search of a theosophy, a teaching upon which all lesser doctrines could be based; like Nachiketa of the Katha Upanishad, they were in quest of That, "by the knowing of which, all things are known."

Apart from a mysterious book entitled *Bahir*, which apparently is based upon earlier sources, it is the *Sefer Yetsirah* or Book of Creation, written sometime between the third and the sixth centuries, that is deemed to be the oldest literary source of the Kabbalah;[12] it is also, as Scholem points out, "the earliest extant speculative text written in the Hebrew language."[13] It is here that the idea of the *Sefiroth* or the ten "primordial numbers," basic to the Kabbalah,

---

12. One must bear in mind, however, that the *oral* transmission is said to go back to the time of Moses.
13. Op. cit., p75.

appears for the first time.[14] But the text proves to be virtually incomprehensible to the uninitiated; what, for instance, do we learn concerning the *Sefiroth* from the following bit of commentary: "Their end is in their beginning, and their beginning is in their end, as the flame is bound to the coal—close your mouth lest it speak, and your heart lest it think." As Scholem observes: "If the author of the book wanted to be obscure, he certainly succeeded beyond his wishes." Be that as it may, the transition from these obscure beginnings to the full-blown literary Kabbalah occupied several centuries, and was moreover facilitated by the emergence of what is known as German Hasidism, a strain of Jewish mysticism which originated in medieval Germany, and is characterized by a shift of emphasis from the transcendent God of the Merkabah mystics to the God immanent in creation, the "God within" who is "the soul of our soul," a concept which apparently the Kabbalists took over from the Hasidim. In any case, Kabbalah emerged as a clearly defined school or movement, characterized by a literature of its own, around the year 1200 in Spain and the Provence, and attained its Golden Age about a century later. Although the name by which this school is designated means literally "reception" or "tradition," it is to be noted that the factor of mystical experience, conceived as divine inspiration, was from the start admitted as a parallel source of doctrine.

The two major schools of thirteenth century Kabbalism are those of Abraham ben Samuel Abulafia and of the pseudepigraphic *Zohar*, which ranks doubtless as the single most influential Kabbalistic treatise ever written. Abulafia's doctrine may be characterized as centered upon the spiritual life, and is closely associated with techniques of mystical contemplation which, according to Scholem, "represent but a Judaized version of that ancient system known as Yoga...."[15] The goal of this teaching is *Devekuth*, a designation which literally means "adherence" and refers to a Judaic conception of the *unio mystica*. It appears that Abulafia conceives of this state in

14. It is not unreasonable to surmise that these are indeed the "numbers" central to the doctrine of Pythagoras. We will return to this question in chapter 4.

15. Op. cit., p139.

nondualist terms; we are told that the adept who has attained to that state of perfection may be called by any of God's Names: "For now he is no longer separated from his Master, and behold, he is his Master, and his Master is he."[16] We shall be mainly interested, however, in the Kabbalism of the *Zohar*, for it is here that we encounter an explicitly theophanic doctrine of creation, satisfying the requirements of a nondualism. One might say that where Abulafia's teaching is centered upon last ends, that of the *Zohar* is focused upon first beginnings; yet one should bear in mind that the last end and the first beginning are, in the final count, one and the same. The two doctrines prove thus to be in a way complementary; and as Scholem notes: "For all their difference, the two belong together, and only if both are understood do we obtain something like a comprehensive picture of Spanish Kabbalism."[17]

II. THE KABBALAH OF THE ZOHAR

The *Zohar* distinguishes between *En-Sof*, the Absolute and Infinite Godhead, and God's Self-Revelation in what may be termed the world of the *Sefiroth*; and whereas *En-Sof* as such remains utterly unknown, the Sefirothic realm proves to be knowable and constitutes in fact the object of the Kabbalistic quest. The latter is in effect identified as the realm beyond the "throne-world" to which the Merkabah mystics had advanced, the veritable "abode of God" beyond the *pargod* or "veil" which now the Kabbalist claims to penetrate. One still senses the charged mystical atmosphere surrounding these "penetrations," which the *Zohar* conveys not only by the power of its speech and the luxuriance of its symbolism, but also by the thoroughly unsystematic format of its presentation. We are yet a long way from the more orderly and "scholastic" compositions of the later schools, where the Kabbalistic doctrine assumes a more "philosophical" face: "For the *Zohar*," writes Scholem, "the *Sefiroth* still had the unbroken reality of mystical experience."

16. Op. cit., p140.
17. Op. cit., p124.

We need, from the start, to bear in mind the essential connection between the Sefirothic world and the Torah, which according to the Kabbalah constitutes its direct manifestation, its "embodiment" one can say. As Scholem explains: "The Torah is conceived as a vast *corpus symbolicum* representative of the hidden life of God which the theory of the *Sefiroth* attempts to describe."[18] Within this *corpus*, he goes on to say, "almost every biblical word corresponds to one of the *Sefiroth.* . . . In the last resort, the whole Torah, as is often stressed by the author [of the *Zohar*], is nothing but the one great and holy Name of God." Here, in this remarkable attestation, we catch a first glimpse of the connection—verging upon "mystical identity"— between the Torah and Christ, "the Word of God made flesh." To enter the world of the *Sefiroth* is thus to gain access to a wisdom without bounds: for that is the Wisdom of Christ himself.

What then, let us ask, are the *Sefiroth?* One can say that they constitute the creative Names of God—the "dynamic archetypes"—by which all that ever was or shall be is made manifest. It needs however to be understood from the outset that this Sefirothic realm—what the Kabbalists term the *alma de-yihuda* or "world of union"—is not simply some celestial sphere high above the world in which we find ourselves, but that it truly *is* that very world: which is evidently the reason why the Sefirothic realm is the only world of which the *Zohar* speaks, at least in its major parts. For all the rest it has the term *alma de-peruda*, "world of separation," a so-called world which in truth does not exist; for as the *Zohar* goes on to say: "If one contemplates things in mystical meditation, everything is revealed as one."[19]

Given this mystical and indeed advaitic perception, one is hard pressed to conceptualize the *Sefiroth*, to define precisely what they are. It would be misleading to refer to them as "attributes" of God, inasmuch as that notion entails too radical a distinction between one *Sefirah* and another: "aspects" of God might be a better term. The *Zohar* itself speaks of "the King's Faces," and employs in addition a multitude of other symbolic expressions. The fact that the *Sefiroth* are enumerated, and thus in a way designated by the integers

18. Op. cit., p209.
19. Op. cit., p222.

1 through 10, suggests the idea of a progression or an unfolding, proceeding from the first *Sefirah*, named *Kether Elyon*, "Supreme Crown," to the tenth, named *Malkhuth* or "Kingdom," a *Sefirah* also known by the feminine designation *Shekhinah*. There can be no doubt, moreover, that the notion of a progressive deployment of what might be termed "the power and the glory of the King" is thoroughly in accord with the Kabbalistic teaching; and yet it is clear that such a notion can have no more than a symbolic validity. In keeping with the idea of an unfolding or growth, the Kabbalah likens the Sefirothic world to a tree, comparable no doubt to the "imperishable Ashvattha"—with its "root above and branches spreading downwards"—spoken of in the Bhagavad Gita. Yet, in a way, the most enlightening symbol of all is that of *Adam Kadmon*, the "imperishable Man," the prototype of man as we know him here below.

It is to be noted next that the first three *Sefiroth* belong together in a special sense, and constitute what can be termed the supreme tri-unity. *Kether Elyon* may be in a way identified with *En-Sof*; for it is "the Root of Roots" which as such remains ever unknown. Indeed, "the Root," properly so called, is *Hokhmah* or "Wisdom," the second *Sefirah*, in keeping with the biblical text "In wisdom hast thou made them all."[20] It constitutes, symbolically speaking, the primal "point" which gives rise to all things in creation. According to the Kabbalah, *Hokhmah* is complemented by *Bina* (generally rendered, rather inadequately, by the term "Intelligence"), the third *Sefirah*, that may be said to constitute its feminine counterpart: the symbolic "circle" which receives the deployment of the "point" that has now become its center. It is as if *Kether Elyon* had become polarized into the bi-unity of a primordial Father and a supernal Mother, not forgetting, however, that according to the *Zohar* "everything is revealed as one." As regards the remaining *Sefiroth*, referred to sometimes as "the Sefiroth of Construction," these constitute a septenary, within which the first six are deemed to be active or masculine, whereas the seventh and last *Sefirah*, the *Shekhinah*, is said to be receptive and feminine, as has been already noted.

It is of major interest that the *Zohar* speaks of the primal Point as

20. Psalm 104:24.

a "fountain" which springs forth, as it were, "out of Nothing," and "waters" the entire Sefirothic realm; as Scholem explains:

> In many places the primordial point is directly identified with this fountain from which all bliss and blessings flow. This is the mystical Eden—Eden meaning literally bliss or joy—and from here the stream of divine life takes its course and flows through all the *Sefiroth* . . . until at last it falls into the "great sea" of the *Shekhinah*, in which God unfolds His totality. The seven *Sefiroth* which flow from the maternal womb of *Bina* are the seven primeval days of creation.[21]

Needless to say, all this is "worlds removed," not only from Protestant fundamentalism, but likewise from the official Catholic reading of what Christians term the Old Testament. One sees that even a cursory exposure to the Kabbalah opens one's eyes to new and altogether unsuspected levels of meaning: for example, when we read, in the second chapter of Genesis, that "a river went out of Eden to water the garden."

It will be expedient to say a few words, at least, concerning what may be termed the "erotic" aspect of the creative process *in divinis*, as conceived in the Kabbalah, an aspect which, understandably, may not have received its due in our theology. Here is how Scholem broaches the subject:

> The mystery of sex, as it appears to the Kabbalist, has a terribly deep significance. This mystery of human existence is for him nothing but a symbol of the love between the divine "I" and the divine "You," the Holy One, blessed be He, and His *Shekhinah*. The *hieros gamos*, the "sacred union" of the King and the Queen, the Celestial Bridegroom and the Celestial Bride, to name a few of the symbols, is the central fact in the whole chain of divine manifestations in the hidden world. In God there is a union of the active and passive, procreation and conception, from which all mundane life and bliss are derived.[22]

21. Op. cit., p220.
22. Op. cit., p227.

It is apparent that considerations of this nature are excluded by the theological perspective as such; what replaces them, in a way, is the Trinitarian concept of "generation," which however is viewed in a different key. We will, of course, have more to say on this question; for the moment it suffices to observe that there is no substantive conflict between the respective positions: the difference is a matter of perspective, of "key," as I say.

Moreover, in keeping with its "unsystematic" format, the *Zohar* itself embodies a medley of perspectives. Thus, despite its overriding nondualism, it does at times speak of the *alma de-peruda* or "world of separation" as a created universe; for instance, when it says:

> The process of creation, too, has taken place on two planes, one above and one below, and for this reason the Torah begins with the letter "Beth," the numerical value of which is two. The lower occurrence corresponds to the higher: one produced the upper world, the other the lower world.[23]

Yet this seeming admission of dualism is in fact followed immediately by the advaitic declaration quoted above: "If one contemplates things in mystical meditation, everything is revealed as one." It all depends upon our state of knowing, how we "see" the world. Yes, there *is* a "second plane"—an *alma de-peruda* or "world of separation"—because there is a "separative" knowing; but to the eye of the mystic—to the eye that "sees true"—that "world below" coincides with the "world above." And that is why the *Zohar* speaks predominantly of *one* creation—of a single creative act, unique and indivisible—which is tantamount to saying that the *alma de-peruda* is but a manifestation of that "one world" in what may be termed *illusory* mode.

Yet "illusory" though it be—to those who "contemplate things in mystical meditation"—that "lower world" needs nonetheless to be taken into account. A theogony cannot stand alone: it demands a

---

23. Quoted by Scholem, op. cit., p222. The reference to the numerical value of the letter "Beth" refers to *Gematria*, a science which, strictly speaking, is not confined to the Kabbalah, but is to be found also in German Hasidism.

cosmogony "to round out the picture." For indeed, illusion too has its reality: "To dismiss the illusion as just an illusion is itself just an illusion" to quote Peter Kingsley again. There are, then, "two planes," because there are, fundamentally, two kinds of knowing, corresponding to the Vedantic distinction between *para* and *aparavidyā*. It is by no means surprising, therefore, that the Kabbalah—which constitutes indeed a theogony—should encompass a cosmogony as well; and as a matter of fact, it encompasses several, which may however be viewed as different expressions of a single cosmogonic doctrine. And this is what we need now to touch upon.

If the primary act of creation gives rise to the Sefirothic world, and if there is indeed no second creative act, then it follows that both man and cosmos originate in that world. The fact, therefore, that presently man and cosmos are *not*—or seem not to be—in the aforesaid world, demands explanation. Now, for the Kabbalist, that explanation is to be found, quite clearly, in what may be termed the myth of Adam's Fall. This means, basically, that the origin of "separation" is to be ascribed to the mystery of "sin," the mystery of evil: it seems that there may yet be truth in the ancient "Gnostic" idea that our world was created, not by the beneficent God, but by a distinctly less-than-beneficent Demiourgos. What is in any case unproblematic and beyond dispute for the Kabbalist is the fact that this "second creation" is to be understood as a disruption—be it real or apparent—of an original harmony; what ultimately caused this catastrophic rupture, on the other hand, that is indeed a mystery—and perhaps, the deepest mystery of all.

The crucial cosmogonic tenet has been stated with exceptional clarity by Joseph Gikatila, a disciple of Abulafia, in a passage which conveys the gist:

> In the beginning of creation, the core of the *Shekhinah* was in the lower regions. And because the *Shekhinah* was below, heaven and earth were one and in perfect harmony. The well springs and channels through which everything in the higher regions flows into the lower were still active, complete and unhindered, and thus God filled everything from above to below. But when Adam came and sinned, the order of things

was turned into disorder, and the heavenly channels were broken.[24]

In the original state, "the *Shekhinah* was below," which clearly means that man was *within* the Sefirothic world. The divine streams said to flow eternally into the *Shekhinah* still flowed through Adam, which is to say that he lived by the Life in God. The material universe—which we behold with our senses and contemplate with our rational mind—did not exist, because Adam had not yet "sinned." What is it, then, that caused the transgression which precipitated his Fall? That is where, for the Kabbalist, the problem of cosmogony resides. To discern the origin of the cosmos, one needs to discover the source of "sin," the *raison d'être*, if you will, of evil;[25] and this, as we have said, is in a way the most unfathomable mystery of all.

It is not surprising, therefore, that the issue of Adam's Fall has been discussed at great length in the Kabbalistic literature; yet, strangely enough, the *Zohar* has little to say in that regard. According to Scholem, its author "considered the subject to be extremely dangerous, as it touched the great question where and how the unity of God's life has been disturbed and whence comes the breach which is now manifest in the whole universe."[26] Scholem points out that Moses de Leon—the great thirteenth-century master of Kabbalah whom he regards as the true author of the *Zohar*—inveighs elsewhere against those Kabbalists "who indulge in too much talk" concerning the mystery of Adam's Fall. Nonetheless, it appears that the Master himself, in some of his Hebrew writings,[27] betrays an affinity for at least one of the doctrines put forth by these "talkative" Kabbalists: the thesis, namely, that Adam "set his mind to worship the *Shekhinah* exclusively, without recognizing its union with the other *Sefiroth*. Thus he interrupted the stream of life which flows

24. Quoted by Scholem, op. cit., p231.
25. I do not know whether the Christian notion of *"felix culpa"* has found expression in the Kabbalah.
26. Op. cit., p232.
27. Whereas the *Zohar* is written in Aramaic, all other writings attributed to Moses de Leon are in Hebrew.

from sphere to sphere, and brought separation and isolation into the world." There are in fact exegetical grounds in support of the view that the *Shekhinah*, thus separated, as it were, from the remaining *Sefiroth*, turns into the reputed Tree of Knowledge, which does indeed bear "forbidden fruit." But the subject proves to be exceedingly difficult—and indeed, "dangerous"—and we will leave it at that. What concerns us is simply the fact that the Kabbalah ascribes the origin of the *ad extra* cosmos, not to a second creative act—not to a *creatio ex nihilo* in the theological sense—but precisely to the Fall of Adam. What comes into being, if one may put it so, as a result of that Fall, is not in truth a new world—a world "outside of God"—but simply a new state of knowing. What happened to Adam when he ate of the "forbidden fruit" is that "his eyes were opened," as we read in Genesis 3:4, and he came to know "good and evil." This marks the birth of a new and lesser mode of knowing characterized by duality, by what the Vedanta terms the *dvandvas* or "pairs of opposites." In a word, what came to birth, at least potentially, are the multiple levels of the *aparavidyā*, together with the corresponding cosmic spheres.

III. THE SCHOOL OF ISAAC LURIA

Following the expulsion of the Jews from Spain in 1492, the center of the Kabbalistic movement shifted from the small Catalonian town of Gerona to Safed in Galilee, where a new school of Kabbalah began to form. Here lived Moses ben Jacob Cordovero, "undoubtedly the greatest theoretician of Jewish mysticism," according to Scholem. I will quote what strikes me as one of the most remarkable Kabbalistic declarations of nondualism; speaking of God as *En-Sof*, Cordovero states:

> He encompasses all existence, but not in the mode of its isolated existence below, but rather in the existence of the substance, for he and existing things are one, and neither separate nor multifarious, nor externally visible, but rather his substance is present in his Sefiroth, and he himself is everything, and nothing exists outside of him.

This is perhaps as "nondualist" a statement as human language permits us to make. But whereas Cordovero affirms that "God is all reality," he adds that "not all reality is God": a reference, evidently, to what the *Zohar* terms "the lower world." The two statements, joined together in seeming paradox, brilliantly epitomize his metaphysics.[28]

The single most towering figure, however, of the Safed school, was Isaac Luria (1534–1572), who seems to have left no written legacy of his own. It appears that his teachings were disseminated mainly in the form of tracts written by his followers, yet circulated under his name, to which, as Scholem informs us, "the Kabbalists always reverently referred as *Kithve Ha-Ari,* 'the writings of the Sacred Lion.'"[29] Isaac Luria's doctrine, as set forth in these writings, is based upon the notion of *Tsimtsum,* "one of the most amazing and far-reaching conceptions ever put forward in the whole history of Kabbalism." By means of metaphors, which might actually be considered crude, Luria formulates a doctrine of *kenosis* purporting to explain how God produced the "space" within which an *ad extra* world could exist. As someone has noted—inaccurately, as it seems to me—the idea of *Tsimtsum* constitutes "the only serious attempt ever made to give substance to the idea of Creation out of Nothing." Scholem himself perceives the *Tsimtsum* doctrine as a bulwark against what he terms "the pantheistic tendency" within Kabbalism, and as providing "an explanation for the existence of something other than God." Yet, for my part, I perceive this so-called "pantheistic tendency" to be simply a recognition of the advaitic truth, to which Isaac Luria himself had presumably attained: I find it unthinkable that he who was "the Sacred Lion" of the Safed School could be ranked among those who take at face value the notion of a world "outside of God." I surmise that the *Tsimtsum* doctrine is to be viewed, rather, as an attempt to account for the illusory "world of separation," which is just the interpretation Scholem rejects when he writes:

> If the *Tsimtsum*—as some later Kabbalists have tried to prove—
> is only a veil which separates the individual consciousness

28. Op. cit., pp 252–53.
29. Op. cit., p 254.

from God in such a way as to give it the illusion of self-con-
sciousness, then only an imperceptible change is needed so
that the heart may perceive the unity of divine subsistence in
all that exists.[30]

How beautifully Scholem has put it: is this not exactly what the
advaitic sages—from the Upanishads right to the Kabbalah—have
always maintained? I am persuaded that the *Tsimtsum*, so far from
standing in opposition to the advaitic claim—what Scholem mis-
leadingly labels "pantheism"—constitutes one of the major symbols
by means of which a nondualist interpretation of the "lower" world
or worlds could be expressed. This is not to say that this pivotal
conception of Lurianic Kabbalism does not also admit of other
readings, or that a dualist understanding of this doctrine is simply
erroneous; for it appears that the highest teachings, in fact, are
those which admit the widest range of interpretation, and prove
indeed to be inexhaustible in their content.

The idea of *Tsimtsum* is complemented in the Lurianic doctrine
by two other pivotal notions, the first of which is *Shevirath Ha-
Kelim*, the so-called "Breaking of the Vessels," which is equally
abstruse, and likewise intended to "explain" the formation of nether
worlds, that is to say, of ontological realms beyond the Sefirothic
order. The other is *Tikkun*, which has to do with "the mending of
the vessels" broken in the *Shevirath*. These two notions, *Shevirath*
and *Tikkun*, correspond thus to Fall and Redemption, and together
encompass the entire drama pertaining to the religious sphere. It is
no wonder that "the influence of these two ideas on the development of later Kabbalistic thought has been as great as that of the
doctrine of *Tsimtsum*,"[31] to which however one might add that it is
the latter concept that renders possible "these two ideas." Yet,
though based upon *Tsimtsum*, the Lurianic teaching is in a way centered upon the idea of *Tikkun*. It culminates, thus, in a doctrine of
Salvation, conceived as a restoration of the ideal order, or more
precisely, a reintegration into the Sefirothic realm; as Scholem

30. Op. cit., p262.
31. Op. cit., p265.

observes: "Naturally enough the mysteries of *Tikkun* are the chief concern of Luria's theosophical system, theoretical and practical."[32] Referring to *Shevirath* and *Tikkun*, he goes on to say: "These parts of the Lurianic Kabbalism undoubtedly represent the greatest victory which anthropomorphic thought has ever won in the history of Jewish mysticism"; and in a statement of utmost significance, he notes that "many of these symbols reflect highly developed mystical meditations, which are almost impenetrable to rational thought." Thus it comes about that the most profound of mystical teachings may indeed appear as the most primitive and the most naïve; one is reminded of the early Upanishads, such as the *Brihadāranyaka*, which seem to be about as "impenetrable to rational thought" as sacred literature can get. In the case of the Lurianic doctrine, the dominant conception emerging from its development is that of God as the *macro-anthropos*, "God in the image of man," if you will. "The whole attempt of Lurianic Kabbalism to describe the theogonic process in God in terms of human existence," writes Scholem, "represents an effort to arrive at a new conception of the personal God."[33]

That fact alone suffices to explain why this profoundly esoteric teaching could exert a powerful influence upon Jewish society at large, and give rise to the impression that a branch or school of Kabbalah had turned into a popular movement. What likewise accounts for this widespread influence, and indeed renders such a "popularization" possible in the first place, is the fact that Kabbalism in its Lurianic form lends itself quite naturally to a dualist interpretation; as Scholem has put it:

> Not only is there a residue of divine manifestation in every being, an idea which might indeed lead to pantheism, but under the aspect of *Tsimtsum* it also acquires a reality of its own which guards it against the danger of dissolution into the non-individual being of the divine "all in all".[34]

---

32. Op. cit., p268.
33. Op. cit., p269.
34. Op. cit., p262.

I would, however, add—from an advaitic point of view—that this so-called "reality of its own" proves in the end to be illusory. And so, too—and for that very reason—there *can be no* "dissolution into the divine 'all in all'"; to put it in terms of the Vedantic metaphor: the "snake" does not in fact "become the rope." Certainly I do not wish to suggest that the thought of Isaac Luria can be adequately expressed in the language of Vedanta—that would be incongruous. I do, however, surmise that the advaitic claim is made just the same, be it in a more implicit form; and of course, we do not know what was actually "spoken in the ear." There appears to be, in any case, no reason to suppose that Isaac Luria would have contested Cordovero's contention to the effect that "nothing exists outside of Him."

The impression of dualism in the Lurianic teaching was further enhanced by the fact that three additional "worlds"—corresponding in fact to the Vedic *tribhuvana*—were added "below" the Sefirothic realm, which was now termed *Atsiluth*. The highest of the three worlds "beneath *Atsiluth*" is called *Beriah*, "world of creation"; it constitutes the supreme angelic sphere and was identified with the "throne-world" of the Merkabah mystics. Next comes *Yetsirah* or "world of formation," which is still angelic and corresponds presumably to the subtle or *sūkshma* domain of the *tribhuvana*; and last comes *Asiyah*, "the world of making," which is not yet our material world, but might be termed its immediate prototype or precursor. As Scholem observes, in a comment which I find highly enlightening: in all these "worlds" the eye of the mystic perceives the Aspects or Faces of God, "albeit shrouded in progressively deeper disguise."[35] Are these not indeed tantamount to the shroudings or concealments of which the Bhagavad Gita speaks, when it declares: "As fire is concealed by smoke, as a mirror by dust, as an unborn babe by the womb, so is Knowledge concealed by ignorance"?[36] Such, in any case, is the nondualist understanding of "the three worlds."

It would take us too far afield to touch upon the anthropology of Lurianic Kabbalism, which is uncommonly explicit and refined. Suffice it to say that the doctrine distinguishes between *Adam Kadmon*

35. Op. cit., p272.
36. III.38.

and *Adam Ha-Rishon*, who represents, so to speak, a lower and more "historical" reading of the biblical Adam, and who originally pertained to *Asiyah* or the "world of making," the third of the lower worlds, which however is yet a paradisiacal realm. It does so distinguish, one may presume, in order to deal with the question of *Tikkun* in the most precise and effective manner possible; in a word, anthropology stands here in the service of eschatology: an eschatology that proves to be one of the most elaborate and "technical" on record. The theory is complex, and entails, among other component elements, a notion of transmigration, called *Gilgul*, which was apparently founded upon mystical experience; for as Scholem relates, it acknowledges that "everyone carries the secret trace of the transmigrations of his soul in the lineaments of his forehead and his hands, and in the aura which radiates from his body," to which he adds that the power to decipher these signs is conceded by Cordovero and Luria only to the great masters of the spiritual life.[37] It is hardly needful to point out, moreover, that this teaching of "transmigration" is incurably esoteric and must not be interpreted in the simplistic terms of "reincarnationist" doctrine. It is in fact to be noted that according to the Kabbalistic teaching, "all transmigrations of souls are in the last resort only migrations of the one soul of *Adam Ha-Rishon*, whose exile atones for his fall."[38] It appears that the notion of self-identity or personhood pertains, in the final count, not to the natural soul or *Nefesh*, but to the *Neshamah*, the "divine spark" in us, which is, as Scholem points out, "substantially the same as God."[39] In keeping with this tenet, Lurianic Kabbalah teaches that "each individual soul retains its individual existence only until the moment when it has worked out its own spiritual restoration."[40] I find it remarkable that a doctrine as profoundly mystical as Lurianic Kabbalism could become "something of a true *theologia mystica* of Judaism," as Scholem informs us.[41]

37. Op. cit., p283.
38. Op. cit., p282.
39. Op. cit., p241.
40. Op. cit., p282.
41. Op. cit., p284.

IV. THE KABBALISTIC VIEW OF CREATION

We turn now to the Kabbalistic exegesis of Genesis 1:1. It is to be noted, in the first place, that this exegesis penetrates to a level of meaning which is lost in *any* translation of the text. We need to realize that in its function as a sacred language, *Hebrew is untranslatable*. Even if a text admits a univocal literal sense, it does not follow that all levels of meaning are preserved in translation, as would be the case if it were a question of "symbolism" in the ordinary sense. In that case, where the text speaks of "water," for example, the exegete could in principle ascend to the notion of a *materia prima*, say, or to any other conception "water" may symbolize. It happens, however, that the highest levels of meaning concealed, as it were, in the Torah, are not thus "symbolic," and cannot in fact be accessed by way of the literal sense. To imagine, therefore, that what Christians term the Old Testament is in effect replaceable by the Septuagint or the Vulgate is to misconstrue the nature of the sacred text: for it is the Hebrew language itself—inclusive of its 22 letter alphabet, in which every letter is endowed with a numerical value—that enshrines its innermost secrets. To access these, one requires keys that have been passed on by way of an oral transmission, which in fact is none other than the formal esoterism of the Judaic tradition: namely, the Kabbalah.

Let us then consider the Hebrew text:

Bereshith bara Elohim eth ha-shmayim ve eth ha-arets.

Following the Kabbalistic approach, we begin with the first three words: *Bereshith bara Elohim.* Now, "*reshith*" means "beginning," and "*bereshith*" means "in the beginning"; the verb "*bara*" means "created"; and "*Elohim*" is a *nomen Dei* which has no "dictionary" meaning at all. This gives "in the beginning created *Elohim*": what does this mean? According to the *Zohar*, "*reshith*" refers to *Hokhmah* or "Wisdom," the second *Sefirah,* and the first to emerge from the *ain* or "nothingness" of *Kether Elyon.* What comes next is a masterstroke: the *Zohar* identifies the subject of the verb *bara* by picking up on a most subtle clue: the subject of the verb, it maintains, is none other than *Kether Elyon,* precisely because this *Sefirah* is not "spoken" at all. That is to say: the *ain*, or "nothing," is implied as the subject by the very fact that the verb appears to *have no* subject![42] The third step is now plain: having identified the subject of the verb, its object can only be *Elohim*. The explicated meaning, then, of the first three words, is this: "In (or by means of) *Hokhmah, Kether Elyon* created *Elohim*."[43]

It should be noted, first of all, that this constitutes what might be termed the esoteric *creatio ex nihilo*, the foundational metaphysical tenet, which the exoteric dogma *inverts*. It does so, actually, in two ways: first, by replacing the super-essential *ain* by the sub-essential *nihil*; and secondly, by taking the object of the verb *bara* as its subject, thus turning "the created" into the Creator. Admittedly, *Elohim* is divine from either point of view; it is only that the esoteric perspective distinguishes between an unknown God or Godhead and his manifestation. It thus presents an incomparably more refined conception of Deity, foreshadowing the distinction between God the Father and God the Son. One might say—speaking from the esoteric point of view—that the exoteric reading has missed the theosophic point of Genesis 1:1, and in so doing, has turned a theogony into a cosmogony.

Everything hinges now upon the interpretation of the term "*Elohim*": who or what, precisely, is this "created God"? To be sure, the word is in plural form, and even a cursory acquaintance with the Kabbalah suffices to disclose the rough answer: the term refers evidently to the remaining *Sefiroth*—it must! Not only, however, does the Hebrew word—this mysterious *nomen Dei*—refer to the *Sefiroth*, but it actually discloses the nature of what may be termed the Sefirothic world. To begin with, we need to recall that Kabbalah distinguishes between the first three *Sefiroth*—said to constitute the supreme tri-unity, consisting of *Kether-Hokhmah-Bina*, referred to as the *arik anpin* or "Great Face"—and the remaining seven, comprising the *zeir anpin* or "Small Face." The *Zohar* now takes a seem-

42. We have here a splendid example of what might be termed "the divine subtlety" of the Mosaic text.

43. Recall the verse (from Psalm 104): "In wisdom [*Hokhmah*] hast thou made them all."

ingly unmotivated step: out of the blue, so to speak, it refers to the former by the curious designation "*mi*," which means "who," and to the latter by the equally puzzling term "*eleh*," meaning "these." By this second master-stroke, the *Zohar* provides an esoteric reading of the verse "Lift up your eyes on high and see who (*mi*) has created these (*eleh*)":[44] the question "Who has created these?" has now become itself the answer, the key to the riddle of creation

The designation *mi* identifies the Great Face—the bi-polarized manifestation of *Kether Elyon*—as the ultimate object of inquiry: we can still ask "who?" but can no longer give answer, can no longer grasp the object of our query as "this" or "that." So too "*eleh*" identifies the Small Face as the source of what Leo Schaya[45] terms "intelligible and analogical determination": that is to say, as comprising what in the fullest possible sense may be referred to as "these." One must not, however, think of the two Faces as distinct—like the faces of an actual coin—if only because the Great Face (as the universal "Who?") constitutes the ultimate object of *all* inquiry.

Having thus introduced the Kabbalistic "*mi*" and "*eleh*," we are ready, at last, to broach the exegesis of "*Elohim*": what then is the meaning of this sacred name? The *Zohar* does not give a detailed or explicit answer: it gives us, rather, a formula, or better said, a key. The formula is simple: *Elohim* is broken into *eleh* + *im*; what are we to make of this? The explanation is given, cryptically, by Leo Schaya in the following words: "*Eleh* (the Small Face) added to *mi* (the Great Face which is turned towards the created as *im*) formed *elohim*."[46] But this, evidently, is not so much an explanation as it is, again, a symbolic formula, again merely a key. There *can* in fact be no "explanation," properly so called, of the Kabbalistic reduction; it is perforce a question of symbolism, and ultimately, of mystical perception.

There are, of course, explanatory observations to be made. To

---

44. Isa. 40:26.

45. What distinguishes Leo Schaya is the overtly advaitic perspective he brings to the exposition of Kabbalistic doctrine.

46. *The Universal Meaning of the Kabbalah* (London: George Allen & Unwin, 1971), p 45.

begin with, it is to be noted that the name "*Elohim*" actually designates the Small Face: it does so, in the first place, because, as "the created," it is "small" in comparison to the Creator; and it does so by virtue of the "*eleh*," which in fact designates the *zeir anpin*, as we have noted before. What, then, is the significance of the "*im*," the second component in the Kabbalistic formula? The shift from "*mi*" to "*im*" is evidently indicative of an inversion, which is to say that the transition from the Great to the Small Face entails a reversal of some kind. This calls to mind the reversal implicit in the Lurianic conception of *Tsimtsum*. One is reminded, too, of the inversion of an object in its mirror image, and of the *metanoia* demanded of those who would ascend to the supreme enlightenment, which constitutes a "reversal" in the direction of the intellective gaze. Whatever the case may be, we catch a glimpse of this mysterious "reversal" in Exodus 33:23, where God reveals himself to Moses "from behind": "but my face shall not be seen." What "shall not be seen" is presumably the Great Face, which is to say that what Moses was permitted to see, at that stage of his *itinerarium in Deum*, is precisely the *zeir anpin* or Small Face. On the other hand, we need to bear in mind that the "*mi*"—inverted though it be—is yet present in the *zeir anpin*. What, in fact, *is* the so-called Small Face, if not a manifestation of the Great! In our eagerness to understand—to "picture" what in fact cannot be "pictured" at all—we are prone to separate, to "cut asunder," what in truth "is one."

"*Eleh* (the Small Face) added to *mi* (the Great Face which is turned towards the created as *im*) formed *elohim*" writes Leo Schaya. Note the words "added to": something has been *added to* the Great Face; and this "addition" is effected by the creative act of God. *Eleh*, then, is what has been created or "added to"; yet it is not, by itself, *Elohim*: for the Great Face—the *mi*—enters into the creation. It does so, however, the way an object enters into its mirror image: "in reverse."

What is it, then, that has been "added"? What is it that is "new"? It is "*eleh*," meaning "these." One might say that what has been "added" are the "seeds" or archetypes of all that exists, of all that *can* exist. However, the designation "these" is subtle. What has been "added" is not a multitude—is not "these things," be they even archetypes—but simply "these": what can this mean? It appears that the "*eleh*" ultimately designates "multiplicity" itself, that is to say, *number*: the *Sefiroth*, after all, are "numbers," as in fact the etymology of the word confirms.[47] To "create" is thus to "unfold into multiplicity": to "make many" what "is one," paradoxical as it may seem. Yet the "one" remains; as Sri Ramakrishna says: "Water is water, whether it is still or in waves." And that is why the "*mi*" enters into *Elohim*.

Such, in brief, is the Kabbalistic interpretation of the name which, esoterically speaking, designates what God created "in the beginning." This brings us, finally, to the concluding words of the verse, the "*eth ha-shmayim ve eth ha-arets*," which literally mean "the heavens and the earth." What are these "heavens" and that "earth"? According to the exoteric interpretation—which identifies the *Elohim* with the *Deus* of the Vulgate—they are of course "the heavens and the earth" of *creatio ex nihilo* theology. What, then, are they according to the esoteric view? To answer this question, let us recall that the *Sefiroth*, beginning with *Hokhmah*, are characterized as masculine or feminine, active or receptive: the entire dynamic of "the life in God" hinges upon this polarity. As Scholem has explained: "The *hieros gamos* . . . is the central fact in the whole chain of divine manifestations in the hidden world." That *hieros gamos*, however, may be conceived on two planes: that of *Hokhmah-Bina*, and that of the Septenary. Now, it is this division, this polarity, which constitutes "the central fact" concerning the Septenary: the "morphology," if you will, that determines its "life." The supernal dynamic of *Hokhmah-Bina* is in a way replicated on the plane of *Elohim*, in keeping with the fact that *Elohim* constitutes a theophany, a Self-Manifestation of God, that is to say, of *Hokhmah-Bina*. There are, of course, many ways in which one may envision the aforesaid "morphology"; for example, one may represent the Septenary by a sphere with a three-dimensional cross inscribed: the six *Sefiroth* comprised in that Face are now represented by the six radii that make up the cross, while the *Shekhinah* is given by the bounding sphere. The center then represents *Hokhmah*, the "primordial Point," which is now deployed in the six directions represented by the radii.

---

47. The word is derived from "*safar*," which means "to count."

What, then, are "the heavens and earth"? The answer, by now, is clear: they must be the active and passive elements, respectively, comprised in *Elohim*. The verse can thus be read, finally, as follows:

"In (or by means of) *Hokhmah, Kether Elyon* created *Elohim*: the heavens and the earth."

These "heavens," then, are the six "active" *Sefiroth* (represented by the six radii in our symbolic sphere), to which *Hokhmah* (depicted by its center) could be added as the seventh; and the "earth" is none other than the *Shekhinah*. If the first three words of the Torah tell us what it means "to create," the last seven characterize—in the most inclusive terms—the creation itself: what it is that God has "made."

There is also, however, a second reason why the text refers to "heavens and earth": for that reference grounds the exoteric interpretation—the theological *creatio ex nihilo* as opposed to the esoteric *creatio ex Deo et in Deo*—which thus enjoys divine sanction as well. It is not a question of "truth versus error," but of a lower and a higher truth; and let us understand it well: the lower has also its *raison d'être*, and its rights. One must remember that the *Sefiroth* do not simply exist, like so many inert entities, but constitute "channels," as it were, through which the life of God himself flows and pulsates. And so they too *create*: *Elohim*—this pantheon of "gods"— though itself created, is in a sense Creator as well; and what, in a way, *Elohim* "creates," replicates its morphology, that is to say: consists again of "heavens and earth."

Let us now consider these lesser "heavens" and this our "earth" from a Kabbalistic point of view. According to Isaac Luria, "the light was weakened to allow the existence of souls, angels and the material world,"[48] a statement many have interpreted in a dualist sense, as affirming the existence of a cosmos "outside of" or "in addition to" the Sefirothic world. Yet it need not be thus construed. This "weakening of the light" can be understood as referring to the birth

48. Quoted by Leo Schaya, op. cit., p 64.

of a lower and imperfect knowing. The idea goes back to the Merk-abah symbolism of the *pargod* or "curtain," conceived as partly translucent: for such a curtain or veil does in fact cause a "weakening of the light," and gives rise to the appearance of things which in truth do not exist. So too one reads in the *Zohar* that the Ancient of Ancients "drew a curtain down before him," in keeping with the words of the Psalmist: "Who coverest thyself with light as with a garment: who stretchest out the heavens like a curtain. . . ."[49] Or again, recalling the familiar words of St. Paul—"now we know as through a glass, darkly"—it becomes apparent that the notion of a "glass" or "mirror" is akin to that of the *pargod*: its significance is quite the same, for what is known "through a glass, darkly," so far from con-stituting a second reality—something "created"—is simply an imperfect presentation of something else, which by the very fact that it is mistaken for the real, proves to be illusory.

This brings us to the Solomonic notion of "*habel*," which is in a way complementary to the idea of the *pargod*, and completes the Kabbalistic understanding of cosmic reality. The term literally means "vanity" or "illusion," and it is precisely in the latter sense that the Kabbalist understands the famous "*habel habalim*" of Eccle-siastes: "Vanity of vanities, says the Koheleth, all is vanity."[50] In these memorable words, King Solomon, the master of gnosis, proclaims the advaitic truth of the Kabbalah; as the *Zohar* comments:

> King Solomon, in his book, treated of the seven "vanities" (*habalim*) upon which the world stands, namely, the seven [Sefirothic] pillars which sustain the world. . . .[51]

Now, this is not to say that the *Sefiroth* in question are in themselves "illusory": that would not only go against the Kabbalistic teaching, but would actually be absurd. The point, rather, is that the aforesaid *Sefiroth* give rise to illusory effects. Ecclesiastes provides in fact two clues which identify the Sefirothic septenary as the "cause" of the cosmic *habel*. The first is given in the words: "There is no new thing

49. Psalm 104:2.
50. I.2.
51. Quoted by Leo Schaya, o. cit., p66.

under the Sun."[52] According to the Kabbalistic reading, the word "Sun" refers here to *Tifereth*, the sixth *Sefirah*, conceived as the "heart" or synthesis of the six active *Sefiroth* (the so-called "*Sefiroth* of Construction"). These *Sefiroth* (which correspond, as we have noted before, to the six Days of creation) are said thus to contain all things: nothing "here below"—nothing "under the Sun"—is "new"; in a word: there *is* no "*creatio ex nihilo*" in the theological sense. Such is the first "clue"; and the second is given, quite inconspicuously, in verse 20 of chapter 3, where it is said that all things "were made of earth," or more accurately, "upon the earth." Now, the term "earth," as we have seen, refers to the *Shekhinah*, the last *Sefirah*, which itself stands "under the Sun": it is here that the mystery of cosmogenesis—this "making" in which nothing "new" is made—finally takes place. The *Shekhinah* is therefore the seventh "pillar" that "sustains the world," the last of the seven accused as the cause of *habel*.

The *pargod*—the "curtain" that is said to "weaken the light"—or the "mirror" that gives rise to a reflected image, are realized precisely in the *Shekhinah*, the "Mother" who, in a sense, gives birth to the integral cosmos: from angels down to the material world. We need however to understand that the *Shekhinah* is not the "*pargod*," nor the "mirror," but that these symbolic designations refer only to Her passive aspect, Her aspect of pure receptivity. And this is none other than *avir*, the "aether" that gives rise to the four subtle elements[53] from which all substance or materiality derives. It is of great interest that the Kabbalah designates this aspect of the *Shekhinah* by the term "*mah*," which means "what": when it comes to the principle or source of materiality—to what the Scholastics called *materia prima*—one can ask "what is it" but cannot answer: cannot say it is "this or that." The *mah* or "what?" is thus reminiscent of the *mi*, the "who" by which the Kabbalah designates the supreme trinity *Kether-Hokhmah-Bina*. Each is expressive of a "nothingness": the *mi* of the *ain*, the "supreme nothingness" of *Kether Elyon*, and

52. I.9.
53. The traditional "four elements"—which the Kabbalah associates with the four letters of the Tetragrammaton—can indeed be "derived" Kabbalistically.

the *mah* of what could almost be characterized as its opposite: the "emptiness" out of which the cosmic manifestation seems to emerge, and which is in a way the *nihil* of the theological *creatio ex nihilo*.

But though the *Shekhinah* admits a passive aspect answering to the designation *mah*, She also reveals an active side, which the Kabbalah designates by the term *Metatron*, the origin of which has been the subject of considerable debate. As Leo Schaya explains: "*Metatron*, the manifestation of *Hokhmah* and the active aspect of the *Shekhinah*, is the principial form from which all created forms emanate...."[54] The triad *Shekhinah-Metatron-avir* corresponds thus in a way to the supreme tri-unity *Kether-Hokhmah-Bina*, which it manifests, so to speak, in "feminine" mode. It is truly in Her that "we live, and move, and have our being"; it is in Her that "the mirage of creation[55] is produced, maintained, and effaced,"[56] writes Schaya. To which, as it were, the *Zohar* adds:

> That is why the beginning of Genesis is concerned exclusively with the *Elohim* designating the *Shekhinah*. Everything created, from the *Hayoth* and the *Serafim* [the highest angels] down to the least worm on the earth lives in *Elohim* and through *Elohim*.... The creation is the work of the *Shekhinah*, who takes care of it as a mother cares for her children.[57]

It appears, from this remarkable text, that the active *Sefiroth* comprised in *Elohim* are not in truth distinct or separated from the *Shekhinah*, who is not simply the tenth *Sefirah*, but may indeed be viewed as the "maternal" aspect of God.

54. Op. cit., p 68. The term "created forms" refers to forms manifested on the cosmic plane.

55. That is to say: "creation" in the sense of *creatio ex nihilo* theology, which, from the standpoint of gnosis, is indeed a "mirage."

56. The student of Hindu mythology will recognize here the *trimūrti* or "three Faces of God" corresponding to Brahmā, Vishnu, and Shiva, respectively.

57. Quoted by Leo Schaya, op. cit., p 67.

Certainly the Kabbalah recognizes what we deem to be cosmic reality; however, it conceives of that "cosmic reality" with the understanding that "there is neither emanation nor [cosmic] manifestation except from the subjective and relative point of view of manifested beings," as Schaya states with the utmost clarity. The "becoming" or *genesis* which constitutes "our" world—the ceaseless "birth and death" comprising what Hindus and Buddhists term *samsāra*—proves thus to be illusory: "*Habel habalim*" the Koheleth declares. It is ultimately a question of *aparavidyā* in its varying degrees; as the Bhagavad Gita expresses it: "*ajñānena avritam jñānam*" ("knowledge is veiled by ignorance"): that is all.[58] It is the *lilā* or "play" of *Mahashakti*: of Her whom the Kabbalah knows as *Shekhinah*. As the *creatio ad intra* springs from the infinite knowledge God has of himself, so the *creatio ad extra* derives from the finite knowledge *we* have of God, that is to say, of his self-revelation in the *creatio ad intra*. Remove the *pargod*—the "veil" that "weakens the light"—and what remains is, finally, God. And this "tearing of the veil" is what constitutes the attainment of *jñāna*, of authentic gnosis; as Schaya has beautifully said: "This cognitive and deifying act is the ultimate fulfillment of the creative work; it is for that—for Himself—that God created the world."[59]

One sees that despite its intrinsic nondualism, the Kabbalah does not simply "deny" the *creatio ad extra*, as one denies, say, the existence of a square circle, or the horns of a hare. Although the *ad extra* cosmos may indeed be "an illusion," it is not "just an illusion." And no one understands this better than the Kabbalists, who have in fact labored from the start to investigate these "worlds," to discover the true science by which the various cosmic domains can not only be known in theory, but can in a way be mastered; for indeed, the Kabbalah opens the door to theurgic and magical practices, with which moreover it has all along been vaguely identified in the popular imagination. That Kabbalistic mastery, however, derives precisely from an ability to grasp the *ad intra* reality within the *ad extra* manifestations, and thus to transcend their illusory aspect. Though the

58. V.15.
59. Op. cit., p63.

Kabbalah may ascend to the supreme tri-unity, and derive its ultimate inspiration from the unspeakable Name of God, it is yet in a way centered upon the Small Face, that is to say, upon the *Shekhinah*. It is here, on the feminine side of Divinity, that the keys to the secrets of Nature are to be found: truly, to those who find access to Her realm, Her Kingdom, "all things shall be added" as Christ declares.[60]

It is, then, by way of the *creatio ad intra* that the so-called *creatio ad extra* is to be known in depth, and mastered: for that *ad extra* universe "known in depth" *is* the *creatio in Deo,* the one and only Creation that ever was and ever shall be. What *is* the world? what *is* the Creation? According to the Kabbalah, it is what Schaya calls "the infinite and indivisible aspects of the One," deployed and realized in the *Shekhinah*. Here at last is to be found the longed-for object of all our seeking: what Goethe, in the penultimate line of *Faust*, calls "*das Ewig-Weibliche*," the "Eternal Feminine," which "draws us onwards" ("*zieht uns hinan*") till the Goal is reached. The Kabbalah speaks of this Eternal Feminine as the Wife and Queen of the King, whose gaze is ever fixed upon Her. All the King's riches—"the infinite and indivisible aspects of the One"—are lavished upon Her: whence the name *Malkhuth*, "Kingdom." And She is called "Mother," because it is She who gives birth to all beings and to all the worlds. She does so, moreover, by virtue of the *mah*, the inscrutable "what" which is said to constitute Her aspect of pure receptivity; and I would add (no matter what philologists may think): it is this *mah* that we find in the words "*mater*" and "*materia*," not forgetting the Vedantic term "*māyā*." It is this *mah*, this *māyā*—and not God!—which in a way gives rise to the *creatio ad extra*, and which moreover proves to be intrinsically unknowable. Of Her who remains forever inscrutable it can indeed be said: "*Nigra sum, sed formosa*" ("I am black, but beautiful," as we read in the Song of Solomon): for She is both in the highest degree.

A concordance or kinship between the *Shekhinah* and the Blessed Virgin Mary, too striking to overlook, has begun to emerge. Take the words of the Angelic Salutation "*Dominus tecum*" ("the Lord is

---

60. Matt. 6:33.

with thee"): can this not also be said of the *Shekhinah*? Or the designation "*gratia plena*" ("full of grace"): does this not apply likewise to Her upon whom the King has bestowed the fullness of his bounty? One can go through the entire litany of Marian perfections and mystical epithets: it seems that all fit the Kabbalistic *Shekhinah* as well. What, then, is the meaning of these concordances, which can hardly be dismissed as "accidental"? It should be noted that even the Catholic dogma of the Immaculate Conception proves to be concordant, and in fact assumes an even deeper significance in light of that concordance. But these are matters beyond the scope of this book.

As we learn from the Kabbalah: All that is manifestable of "the infinite and indivisible aspects of the One" is given, once and for all, in *Malkhuth*, the Kingdom of God, in the glory bestowed upon Her who is *gratia plena*; as Moses de Leon, the great master, writes:

> When God gave the Torah to the Israelites, He opened the seven heavens to them and they saw that nothing was really there but His glory; He opened the seven worlds (or "earths") to them and they saw nothing there but His glory; He opened the seven abysses (or "hells") before their eyes and they saw nothing there but His glory.[61]

---

61. From the *Sefer Harimmon*, one of his Hebrew writings; quoted by Leo Schaya, op. cit., p166.

4

THE WISDOM OF
CHRISTIAN KABBALAH

THE GREAT QUESTION, now, is whether the pivotal Christian conceptions—"*Trinity*" and "*Incarnation*"—can be interpreted in Kabbalistic terms; and as a matter of fact, soon after the Kabbalah "surfaced" in the form of its early mystical tracts, the issue was raised and actively pursued. Thus began a movement, known to historians as Christian Kabbalah, which for a period of about four hundred years exerted considerable influence in Europe and America. Persons of diverse occupation and rank—notably artisans and physicians, scientists and literati, not forgetting men of the cloth, all gifted evidently with a certain philosophical acumen or mystical bent—felt drawn into its fold. The roster includes a Cardinal, and even a German Princess! What concerns us, however, is not the history of Christian Kabbalah, however colorful, but its doctrine, its central claims: we wish to know what the leading Christian Kabbalists have to say in answer to "the great question" posed above.

It is customary to suppose that Christian Kabbalah came to birth in the year 1486, when a 23-year-old Count, named Pico de la Mirandola, proposed 900 Conclusions to be examined by scholars and publicly debated in Rome. The latter included 119 specifically Kabbalistic tenets, divided into a group of 47 drawn from Hebrew sources, plus a group of 72 said to be "*secundum opinionem propriam,*" that is to say, his own. Pico's objective is to demonstrate that the teachings of Christianity, beginning with the twin mysteries "Trinity" and "Incarnation," can be confirmed on Kabbalistic grounds. What is more, the Count wishes to show, by the combined strength of his 900 tenets, that the sacred beliefs of all nations are consonant with the Christian religion, which he conceives to be the end and culmination of them all. What Pico de la Mirandola advocates is basically what in our day has come to be known as "the transcendent unity of religions," but with a distinctively Christian turn.

It is however to be noted that documented contact between Kabbalah and Christianity antedates the year 1486 considerably, and in fact goes back to the thirteenth century. Perhaps the earliest figure of note, in this regard, is Arnold of Villanova (1238–1312), a physician, alchemist, and Franciscan no less. Driven, apparently, by aspirations not unlike those motivating Pico de la Mirandola, Arnoldus proposed a Kabbalistic "derivation" of the Trinity which altogether accords with conclusions reached centuries later in the heyday of Christian Kabbalah.[1] As might be expected, most documents of this genre, produced in the fourteenth and fifteenth centuries, are the work of Jewish converts to Christianity, who wished, presumably, to justify their conversion and defend themselves against the charge of apostasy. One knows today that these endeavors have at times resulted in the falsification of Kabbalistic treatises, and the question has been raised to what extent Christian Kabbalists of a later era, beginning with Pico de la Mirandola, may have been misled by such "doctored" texts. In any case, while Jewish converts were claiming to have confirmed their Christian beliefs on Kabbalistic grounds, Talmudic Jews opposed to Christianity responded with a polemic of their own, arguing in effect that the Kabbalah constitutes a Christian heresy. By the middle of the fifteenth century, moreover, a third group of documents began to emerge, consisting of Latin translations of Kabbalistic texts, produced in the name of the Church. As we learn from Pico himself, seventy such translations were made by order of Pope Sixtus IV (1471–1484).

In light of this pre-history, one may well ask what Pico brings to the table that is new. In the first place, let it be said, he brings him-

---

1. To be precise, he associates the *Yod* in the Tetragrammaton with the Father, the *Vav* with the Son, and the *He* with the Holy Spirit. See Gerschom Scholem, "Considérations sur l'histoire des débuts de la Kabbale chrétienne," in *Kabbalistes Chrétiens*, Edited by Antoine Faivre and Frederick Tristan, Cahiers de l'Hermétisme (Paris: Albin Michel, 1979), p 26.

self: a native Christian, a Count, and a genius; and this combination, most assuredly, *is* something new. One may recall, in that connection, that Pico's *Conclusiones* were condemned by Pope Innocent VIII (1484–1492)—at first 13 tenets, then all 900 *en bloc*—following which Pico fled to France, was arrested and imprisoned by the Pope's men in Lyon, and might well have died at the stake if it had not been for the protection of his friend, Lorenzo de Medici, who secured his release. Here was someone who could not be suppressed, could not be silenced, a man, above all, totally dedicated to a single purpose: namely, to expound "the true Kabbalah" before the Christian world as its first protagonist; and let us add that he was in fact perceived as such by succeeding generations of Christian Kabbalists. What fascinated Pico, and inflamed him, was the prospect of demonstrating the consonance and perfect harmony of the Jewish, Greek, Islamic and Christian traditions with the aid of Kabbalistic means.[2] Persuaded that Hebrew constitutes indeed the primordial tongue, and that what he termed "*prima et vera Cabala*" was revealed to Moses by God himself, he believed that this supreme doctrine enables one to penetrate to the very core of every sacred tradition given to mankind. One catches a glimpse of these sentiments—and of the ardor with which they were held—in a remarkable passage (from *De Hominis Dignitate*), provoked by his encounter with certain rare Hebrew books of Kabbalistic provenance:

> When I procured these works, at a very high price, and had studied them with great concentration and without interruption, I recognized in them—and God is my witness—a confirmation not only of the Mosaic faith, but of the Christian. Here is to be found the secret of the Trinity, the Incarnation of the Word, the divine nature of the Messiah; here one speaks to us of original sin and its atonement through Christ, of the heavenly Jerusalem, of the fall of the demons, of the angelic hierarchies, of purgatory and the pains of hell, in the same way as we

2. One might mention that the Florentine Academy, to which Pico belonged, was founded by Marsiglio Ficino—the proponent of "*prisca theologia*"—a person similarly inclined towards "ecumenical" goals.

read daily in the writings of Paul and Dionysius, of Jerome and Augustine. And as concerns the philosophic content of these books, one has the impression of finding there, quite simply, the thought of Pythagoras and Plato. Now, one knows well that the doctrines of these thinkers are near to the Christian faith to such a degree that Augustine thanked God profusely for permitting him to gain acquaintance with the Platonist books. In brief, in that which separates us from the Jews there is hardly a disputed point on which we cannot, with the help of the Kabbalah, refute them so cogently that they have no more ground upon which to stand.[3]

It is traditional to conceive of Kabbalah as comprised of two parts—the doctrine of the *Sefiroth*, namely, which we have summarized in the previous chapter, and the science of Divine Names, which remains yet to be considered—and Pico, as we shall see, has his eye on both. Let us begin with the fourth tenet of his second list of Kabbalistic propositions, the one said to be "*secundum opinionem propriam*," which addresses the question how the *Sefiroth* stand in relation to *En-Sof*, the absolute and infinite Godhead. The text reads as follows:

> *En-Sof* cannot be counted among the numerations [*Sefiroth*] because it constitutes their unity, abstract and additional, and not the unity associated with these numerations.

Pico distinguishes here between two kinds of unity: that of *En-Sof*, and that of each *Sefirah*, taken in itself. Every *Sefirah* has of course a unity of its own; but the unity of *En-Sof* transcends each of these unities: it is "abstract and additional." What, then, does it unify? Clearly, it unifies the ten *Sefiroth*, or the "world" comprised of these ten emanations. But whereas *En-Sof*, as the non-emanated origin of the ten *Sefiroth*, transcends not only each *Sefirah*, but the entire ensemble of ten, it is nonetheless "non-separate" from them, inasmuch as it constitutes their unity, "abstract and additional" though

3. It is hardly surprising that Talmudic Jews countered by attacking the Kabbalah itself.

that unity may be. Thus, what Pico affirms in II.4[4] amounts evidently to a Kabbalistic formulation of nondualism, a Kabbalistic *advaita*.

Let us consider next how Pico responds to what is doubtless the most burning question of all: the problem of interpreting the Christian Trinity—if such be possible—in Sefirothic terms. To begin with, Pico informs us, in II.20, that the Hebrew word *az*, when "interpreted by the Kabbalists," throws light upon the Trinity: "*de trinitatis mysterio multum illuminabuntur.*" Now, this Hebrew word of two letters, so far from constituting a *nomen Dei*, is simply the common adverb "then," which, on the face of it, has nothing in particular to do with the *mysterium trinitatis*—unless, that is, the word be interpreted according to the Kabbalistic art.[5] Such an interpretation is in fact to be found in the *Book of Foundations*, a Hebrew text which, as Chaim Wirszubski has shown, was known to Pico in a Latin translation.[6] It states that the letter *Aleph* in the word *az* "refers to the three superior *Sefiroth*," whereas the letter *Zayin* refers to the remaining septenary. It is clear, therefore, that the concordance to which Pico alludes associates *Kether Elyon* ("Supreme Crown") with the Father, *Hokhmah* ("Wisdom") with the Son, and *Bina* (generally rendered as "Intelligence") with the Holy Spirit. One might add that this is evidently the most natural among all conceivable Sefirothic interpretations of the Trinity, and the one most commonly encountered in the writings of Christian Kabbalists. The partition of the ten *Sefiroth* into a supreme triad followed by a septenary conforms, moreover, to the esoteric reading of Genesis 1.1, outlined in Chapter 3. The seven lower *Sefiroth*—commonly referred to as the *Sefiroth* of Construction, which correspond in fact to the Seven Days of

4. We shall henceforth designate the first and second lists of Kabbalistic tenets included in Pico's 900 *Conclusiones* (consisting of 47 and 72 propositions, respectively) by Roman numerals. The designation II.4 refers thus to proposition number 4 of the second series.

5. It is not unusual, in Kabbalah, to assign an esoteric sense to a common word: think of the words *mi* ("who"), *eleh* ("these"), and *mah* ("what") encountered in chapter 3.

6. "L'Ancien et le Nouveau dans la confirmation kabbalistique du christianisme par Pic de la Mirandole," in *Kabbalistes Chrétiens*, op. cit., p187.

Genesis—constitute thus the created and in turn "creative" order, that is to say, the Sefirothic world.

But does the aforesaid concordance between the Christian Trinity and the supreme Sefirothic triad imply that the two are simply one and the same? There are those who think that it does; Joseph Blau, for example, has made the point quite clearly:

> From the time of Pico [the doctrine of the *Sefiroth*] was adapted into the Christian system by considering the three highest *Sefiroth, Kether, Hokhmah,* and *Bina,* as the representation of the Trinity... The only other emanation [i.e., *Sefirah*] which was treated with any thoroughness was the sixth of the *Sefiroth, Tifereth* ("Glory"), which was conceived as the representation of Jesus Incarnate. Thus, if anything, the doctrine of the *Sefiroth* aided the Christian interpreters of the Kabbalah, for it gave them the opportunity to distinguish between the Son as divine Wisdom and the Son as the incarnate Redeemer; it also resolved the difficulty of explaining the triune God by making the Persons of the Trinity manifestations or emanations of the Limitless God, by considering the Father, the Son, and the Holy Ghost as Three out of One, rather than Three in One.[7]

Now, it is true enough that the conception of the Trinity would indeed be greatly simplified were one to adopt the stipulated identification; yet it is by no means clear that Pico, for one, does adopt it. Nowhere does he say so. What he does say, in II.20, is that the given concordance sheds light on the *mysterium trinitatis*. But that is all; the rest is speculation on our part. It is of interest to note, in this connection, that the letter *Aleph,* which is said to refer to the supreme Sefirothic triad, has the numerical value 1, whereas the *Zayin,* which refers to the septenary, has in fact the value 7. This appears to indicate that the Sefirothic triad may actually be viewed *as one*. Could this mean that the Christian Trinity is to be conceived—not as a triad, but as that "oneness," which is indeed "abstract and additional"? Again, Pico does not say.

---

7. *The Christian Interpretation of the Cabala in the Renaissance* (Port Washington, NY: Kennikar Press, 1965), p15.

He does however affirm something else which speaks against Blau's "Three out of One" interpretation: in II.6, namely, he propounds a second concordance between the Persons of the Trinity and a Sefirothic triad, this time composed of the first, sixth and tenth *Sefirah*. The text reads as follows:

> The three great Divine Names comprised of four letters, which pertain to the secrets of the Kabbalah, are to be associated unequivocally with the Persons of the Trinity, so that the name EHYE corresponds to the Father, the name YHVH to the Son, and the name ADNY to the Holy Spirit; whosoever is versed in the Kabbalistic science will understand this.

Now, the first of these Names is none other than the "I AM" of Exodus 3.14; the second is the "unspeakable" Name commonly referred to as the Tetragrammaton; and the third is *Adonai*, perhaps the most beloved Name of God among the Jews. There can be no doubt, moreover, that the reference to "whosoever is versed in the Kabbalistic science" alludes to the identification of the three Names with *Kether Elyon*, *Tifereth*, and *Malkhuth*, the tenth *Sefirah*, also known as *Shekhinah*, a correspondence which is in fact based upon Kabbalistic principles. What is especially enlightening, here, is the association of the Son with *Tifereth*, whom Kabbalists are wont to identify with *Adam Kadmon*, primordial and universal Man. To be sure, this correspondence does prepare the way for a Kabbalistic understanding of the Incarnation; yet what Pico enunciates in II.6 is a rendering of the Trinity, howbeit one based upon a different Sefirothic triad than is stipulated in II.20. We may therefore conclude that whatever Pico's "Kabbalistic interpretation" of the *mysterium trinitatis* may finally be, he does not simply identify the Trinity with a particular Sefirothic triad, nor "explain it away" in keeping with Blau's "Three out of One" hypothesis.

In addition to the two aforesaid representations of the Trinity, Pico proposes a Kabbalistic view of the Incarnation, that is to say, of Jesus Christ, which he bases upon the Hebrew name *Yeshou* (from which the name "Jesus" is derived). Thus, having associated the Son with *Tiefereth* (in II.6), he goes on to say (in II.7):

No Jewish Kabbalist can deny that the name *Jesus*, when interpreted according to the principles of Kabbalah, means precisely
and unequivocally God, the Son of God and Wisdom of the
Father, related to human nature in the unity of the Person by the
third *Person* of the Deity, which is the most ardent fire of Love.

We need thus to consider how the name *Yeshou* lends itself to this
interpretation. Pico gives us a clue in II.14: "By the letter *Shin*, found
in the center of the name of Jesus, it is indicated to us, in Kabbalistic
mode, that the world finds complete repose in its perfection when
the *Yod* is related to the *Vav*, which is realized in Christ, who is at
once authentic Son of God and man." Despite the enigmatic nature
of this statement, one thing, at least, is clear: the "repose" of which
Pico speaks can be none other than what the Kabbalah knows as the
Sabbath resulting from *Tikkun*, the Restoration of all things in
Malkhuth, the Kingdom of God. But the question remains, of
course, how Pico's contention, as stated in II.14, can be justified by
Kabbalistic means. Now, it happens that the key to this riddle was
discovered by Hermann Greive in a footnote to a 1596 edition of the
Adversus Haereses of St. Irenaeus.[8] The annotated text reads as fol-
lows: "According to the original language of the Jews, the name of
Jesus is composed of two letters surrounding a central letter, as say
their scholars, and denotes the Lord who embraces heaven and
earth"; and this is what the footnote states by way of explanation:

> However, in order that it [the name of Jesus] designates the
> Lord of heaven and earth, it is necessary to write it, in the
> manner of the ancients, with three letters, *Yod-Shin-Vav*, and
> interpret it by means of Notarikon,[9] which consists of inter-
> preting the individual letters as expressing entire words, so that
> *Yod*, which is the first letter of the Tetragrammaton YHVH,
> expresses the word "Lord." Moreover, the *Shin* is the first letter

8. "La Kabbale chrétienne de Jean Pic de la Mirandole," in *Kabbalistes Chrétiens*,
op. cit., pp169–70.
9. Notarikon, along with Gematria and Themura, pertain to the Kabbalistic
modus operandi, and plays a central role in Kabbalah. We shall have more to say on
this subject presently, in connection with the Christian Kabbalist Johann Reuchlin.

of the word *Shamayim,* which means "heaven"; and finally, the *Vav* stands at the beginning of the word *Vaarets,* which means "and earth." In this manner, the three letters of the name *Yod-Shin-Vav,* when interpreted with the aid of Notarikon, designate the Lord of heaven and earth.

Clearly, this not only justifies Pico's central contention in II.14, but also, in a way, confirms the connection between the Second Person of the Trinity and the Tetragrammaton, proposed in II.6.

However, as Greive likewise points out, it happens that one can also interpret II.14 by an alternative approach, based upon the numerical values of the letters *Yod* and *Vav*: for these values, which are 10 and 6, designate God and man, respectively. If, now, one takes the letter *Shin* to stand for the Hebrew word *she* (meaning "which"), one sees that *Yod-Shin-Vav* can be read as "the God which is man." This also explains, no doubt, what Pico has in mind when he writes, in II.43, that "by the mystery of the two letters *Vav* and *Yod,* one is able to understand how the Messiah, as God, is his own proper principle as man." By means of this simple Kabbalistic *modus operandi,* the intended meaning of both assertions (namely, II.14 and II.43) has evidently become manifest. As Eugenio Anagnine observes: "The mystery of the Incarnation of the Word is represented in the Kabbalah by means of the union of the letters *Vav* and *Yod*."[10]

Now, that union was effected in principle by Jesus Christ, the promised Messiah: I say "in principle," because the plenary manifestation of that union remains for us unrealized. What stands at issue, here, is precisely the distinction between what theology knows as the First and Second Coming of Christ: the former took place when Mary conceived and bore a Son, whereas the latter will be effected when Christ shall return in glory. The fact, moreover, that the name "Jesus" emerges out of the Tetragrammaton through the addition of the letter *Shin,* signifies that Jesus is indeed the manifestation or "utterance" of the Tetragrammaton. The latter thus becomes "effable" through the union of *Yod* and *Vav,* as Pico himself suggests (in II.15). Prior to the historical birth of Christ, the Tetragrammaton

10. *Pico della Mirandola* (Bari, 1937), p183.

was "ineffable" in a twofold sense (corresponding to the two Advents, neither of which had yet taken place), whereas presently it is in a way "effable" and "ineffable" at once, and will remain so until the Parousia. Yet the name of Jesus is in truth the "utterance" of the Tetragrammaton; and that is manifestly the reason why that Name is "above every name," and why, before the name of Jesus, "every knee must bend."[11] One can thus understand, on Kabbalistic grounds, why the name "Jesus" is endowed with power to heal, to sanctify, and to enlighten, and why, as St. Peter declares, it is the Name "whereby we must be saved."[12]

We turn now to the Fall of Adam and the Redemption wrought by Christ. Pico broaches the subject almost immediately, namely in I.4, which reads: "*Peccatum Ade fuit truncate regni a ceteris plantis*" ("The Sin of Adam has severed the Kingdom from the other plants"). Now, in the first place, one sometimes refers to the *Sefiroth* as "plants," a usage Pico evidently adopts in this passage. What he says is that the Sin of Adam has caused the tenth *Sefirah*, named *Malkhuth* ("Kingdom") or *Shekhinah*, to be cut off, as it were, from the remaining nine *Sefiroth*.[13] It appears that despite its esoteric nature, this Kabbalistic tenet—which Moses de Leon, as we have seen, considered dangerous for the unprepared—had become widely disseminated among scholars of the Renaissance: even Leibniz speaks somewhere of Adam's Fall as "a severance of *Malkhuth* from the other plants."

One sees, from what Pico tells us in I.4, that he aligns himself from the start with the Kabbalistic view of man: an anthropology, namely, based on the Kabbalistic *creatio in Deo*. What in effect replaces the theological *creatio ex nihilo* is precisely the aforesaid "severance of *Malkhuth*," which brings into being what we take to

11. Phil. 2:9, 10.
12. Acts 4:12.
13. This is what stands at issue when one speaks of the so-called "Exile of the Shekhinah."

be the world. Moreover, since there is in truth no "second creation," but only a severance from the first, it follows that the resultant "world" cannot be distinct in essence from its Sefirothic predecessor or counterpart. Redemption may therefore be conceived in principle as a *cognitive* ascent into the Sefirothic realm, that is to say, an ascent culminating in gnosis: a gnosis that takes the knower "above the sphere of creation," as Clement of Alexandria declares. Pico refers to this cognitive ascent—in terms at once Platonist and Kabbalistic—when he writes (in I.44):

> If the soul grasps that which she is capable of grasping, and unites herself thus with the superior soul, she casts off her terrestrial robe, so that she becomes thereby severed from her earthly ambience and united with God.

The superior soul, of which Pico speaks, is what the Kabbalah knows as *Neshamah,* and conceives as being "substantially the same as God."[14] This soul is thus in reality never separated from God, that is to say, from the Sefirothic world. To be "united with" that "superior soul" is therefore to "enter" the plenary realm of the Sefirothic septenary, which in fact may be identified with Paradise; for as Pico himself explains (in I.10): "It is more correct to say that Paradise is the entire edifice, and not only the tenth [*Sefirah*]." And let us not fail to note, with regard to this "edifice," that in its center "there resides the great Adam, who is *Tifereth*," as Pico goes on to say. Such, then, is the Kabbalistic conception of Redemption and of Paradise, which the Count has made his own.

It is apparent that Pico speaks of the spiritual ascent in initiatic terms: for example, when he distinguishes (in II.11) between the separation of the body from the soul which takes place in ordinary death, and a so-called separation of the soul from the body—constituting what has sometimes been called "death by a kiss"—which consummates the spiritual quest. The latter is something very different from ordinary death; and as one reads in a Jewish text: "Precious in the eyes of the Lord is the death of his saints." I

---

14. Gerschom Scholem, *Major Trends of Jewish Mysticism* (New York: Schocken Books, 1954), p241.

will note, parenthetically, that this explains the Hindu practice of preserving the body of an enlightened Master: for a sage who has entered into *mahāsamādhi* is not *ipso facto* separated from his or her earthly remains, and may employ that erstwhile body as a vehicle of spiritual influence. The subject of death "by a kiss" is brought up again in II.13, where Pico observes that those who "operate in Kabbalah" over a long period of time, without recourse to "that which is strange," will attain this coveted end, whereas those Kabbalists who fall into error, or who engage in this work without the requisite purification, will be "devoured by the fire of Azazel, on account of the rigor of judgment."

But whereas Pico's conception of the spiritual ascent is evidently both Platonist and Kabbalistic, it is also Christian, by virtue of the fact that he identifies the Eschaton with Jesus Christ, the Incarnate Son of God: it is in him and through him that we are to be united with God. That Redemption, however, is destined to include the cosmos in its entirety: this is what the Kabbalah knows as the Great Jubilee, and what St. Peter refers to as *apocatastasis*, "the restitution of all things."[15] Pico conceives of it Kabbalistically as the perfect union of the *Yod* and the *Vav* realized in Jesus Christ.

One more point needs to be considered: Pico has not only given a Kabbalistic interpretation of Christian tenets, but has applied Kabbalistic principles to the exegesis of New Testament texts. Consider John 8.56, for example, the verse which quotes Jesus as saying: "Your father Abraham rejoiced to see my day; and he saw it, and was glad." Pico gives us the requisite key in II.37, where he speaks of a "subordination of Piety to Wisdom on the right." As Wirszubski points out, the Kabbalah associates Abraham with *Hesed*, the fourth *Sefirah*, which Pico designates by the term *Pietas*.[16] If now we call to mind the customary representation of the Sefirothic Tree, one sees that *Hesed* is situated directly below *Hokhmah* ("Wisdom") *on the right*. All that is yet needed to "decode" what Pico writes is to recall that the *Sefiroth* are also referred to as "days." It then becomes clear that "the day of Christ" can be none other than *Hokhmah*, the Wis-

15. Acts 3:21.
16. Op. cit., pp174–76.

dom of God, which moreover explains why Abraham, "in his day," saw "the day of Christ," as Pico says, *"per rectam lineam"* ("along a straight line"): it is evidently the very line connecting *Hesed* to *Hokhmah* in the Kabbalistic diagram to which we have referred! Now, this reading of John 8:56, which Pico was apparently the first to propose, far exceeds in depth the exegesis of even St. Irenaeus and Origen, who perceived the text as referring to a premonition, on the part of Abraham, concerning the future Messiah. It would be hard to overstate the significance of this breakthrough: for it demonstrates that there are levels of meaning in the New Testament as well which prove to be accessible only by way of Kabbalistic means. Christian Kabbalah, as Pico conceived of it, so far from being a "marginal" discipline, proves thus to be of primary interest: it is here, quite possibly, that the veritable "key of gnosis" is to be found.

The movement initiated by Pico de la Mirandola spread almost immediately to France, Germany and England. Following the untimely death of Pico—at the age of 31!—his mantle fell on Johann Reuchlin (1455–1522), a Swabian disciple of the Count, who rose to become the leading Christian Kabbalist as well as the most distinguished Christian Hebraist of his time. He too is imbued with the ideal of *"prisca theologia"* emanating from the Florentine Academy, and like his predecessor, regards Hebrew as the primordial tongue, in essence the Language by means of which God created the world. But his thought is more orderly, more systematic and rigorous than that of the meteoric genius who opened his eyes to the splendors of the Kabbalah: where Pico gives us inspired fragments, the Swabian expounds a doctrine, a science in fact. Reuchlin is moreover endowed with a deep and abiding interest in the Pythagorean tradition, which he takes to be of Kabbalistic origin. He has no doubt that the "numbers" to which, according to Pythagorean lore, the things in creation are reducible, are none other than the *Sefiroth*.[17] In line with this belief, he associates the Pythagorean tetractys not

17. As noted in the preceding chapter, the word derives from *safar*, "to count."

only with the ten *Sefiroth*, but also with the Tetragrammaton, the Name said to embody the mystery of their origin.

Reuchlin's major work, *De arte cabalistica* (1517), takes the form of a dialogue, a genre much used in those days, perhaps partly to protect the author against the dreaded charge of heresy. The colloquy has a cast of three characters: Philolaus, a Pythagorean; Marranus, a Muslim; and Simon, a Jewish Kabbalist, who evidently speaks for Reuchlin himself. The discourse is amiable, and as we would say nowadays, "ecumenical" in the extreme. The positions assumed by the disputants blend, and seem to merge on the exalted plane of Kabbalistic wisdom. Philolaus begins the discourse by expounding the symbolism of the Pythagorean doctrine, which he declares to be based upon "number," and Murranus closes the discussion of the first day in the words: "Out of the infinite sea of the Kabbalah, Pythagoras brought his river into the bounds of the Grecian fields."[18]

What strikes one the most in Reuchlin's thought is that, in the end, everything becomes reduced, somehow, to a Divine Name, and that all Divine Names reduce in principle to the Tetragrammaton, conceived as representing the Essence of God. The *Sefiroth*, too, come thus to be viewed as Names: "They are the ten Divine Names we mortals conceive of God" we are told. And since they are also "numerations," or "numbers," if you will, this means that these "numbers" are themselves Divine Names. It is presumably this transcendent identity of "numbers" and "names" which underlies the very concrete association between actual integers and the letters of the Hebrew alphabet, or the Hebrew words comprised thereof, and which moreover permits the Kabbalist to identify one Divine Name with another having the same numerical value.

Reuchlin's *magnum opus* is well titled: for it deals precisely with the Kabbalistic "art," which however can equally well be described as a "science." The objective of this art, or science, is ostensibly to derive the Names of God—the multiplicity of which is beyond reckoning— from the one supreme and "ineffable" Name, which is the Tetragrammaton. And because we mortals are able to conceive of this Name only by way of its four component letters, these derivations

18. Joseph Blau, op. cit., pp 49–59.

require an inherently *algebraic* procedure, involving letters and their numerical values. One is reminded of the mathematical physics practiced in our day, which likewise operates with symbols that admit of interpretation only at the end of a calculation, in the predicted value of an observable. What in Kabbalah corresponds to these observables are the "utterable" Names of God, which take the form of a Hebrew word found in the Torah. As concerns the Kabbalistic calculus, suffice it to say that there are three basic operations, namely Gematria, which consists of replacing a word by another having the same numerical value; Notarikon, which proceeds from the letters of a word to a group of words, in which the letters of the first appear as the first letters of the successive words, or which operates in the reverse direction, by collapsing each word in a group into its first letter; and finally, Themura, which operates through the permutation of letters according to certain rules. By means of these operations, which are indeed "algebraic," the Kabbalist is enabled, in principle, to make his way up or down the arborescent progression of divine Names; as Paul Ricci (another sixteenth-century Christian Kabbalist) states explicitly: "All the other Names insert into the Tetragrammaton even as the branches and leaves of a tree insert into the trunk."[19]

The Kabbalistic art may thus be viewed as a means of uncovering the occult unity beneath the formal diversity of manifestation, as given in the "effable" Names of God. That unity, however, is not itself "effable," but pertains to the Divine Essence, which, *qua* creature, we cannot know. Now, for the Kabbalist—and most assuredly, for Reuchlin—that unity is represented by the Tetragrammaton, upon which his "art" is based. The Tetragrammaton is thus, for the Kabbalist, what an axiom system is for the mathematician: there is, in Kabbalah, no probing into the Tetragrammaton, no "getting behind" that most basic of Names, even as there is, for the mathematician, no probing into his axioms. This is where the ("pure") mathematician is obliged to start, and this is also where perforce he ends: for the theorems he labors to discover are all, in a way, contained beforehand in that foundation. So it is, logically speaking, for the rigorous

19. See Geneviève Javary, "A propos du thème de la Sekina: variations sur le nom de Dieu," in *Kabbalistes Chrétiens,* op. cit., p 290.

Kabbalist, for whom there is nothing prior to the Tetragrammaton, and nothing which is not, in a sense, contained therein.

It appears that Reuchlin "situates" the Tetragrammaton on the supreme level of *En-Sof*, the Unknown God as he is "before" manifesting himself in Creation, which for the Swabian Kabbalist is none other than the eternal "world" comprised of the "effable" Names of God, what the Kabbalah knows as *Atsiluth*, "the world of emanation." This leaves a total of three conceptual domains: the Absolute Godhead, comprising the "ineffable" Tetragrammaton; *Atsiluth*, the eternal world *in Deo*, represented by the "effable" Names of God; and lastly, the realm of what Reuchlin sometimes terms "the things that are not," which in fact includes all that we normally conceive as comprising the created universe. It goes without saying that the Swabian Kabbalist does not attribute that universe to a *creatio ex nihilo*, since from his point of view this so-called universe does not in fact exist; in a word, Reuchlin is a nondualist.

This brings us to the great question how the Unknown God, the *En-Sof* of the Kabbalah, is related to the Christian Trinity, a question to which Reuchlin responds, through the mouth of Simon, in words ostensibly addressed to Christians:

> It is, in effect, written in the book *Bahir*: there is no principle besides Wisdom. To which it seems well to reply by saying that the Infinitude of the three highest numerations, which you are wont to call the three Divine Persons, is the Absolute Essence, since it is hidden in the abyss of darkness.... Likewise one calls it Nothing, or Non-Being and Without End, that is to say, *En-Sof*, because we, who are smitten with such feebleness of intelligence in regard to divine realities, do not judge of realities which do not manifest otherwise than of those that do not exist. But when they present themselves as something that really exists, then the *Aleph* that is dark is changed into the *Aleph* that is luminous.[20]

20. The passage is quoted by Geneviève Javary in her excellent article (op. cit., p291), based on the French translation of *De arte cabalistica* by François Secret (*La Kabbale*, Paris, Aubier-Montaigne, 1973).

In the first place, "there is no principle besides Wisdom": that is to say, besides *Hokhmah*, the second *Sefirah*. This is indeed the "trunk" or "root" from which "the branches and leaves" of the Sefirothic Tree take their rise; as the Psalmist declares: "In wisdom hast thou made them all." But for us, "feeble" as we are, that "root" itself remains concealed. For us manifestation begins with the Sefirothic septenary, that is to say, with the *Elohim*, the Seven Days. The supreme Sefirothic tri-unity, therefore, stands for us on the side of the Unknown God, the Absolute Essence "hidden in the abyss of darkness." The crucial point, now, is this: Reuchlin does evidently identify the first three *Sefiroth* with the corresponding Persons of the Trinity, conceived however, not as "Three out of One," as Joseph Blau assumes, but indeed as "Three *in* One," as Christian theology insists. As Reuchlin tells us, the Divine Persons stand on the side of the Unknown God. The Three are consequently "*in* One," because they have not come "*out of* One": have not emerged from the Absolute Essence. The point, let us note, is as subtle as it is decisive: for indeed, the mystery of Christianity hangs on that point.

It is however to be noted that Simon tells us more: having identified the Three with the Divine Essence, he goes on to say: "But when they present themselves as something that really subsists, then the *Aleph* that is dark is changed into the *Aleph* that is luminous." What exactly does this mean? There can be no doubt, in the present context, that the *Aleph* of which Simon speaks is none other than *Hokhmah*, the Wisdom of God, besides which "there is no principle."[21] Given that *Hokhmah* has been identified with the Second Person of the Trinity, one sees that "the *Aleph* that is dark" can only be Christ, the Son of God, as he is "in the Father." The "*Aleph* that is luminous" must therefore be the Incarnate Christ. Having given a Kabbalistic interpretation of the Trinity, Simon thus goes on to interpret the second Christian mystery: that of the Incarnation. What stands at issue, however, is primarily a "Sefirothic" Incarnation, one that "precedes" the human birth of Jesus, and differs profoundly from the "historical" upon which the theologian has his eye. Yet despite

21. It is true that the letter *Aleph* can also be associated with the Tetragrammaton and with *Kether Elyon*, depending on the context.

this fundamental discrepancy, the Christian Kabbalist is able to understand and interpret, from his own point of view, all that theology teaches concerning the Incarnation, "historical" though it be. Getting back to Simon, "the *Aleph* that is luminous" refers thus to the "Sefirothic" Christ, the Son of God manifesting in infinite splendor: in the very Light of which Peter, James, and John caught a glimpse on Mount Tabor. And it is of interest to note that the Orthodox consider that Light to be "uncreated," which in fact it is: for that Light pertains to the Sefirothic world, the eternal *creatio ex Deo* as opposed to the temporal *creatio ex nihilo*. Anticipating Jacob Boehme, one can say that this Light constitutes the "precious Substance" out of which the Body of the Incarnate Christ is composed.

The question presents itself: if the Tetragrammaton stands for the Unknown God, or for the "*Aleph* that is dark," what Name designates "the *Aleph* that is luminous"? Reuchlin answers, as every Christian would, that it is the holy name "Jesus." But now two further questions arise: what is the Hebrew orthography of that Name? and how can it be derived Kabbalistically from the Tetragrammaton? Reuchlin responds by taking the name "Jesus" to be the Tetragrammaton with the letter *Shin* inserted between the YH and the VH. The Tetragrammaton is thus transformed into the Pentagrammaton YHSVH, an "effable" name that has come down to us as "Jesus." We need not concern ourselves with Reuchlin's Kabbalistic derivation of that Name; suffice it to say that the Tetragrammaton turns into the Name of the Incarnate Christ by way of the letter *Shin*.[22]

Let us recall, at this point, that Pico de la Mirandola conceives of these matters somewhat differently. In the first place, as we have seen, he associates the Tetragrammaton, not with the Unknown God, or with the Trinity, as Reuchlin does, but with the Son, now identified with *Tifereth*, the sixth *Sefirah*, representing *Adam Kadmon*, or Universal Man. Pico also employs a different orthography for the name "Jesus," which he takes to be YSV. One needs, however, to understand that this is not a matter of "right or wrong," but a question of standpoint. One can say that Reuchlin has his eye primarily upon

---

22. The letter *Shin* itself can be associated Kabbalistically with "fire" and thus with the Holy Spirit.

the emergence of the Sefirothic Incarnation, as represented by *Tifereth*, of which the Trinity is the principle, whereas Pico is chiefly concerned with the historical Incarnation, of which *Tifereth* is the prototype. If one measures the depth of a Kabbalistic doctrine by the level at which the Tetragrammaton is conceived, then Reuchlin's outlook is the deeper of the two; one might say that Pico "starts" where Reuchlin "ends." Essentially the same consideration, moreover, accounts for the difference between the two spellings of the name "Jesus": why that Name takes the form YHSVH when conceived as emerging out of the "ineffable" Tetragrammaton ("the *Aleph* that is dark"), but takes the form YSV when conceived as emanating from the Sefirothic septenary ("the *Aleph* that is luminous"), whose Kabbalistic designation is indeed SV, meaning "heaven and earth." It is also to be noted that the respective positions entail different conceptions of ineffability: for Reuchlin, the Tetragrammaton is "ineffable" because it represents God "before" his manifestation on the plane of the Sefirothic septenary, whereas for Pico it is "ineffable" so long as Heaven and Earth have not been united by the Messiah, a union which is to be realized fully at the Second Coming of Christ.

A few words, finally, concerning the reception of Reuchlin's thought. So far as Christian Kabbalists are concerned, his influence has been profound, and can be traced well into the eighteenth century;[23] on the other hand, it appears that the guardians of the Church were not equally pleased. The Dominicans of Cologne, in particular, took pains to persecute the Swabian Kabbalist, going so far as to order the destruction of his books. This explains presumably why the *De arte cabalistica* is prefaced by a dedication to Pope Leo X, a Medici with a more liberal outlook than was typical in those days, in which Reuchlin does in fact allude to "the Battle of

---

23. Reuchlin's influence is apparent in the case of the previously mentioned Princess, named Anatonia (1613–1679). Evidently an ardent Kabbalist, she is known chiefly on account of a remarkable plaque she ordered to be installed in a small church in Würtenburg. Now famous as the *Lehrtafel* or Master Tablet of the Princess Anatonia, it contains an elaborate symbolization of Kabbalistic doctrine. The impact of Reuchlin's thought is yet discernible in the Christian Kabbalist and "Boehme friend," Friedrich Christoph Oetinger (1702–1782), about whom we shall have more to tell.

the Books," in what is evidently a plea for papal protection against his Dominican antagonists. It is of interest to note that unlike the confrères and disciples of Aquinas, the Franciscans of the Renaissance seem not to have been hostile to Christian Kabbalah; and as a matter of fact, beginning with the aforementioned Arnold of Villanova, the Order itself has contributed an impressive array of Christian Kabbalists, the best known of which are Archangelus of Borgo Nuovo and Jean Thenaud. It is tempting to wonder how the Church might have fared if the authority of the Dominicans, and later of the Jesuits, had been tempered by a milder Franciscan influence.

We turn now to Egidio di Viterbo (1465–1532), a Cardinal and Superior General of the Augustinians, who ranks among the greatest Christian Kabbalists of all time. A man of many parts, ranging from papal confidant and emissary to preacher and shepherd of souls, Egidio was also an eminent scholar and linguist, having acquired proficiency in Hebrew, Aramaic, and Arabic. It is known that he assembled an outstanding collection of rare books and manuscripts, a remnant of which is now housed at the National Library in Paris; and one knows also that the Cardinal himself translated into Latin a number of major Kabbalistic texts, and employed a sizable staff, comprised mainly of Jewish converts, to produce an entire Kabbalistic library in translation. A great admirer of Johann Reuchlin, he too looks upon Hebrew as the *Ursprache*, the primordial tongue, and regards Kabbalah as the God-given means to uncover the secrets encrypted in the Mosaic text. He moreover declares this sacred science to be "not foreign, but domestic," meaning thereby that the Kabbalah pertains by right to Christianity as well. The Cardinal seems to imply that "on the level of Kabbalah" the two traditions merge, that in essence they are one. A man of distinctly lyrical cast and devotional temperament, Egidio di Viterbo brings to his Christian Kabbalah a poetic beauty and human warmth not to be found in the austere speculations of his Swabian predecessor; if Reuchlin represents the jnanic side of the movement, the Italian Cardinal personifies its bhaktic complement. So too, his "focus" is different: whereas Reuchlin's mystical inquiries were centered upon the Tetragrammaton, the unspeakable Name of the Unknown God, Egidio appears to have his heart set upon the *Shekhinah*: upon Her "whose delights were with the sons of men."[24]

We recall that the *Shekhinah* constitutes, formally speaking, the tenth and last *Sefirah*, also known as *Malkhuth* ("Kingdom"), envisaged as the feminine and indeed maternal aspect of God. The term itself traces back no further than to the first century AD, and derives apparently from the Hebrew root SKN, which means "to reside." It refers, then, to God conceived as "residing" in Creation, and connotes the fullness and splendor of the *manifested* Deity. But whereas, in reality, the *Shekhinah* resides in the divine or Sefirothic world, in what the *Zohar* terms the *alma de-yihuda* or "world of union," Judaic tradition speaks of Her "exile," that is to say, as residing here below, in the world of fallen humanity. She is thus Emmanuel, "God with us." Now, it is to Her that Egidio devotes his *magnum opus*, a voluminous work entitled simply "*Scechina*," which is clearly a labor of love, completed two years before his death.[25] The Cardinal beholds the *Shekhinah* in virtually all the divine manifestations recorded in Scripture, from the Burning Bush and Ark of the Covenant to the theophanies of the New Dispensation and the Celestial Jerusalem. These perceptions, moreover, affect him deeply, and inspire an abundance of literary allusions; as Jacques Fabry has expressed it: "The work of Egidio di Viterbo is traversed by a stream of images and symbols drawn from the Kabbalistic literature as well as from the Greek and Latin poets and the Neo-Platonist philosophers."[26]

It is of prime importance to note that the Cardinal perceives the *Shekhinah* as the plenary manifestation of *Bina*, the third *Sefirah*, whom Christian Kabbalists identify, in a way, with the Third Person

24. Prov. 8:31.
25. The work was published by Françoise Secret, along with Egidio di Viterbo's *Libellus de Litteris hebraicis* (Rome: Centro Internazionale di Studi Unamistici, 1959).
26. "La Kabbale chrétienne en Italie au XVIe siècles," in *Kabbalistes Chrétiens*, op. cit., p59.

of the Trinity.[27] It is likewise crucial to observe that he associates *Bina* with the Hebrew letter *He*—depicted by a horizontal stroke, followed on the right by a vertical, and on the left by a small vertical mark—a fact which he proceeds to interpret in words attributed to the *Shekhinah* herself:

> The point adjoined to it [the letter *He*] represents me, who am She that is submissive to Her [*Bina*] as to a mother, and who am submissive to the other *Sefiroth* as to brothers. A proof of this is what is written concerning the Messiah: "and he was subject unto them."[28]

The passage is clearly of major interest, first of all, because in it the *Shekhinah* identifies Herself with the Messiah. What is however of equal significance are the words relating to the letter *He*, which evidently connect with the mystery of the Tetragrammaton: for the latter consists of three letters, one of which—namely *He*—occurs twice. Could it be that the alphabetical triad (Y,V,H) represents the Persons of the Trinity, whereas "the second *He*" stands for the *Shekhinah*, who in a sense "completes" the Trinity? It appears that the Cardinal does uphold this view: "Even though there is no Fourth Person," he writes, "if you understand things correctly, it is necessary ... to suppose that in a way there is."[29] To "understand things correctly" means evidently to perceive the matter from an esoteric—that is to say, a Kabbalistic—point of view. One then sees that the Tetragrammaton holds the key to both mysteries of Christianity: that of the Trinity and that of the Incarnation, which according to the Cardinal is indeed the mystery of the *Shekhinah*. Who, then, *is* the *Shekhinah*? Is She perhaps a Fourth Person? Not exactly, Egidio goes on to explain: She is a "blessed nature" which "neither engenders nor is engendered," but embodies and makes its own something that "has not been given to the Three, but which they

27. According to the Kabbalah, it is *Bina* who gives birth to the Sefirothic septenary, which thus corresponds to what theology conceives as the Seven Gifts of the Holy Spirit. See Stratford Caldecott, *The Seven Sacraments* (New York: Crossroads, 2006), chap. 6.
28. Fol. 328 in the 1959 edition, cited above. The reference here is to Luke 2:51.
29. Op. cit., Fol. 328.

possess in common...." The Cardinal is manifestly straining to express in terms of human conceptions a truth which is perhaps inherently inexpressible: it may not be possible, in the final count, to "de-symbolize" the Tetragrammaton, to formulate what it signifies in conceptual or theologically explicit terms. What is however beyond doubt, for those who "understand things correctly," is that the Tetragrammaton bears witness to the fundamental truths of Christianity: to the Trinity by its alphabetical triad, and to the Incarnation by virtue of "the second *He*."[30]

What stands at issue in this "splitting of the *He*" is a separation, or seeming separation, of *Bina* and *Shekhinah*: the transcendent and the immanent Mother of all. And let us note that this "separation" appears to repeat itself, on the level of the *Shekhinah*, in the split between the Sefirothic and the cosmic realms—the eternal and the temporal worlds—and that the *Shekhinah* resides in both: in the former as in Her native domain, and here below as "in exile." In conformity with these respective divisions, the Cardinal distinguishes (as Reuchlin had done before him) between the transcendent "world" of *Bina*, the eternal world of the *Shekhinah*, and the temporal world; but he does so from a different point of view, which one might characterize as "theological." Here is what he makes the *Shekhinah* say:

But *Bina* represents the incorporeal world, I the corporeal; She the immortal world, I the mortal world; She the world that was, I the world that is to come. That is why She is the mother of all, and I, as the Apostle says, am yours.[31]

The "world" associated with *Bina* is indeed "incorporeal" and "immortal": the former, because it is unmanifest, and the latter, because it is above time, and above even what the Scholastics term aeviternity. It is the "world" in which nothing "other than" the Holy Trinity exists. But then, what is the "world" the *Shekhinah* claims as

30. It is significant and indeed fascinating that this "splitting of the *He*" is depicted in the very form of the Hebrew character, wherein "the point"—as the Cardinal keenly observes—refers to the *Shekhinah*.
31. Op. cit., Fol. 328.

Her own: is it the *Sefirothic*, or is it *our* world? The first adjective, "corporeal," could be interpreted in either sense;[32] but the second can not: mortality pertains to this nether world alone. It is therefore apparent that the Cardinal conceives of the *Shekhinah* as now residing with us here below. Yet he does also envisage the Sefirothic world; but in keeping with the theological point of view, he conceives of it as "the world to come." And that "world to come" the *Shekhinah* likewise claims as Her own. Similarly, he conceives of the transcendent "world" as "the world that was," since it is the source of all that exists; and that is why *Bina* is "the mother of all," as he makes the *Shekhinah* say. Only one thing remains yet to be explained: why does She add "and I, as the Apostle says, am yours."

The explanation is simple: the *Shekhinah* is "our" mother, because it is She who brings us into "the world to come" by our "second birth," which is the birth of Christ in us. And this is the birth of which St. Paul speaks in the passage to which the *Shekhinah* alludes, a discourse that begins with the words: "My little children, of whom I travail in birth again until Christ be formed in you."[33] As every Kabbalist understands full well, the Apostle is here speaking as the *Shekhinah* Herself. Moreover, in terms which could almost be called Kabbalistic, he goes on to distinguish between two "mothers" and two "births": there is Agar, the "bondwoman," who gives birth "after the flesh," and there is the "freewoman," who gives birth "after the spirit." The Apostle goes so far as to liken the latter to "Jerusalem which is above," of which he declares that it is "the mother of us all": a more unequivocal reference to the *Shekhinah* as "our mother" could hardly be conceived!

Having duly considered how the *Shekhinah* is related to *Bina*, it remains to consider Her relation with *Tifereth*, which is of a different kind. To begin with, let us recall that the Sefirothic septenary is

32. On this question I refer to *Ancient Wisdom and Modern Misconceptions* op. cit., the chapter on "Celestial Corporeality."
33. Gal. 4:19.

conceived to consist of six "masculine" plus one "feminine" *Sefiroth*, the latter being the *Shekhinah*. It is moreover traditional to regard *Tifereth*—the third in the septenary—as the "heart" and mystical center of the six, which in effect reduces the septenary to the couple *Tifereth-Shekhinah*. This Divine Couple consequently manifests, on the plane of the eternal Creation, the transcendent bi-unity of *Hokhmah-Bina*; and as the Kabbalah has always recognized, it is from that utterly transcendent bi-unity that all worlds, all bliss, and all blessedness are ultimately derived. The supreme Eros, then, which resides in *Hokhmah-Bina*, is manifested on the Sefirothic plane in the relation of *Tifereth* to *Shekhinah*, which is, mystically speaking, that of Bridegroom to Bride; and that is why, in the Cardinal's treatise, the *Shekhinah* refers to *Tifereth* as "my spouse." Like *Hokhmah* and *Bina*, *Tiefereth* and *Shekhihnah* are likewise conjoined; they too comprise a bi-unity.

To the eye of a Christian Kabbalist, not only the Torah, but the New Testament as well, is replete with allusions to that bi-unity or non-separation of *Tifereth* and *Shekhinah*, beginning with the words of St. John in his Prologue: "and the Word was made flesh, *and dwelt among us.*" For whereas the Evangelist, by the first affirmation, identifies Jesus with the Word, and therefore with *Tifereth*, who personifies the Word on the plane of eternal manifestation, he identifies him, by the second, with the *Shekhinah*: the Word that was "in the beginning," that was "with God" and "was God," has become the God who "dwells among us." Admittedly, however, passages in the New Testament which identify Jesus with the *Shekhinah* seem to be few compared to those that identify him as the Son of God, and the ones that do are discernable chiefly to the Kabbalist. Consider, for example, the words of Jesus himself, when he says: "Take my yoke upon you, and learn from me; for I am meek and lowly in heart, and ye shall find rest unto your souls."[34] To those who "have ears to hear," almost every second word in this text speaks of the *Shekhinah*: it is She who is "meek and lowly in heart," who is "submissive"; and it is in Her that the meek and lowly "shall find rest unto their souls." Even the words "my yoke" evoke Her, since the expression "the yoke of the

34. Matt. 11:29.

Shekhinah" is a byword in the Judaic world. So too all Christian Kabbalists, as Geneviève Javry points out,[35] have perceived a reference to the Shekhinah in Matthew 23:37, where Jesus cries out: "O Jerusalem, Jerusalem! . . . how often would I have gathered thy children together, even as a hen gathers her chicks under her wings!" For again, "under the wings of the Shekhinah" is a common expression among the Jews. We find in Jesus a perfect balance of masculine and feminine virtues: he is the King who rules, and yet is "meek and lowly in heart," who commands, and is yet "submissive" to all, the Judge of kings and the Friend of sinners. Wise men perceive him as the Divine Androgyne, "in whom dwelleth all the fullness of the Godhead bodily"; but though, in a way, Jesus embodies both Tifereth and Shekhinah, he nonetheless personifies the Word that "was in the beginning," the Word that is God.

But, if Jesus is the Word of God, who then is the Shekhinah? The answer is clear: She is his Bride. And therefore, when theologians speak of the Church as "the Bride of Christ," they are actually speaking in Kabbalistic terms. Yet what, for the theologian, is a kind of sacred metaphor, is for the Kabbalist a fact on the Sefirothic plane: here "poetry" becomes "science," if you will. For the Kabbalist, the Church is the Bride of Christ, because the Church is the Shekhinah: all sacredness, here below, derives from Her presence, from Her "indwelling." It is She that founds every sacred rite and bestows every sacrament: the sacramental order rests in Her. It can indeed be said: where Christ is, there is the Shekhinah, and where She is, there is the Church.

Such is the vision of Christianity—the Christian Kabbalah— bequeathed to posterity by Egidio di Viterbo in his magnum opus; and let us note that the doctrine could evidently not have passed muster before the Roman authorities. This explains why that treatise—which was written at the request of Pope Clement VIII, to whom it is dedicated—was left unpublished: one might say that the teachings of the Cardinal, as set forth in his Scechina, are inherently "esoteric" in relation to the official theology, to which they stand somewhat as the Kabbalah itself stands to mainstream Judaism.

35. Op. cit., p 300.

5

THE GNOSIS
OF JACOB BOEHME

WHEN the young F.C.Oetinger (1702–1782) approached the renowned Kabbalist Koppel Hecht for guidance, the latter referred him to a Christian author who, according to Hecht, spoke of the Kabbalistic secrets "more openly than the *Zohar.*"[1] And thus began a life-long dedication, on the part of Oetinger, to the teachings of Jacob Boehme (1575–1624).

It is doubtful that Boehme ever read a single Kabbalistic text. His chief literary source, to be sure, was the Bible in Luther's translation. He did also take an interest in certain German authors, notably the Hermeticist Valentin Weigel (1533–1588), with whom he disagreed on various issues, and the great Paracelsus (1493–1541), who taught him much about alchemy, and from whom he derived some of his terminology. One knows that, in addition to the printed word, Boehme had access to the learning of his friends, some of whom were well traveled and erudite. One of these, Dr. Balthasar Walther, for instance, had sojourned six years in Arabia, Syria, and Egypt, and was conversant with writings in Latin, Greek, and Hebrew. But while Boehme himself apparently knew no language besides his native German, he possessed a remarkable receptivity to the spoken word, which enabled him at times to respond with understanding to languages he did not know. One day, for example, when someone spoke the Greek word "*Idea,*" he was filled with joy,

---

1. Gershom Scholem, *Major Trends in Jewish Mysticism* (New York: Schocken, 1946), pp237–8.

and said that this word awakened in him the image of a graceful, pure, and celestial virgin.[2]

One of the earliest recorded incidents took place when he was yet a cobbler's apprentice in the small town of Görlitz. One day, when the boy was alone in the shop, a stranger, dignified and well dressed, came in to buy a pair of shoes. After he had left, he stopped, turned back, and called in a loud voice: "Jacob, come out!" The boy was surprised that the stranger knew his name; and when he came out, the man took his right hand in his own, looked deep into his eyes, and spoke to him. "Jacob, you are small," he said, "but you will become so great that the world will be astonished over you." After enjoining young Jacob to remain ever pious, to fear God and honor His Word, and not to be dismayed by adversity, the stranger went his way. One catches here a glimpse of what might be termed the "Friends of God," a scattered community not set up by human convention, of which the world, inclusive of its visible religious institutions, knows nothing at all.

Not long after this incident, Boehme left Görlitz to become a wandering apprentice, as was the custom in those days. It was a time of great religious ferment, especially in the German lands. Everywhere debates were raging between Catholics and Protestants, or Lutherans and Calvinists, which as these things go, tended to generate more heat than enlightenment. One knows that this ongoing religious strife troubled the young Boehme deeply. It was in that early period of his life, while yet residing as an apprentice at the house of a master cobbler, that he had a mystical experience, which appears to have lifted him far above the din of these conflicts: for seven days, as he later confided to a friend, he was "enveloped in a celestial light."

In due time Boehme returned to Görlitz, became a master cobbler himself, and in the same year (1594) took a wife, with whom he lived the remaining thirty years of his earthly sojourn. The couple had four sons, who likewise took to the cobbler trade. While thus living a normal life, Boehme had a second mystical experience. It took place in his twenty-fifth year, on the threshold of the seven-

2. Julius Hamberger, *Die Lehre des Deutschen Philosophen Jakob Boehme* (München, 1844), p xvii.

teenth century, and lasted about fifteen minutes. As Boehme relates in his first book, the *Aurora*:

> Forthwith, after many hard storms, my spirit broke through the Gates of Hell to the innermost birth of God, and was there received with love, as a bridegroom embraces his bride. But what exulting in spirit took place then, I cannot write or say; it also cannot be compared with anything but this, where, in the midst of death, life is born, and is comparable to the Resurrection from the Dead. In this Light my spirit forthwith saw through all things, and in all creatures, even in weeds and grass, recognized God: who he is, and how he is, and what be his will.[3]

The event was followed by a period of gestation, lasting some ten years, during which the Seer apparently gave little if any indication as to what was happening in his soul. He continued to live a normal and seemingly ordinary life as a tradesman and head of a family. Another great revelation, however, came to him in the year 1610. Again his spirit broke through "to the innermost birth of God," and again he perceived the entire universe, with all its creatures, as a theophany, a divine self-revelation. But this time the vision was apparently more explicit, more "structured" as it were, and there arose in him a desire to write, to share the revelation which had now in a way become his own.

Yet it seems that his first book, completed in 1612, was not intended for publication: like Egidio di Viterbo a century before, Boehme was apparently satisfied to share his treatise with a few intimate friends. A copy, however, fell into the hands of Gregorius Richter, the presiding Lutheran minister at Görlitz, who lost no time to denounce its author and send Boehme into exile. He was permitted to return on condition of withdrawing his book and writing no more. Only after six years did he begin to write again, prompted by his friends, some of whom were influential enough to offer protection against his adversaries. With the help of well-to-do patrons Boehme could now retire from his trade and devote himself

---

3. *Aurora*, 19.11–13. I shall use the Latin titles of Boehme's works, as given in the Gichtel edition, published in 1715.

full-time to his literary apostolate. Thus he was able, in the remaining six years of his life, to produce some twenty major treatises, not counting his minor writings, an output which is formidable even in point of sheer volume. He departed from this world peacefully, in the fiftieth year of his life, with the words: "*Nun fahre ich hin ins Paradies!*" ("Now I go forth into Paradise").

The primary distinction upon which Boehme founds his thought relates to the conception of the Unknown God, the *En-Sof* of the Kabbalah, which Boehme terms *Ungrund*: all else, beginning with God himself, is *manifestation*, and can only be conceived as a theophany of the *Ungrund* itself. The Absolute comes thus to be viewed as the "hidden treasure" that "desires to be known,"[4] a premise which defines the theosophic point of view. Boehme's doctrine, thus, like the Kabbalah, constitutes a theosophy. Yet, though Boehme may speak of Kabbalistic secrets "more openly than the *Zohar*," he does so from a point of view distinctly his own; and even though the respective doctrines are profoundly concordant, one must take care not to confound the two. Both are focused upon the Work of Creation culminating in the eternal world, at the center of which God himself stands revealed; but where the Kabbalah speaks of a Sefirothic septenary, Boehme envisions a seven-part cycle which, as we shall see, is not quite the same thing.

One may find it surprising that he speaks of that "seven-part cycle" in temporal terms, as if it were indeed a transformative process, consisting of seven distinct and successive parts. Yet how else can one speak of it? As Boehme explains in the *Aurora*:

> If I am to render the Birth of God out of himself comprehensible to you, I must indeed speak in a devilish manner, as if the eternal Light had been ignited out of the Darkness, as if God had a beginning; otherwise I cannot teach you, so that you will understand.[5]

4. These words are taken from a celebrated *hadith*.
5. Ibid., 23:18.

Elsewhere, however, he tells us that God gives birth to himself in eternity, where "the First is also the Last, and the Last is again the First," which is almost verbatim what the *Sefer Yetsirah* tells of the *Sefiroth*, when it says that "their end is in their beginning, and their beginning is in their end."[6] In conformity with this principle, Boehme maintains that the term of the seven-part cycle contains the preceding six phases; as Pierre Deghaye observes: "The seventh degree reunites the totality of the emanation. At this stage, the degrees no longer succeed each other, but are simultaneous."[7] This obviously does not mean that the degrees were at first successive, and became simultaneous at the end; what has changed is simply the perspective in which the cycle is viewed. Boehme begins his description from a temporal point of view, which however he discards at the final stage, at which point he views the cycle *sub specie aeternitatis*, as the Scholastics would say.

Yet despite its inadequacy, the temporal description of the seven-part cycle is not without merit, given that this so-called cycle, eternal though it be, is indeed the archetype of time. Not of a homogeneous time, as conceived by philosophers, which is only an abstraction, but of real time, as one might say, which is structured, and is in fact made up of seven phases corresponding to the seven days of a week. And let it be noted that this is in truth the cycle all of us are called to complete: a journey which, from the standpoint of the *viator*, begins in time, but ends in the Sabbath, where time is transfigured into eternity.

Getting back to the primary cycle: Boehme traces the stipulated Birth of God through its seven stages, each of which he describes meticulously in symbolic terms distinctly his own. The cycle begins in Darkness and terminates in Light: Boehme insists that Darkness precedes Light, that Death in fact precedes Life. The first three phases, we are told, transpire in Darkness and culminate in Strife and Anguish too terrifying for mortals to contemplate. We are, at this point, light-years removed from the rosy picture of God to which conventional theology has accustomed us: at this stage, the

6. Scholem, op. cit., p75.
7. *La Naissance de Dieu* (Paris: Albin Michel, 1985), p40.

God of theology has not yet come to birth. What we are witnessing, in a way, is the Travail of that Birth: for indeed, there is no birth without travail. It is precisely at the fourth stage that the impasse of the third—which Boehme describes as a "wheel of anguish"—is broken by the first emergence of Light: the Darkness has now been rent, as if by a bolt of Lightning. And this marks the eternal Victory which prefigures that of Christ upon the Cross: the Victory all Christians aspire to share.

Eternal Light has now emerged, yet the Darkness remains; it is not annihilated, it does not simply disappear: it too is eternal. Boehme speaks of it as a Dark Fire, the Fire that burns in Hell. He calls it the First Principle, because from it all manifestation is derived. And the Second Principle is Light, which comes to birth at the fourth degree and attains its plenitude at the term of the cycle. What now stands revealed—in Light too dazzling for mortal eyes to behold—is the "hidden treasure," clothed as it were in what Boehme calls Eternal Nature, composed of what he refers to as the Precious Substance: a substance "made of Light." According to this view, manifestation is embodiment: it is *incarnation*. What incarnates, however, is precisely the Second Principle; as Deghaye explains: "The dark life does not incarnate. Only the Light is substantial. The Darkness has no true substance."[8]

It is by "taking flesh" that Spirit becomes "visible." A century after Boehme, Friedrich Christoph Oetinger epitomized the Master's thought in the dictum: *"Leiblichkeit ist das Ende der Werke Gottes"* ("Corporeality is the end of God's works"). One needs to bear in mind, however, that the "corporeality" in question is something far different from what we normally understand by that term: what stands at issue is indeed a *celestial* corporeality.[9] It is by means of that celestial *Leiblichkeit* that God reveals himself. That is to say: he assumes a celestial Body, which he "inhabits" as Spirit inhabits Soul.

---

8. Op. cit., p53.

9. Based on ideas of Julius Hamberger, a Boehme follower and disciple of Franz von Baader, I have elaborated upon that notion. See the chapter on "Celestial Corporeality" in *Ancient Wisdom and Modern Misconceptions*, op. cit.

And that Incarnation is consummated in the final phase of the seven-part cycle, in what the Kabbalah terms *Malkhuth*, and what in Christian terms is the Kingdom of God. Now, the God who resides in that Kingdom—whom the Kabbalah, as we have seen, designates by the names "*Tiefereth*" and "*Shekhinah*"—is for Boehme none other than Christ.

But does this mean that the Kingdom is inhabited by Christ alone? Not exactly. Along with Christ, the Incarnate Son of God, what comes to birth in the terminal phase of the seven-part cycle is the angelic order, the celestial world. God does not manifest himself without a world, a celestial sphere: there can be no King without a Kingdom, no Center without a Periphery. The angelic orders are part of the Self-Revelation of God; as Deghaye has expressed it: "The angels are the thoughts of God incarnated in the celestial flesh."[10] But then—since "flesh" alone, no matter how celestial, does not make a body—what "form" do these various incarnations take? In keeping with Boehme's thought one is bound to answer that all these bodies, from that of Christ to that of the lowest angel, are inherently *anthropic*, which is to say that all exemplify the same archetype, the same universal form, which is that of *Adam Kadmon*, primordial Man. It must not be thought, however, that all these angels, in their anthropic bodies, inhabit the Kingdom "in addition to" Christ, as depicted, say, by artists of the Renaissance; for it can indeed be said that the angels—without losing their self-identity!— make up one Body, which is the Mystical Body of Christ: the Body of him "in whom dwelleth all the fullness of the Godhead *bodily*."[11] These words of St. Paul, as we have come to see, are not to be construed as mere "poetry," but apply with supreme accuracy to the celestial Christ, in what the *Zohar* terms the *alma de-yihuda* or "world of union." An angel, then, is not, in reality separated from Christ, even as a cell in a living body is not separated from the soul. Yet all comparison, helpful though it may be, is still only a metaphor, which in the final count falls short of the truth. Deghaye, dispensing with metaphor, defines the principle in question directly: in

10. Op. cit., p47.
11. Col. 2:9, the Greek term being indeed "*somatikos*."

the celestial world, he says, "the point is the equal of the totality."[12] Here, in the Kingdom of God, all *are one*; and that One is Christ.

Yet we do not find ourselves in that *alma de-yihuda* or "world of union": we live evidently in a world in which union is abrogated by separation. How, then, does Boehme conceive the genesis of that "second" world? The story begins with the Fall of Lucifer, the most resplendent among angels, who wanted to be "like God." Having attained to the perfection of embodiment, he desired more. Thus rejecting his own *Leiblichkeit*, Lucifer lost his body of Light and fell back into the primordial Darkness, which thereby became objectified. Now, Lucifer's Fall—his exile from the Kingdom of God—resulted in a certain lack, a kind of vacant space or emptiness, which *our* world is meant to "fill": such is its *raison d'être*. [13] Yet to accomplish its purpose, that world needs itself to pass through the seven-part cycle: to *re-enact* it, if you will. And that is why this world presents itself as temporal, as "a world in process" which has not yet attained its Sabbath, its true end. Though more than a Darkness, the Darkness has not yet been vanquished by Light. And because our world is thus made up of both Darkness and Light, Boehme refers to it as the Third Principle. It is consequently a world of duality, a world of "good and evil," and therefore also a realm of ceaseless strife. Boehme evidently concurs with Heraclitus to the effect that "War is the father of all things."

Boehme's conception of the Third Principle is however subtle in the extreme: we must remember that when he conceives of the so-called seven-part cycle in temporal terms, he is speaking "in a devilish manner." In reality the Light—the Sefirothic world—is present from the beginning: it is truly the Light "that shineth in darkness, and the darkness comprehended it not."[14] What Boehme terms the

12. Op. cit., p 47.
13. The idea is strongly reminiscent of *Tsimtsum*, the concept which stands at the foundation of Lurianic Kabbalah.
14. John 1:5.

Second Principle, though "in" our world, is not "of" that world: which is precisely why Boehme refers to the latter as a Third Principle. The Light "shines" in the darkness of our world: the eternal pervades the temporal. It does so, however, without mixture or fusion, somewhat as soul pervades body or spirit pervades soul. I would like to emphasize that these ideas, though "abstruse" in the extreme, have consequences: that in its conception of the Third Principle, Boehme's doctrine constitutes a *Naturphilosophie* of the deepest kind, a fact which has been recognized not only by philosophers, beginning with Hegel, but also occasionally by members of the scientific community. One knows that Newton himself was influenced by the German theosophist, and even in our day there is the example of Basarab Nicolescu, a scientist who has turned to the teachings of Boehme for insight bearing upon particle physics.[15]

Among authentic Boehme followers, F.C. Oetinger was presumably the first to recognize, however dimly, the scientific implications of the Master's doctrine. Oetinger was right, I believe, when he perceived "polarity" (positive and negative electric charge, for instance), and the undulatory phenomena to which polarity gives rise, as distant exemplifications of the Third Principle, a point which can in fact be greatly sharpened in light of quantum theory. For indeed, by virtue of the so-called phase factor—the ubiquitous multiplier $e^{-2\pi iEt/h}$—one knows that all physical processes are in a way "wave-like," which is after all the reason why one speaks of quantum theory as "wave mechanics."[16]

We have said that the eternal world pervades the temporal; one should however add that the temporal exemplifies the eternal: "As above, so below." This means, in the first place, that all things here below derive their essential nature and dynamic tendencies from

---

15. See *Meaning and Evolution: The Cosmology of Jacob Boehme* (New York: Parabola Books, 1991). On Boehme and Newton, see Serge Hutin, "Note sur la création chez trois Kabbalistes chrétiens anglais," in *Kabbalistes Chrétiens* (Paris, Albin Michel, 1979).

16. An introduction to the formalism of quantum theory, suited to the "non-mathematical" reader, may be found in *The Quantum Enigma* (San Rafael, CA: Angelico Press/Sophia Perennis, 2011), pp 127–151.

what the Kabbalah refers to as the seven *Sefiroth* of Construction: the latter constitute the "manifesting archetypes" which in a way drive and control the flux of events "from within." Moreover, strange as it may seem to the contemporary mind, these *Sefiroth* are represented in our macrocosm precisely by the seven classical planets, beginning with Saturn, the outermost, and ending with the Sun, which corresponds to the last.[17] The Sun shares thus in the ambivalence of the *Shekhinah*, which is counted as the seventh *Sefirah* but is also conceived as "the one who resides" within the Sefirothic edifice. In keeping with the latter conception, Boehme views the Sun (in the *Aurora*) as the transcendent Center of our world, and thus as the visible representation of God, whereas elsewhere—that is to say, in his later works—he adopts the former point of view, counting the Sun as one of the planets.

One must, of course, bear in mind that, for Boehme, a planet is not simply a "body in space," as it is for the contemporary astronomer: we need to divest ourselves of abstractions evolved over centuries before we can enter into the conception of Boehme's universe. The latter differs radically from the universe of classical physics, in particular, first of all, because it conceives the whole to be more than the sum of its parts: we must remember that in the "world of union" which constitutes the prototype of Boehme's universe, there *are no parts*, properly so called. And let us note that, on this issue, contemporary science stands squarely with Boehme, which is in fact precisely what distinguishes quantum mechanics from classical physics, and implies that the former is not actually a "mechanics" at all. In Boehme's universe, moreover, things are connected, not simply the way points in space are connected by lines, or particles by forces acting from one to the other, but "inwardly," by virtue of the fact that the *alma de-peruda* or "world of separation" rests upon the "world of union" in which there is no "separation" at all. And here, again, Boehme's doctrine evinces a kinship with quantum theory,

17. Although the *Sefiroth* "precede" space and cannot be localized, they have nonetheless a special connection with the respective planetary bodies, even as certain powers of the soul have a special connection with corresponding organs of the body: the power of sight, for example, with the eye.

this time with its notion of "non-locality": the fact that quantum theory permits particles to interact "instantaneously," in ways that cannot be explained on the basis of forces acting through space. It can be argued that Boehme's doctrine enables us to resolve the enigma of "non-locality" on a metaphysical basis.[18]

But if Boehme's world-view proves thus to be incurably *astrological*, it turns out to be *alchemical* as well: his *Naturphilosophie*, after all, is the science of a seven-part cycle, destined to transform the "lead" of things here below into the celestial "gold," which is none other than the Precious Substance out of which the bodies of angels are made. And as is to be expected, Boehme is concerned, above all, with one "alchemical transformation" in particular: the one, namely, which constitutes our "second birth." It is this "birth of Christ in us" that stands at the center of his discourse as the primary truth he labors to convey.

One sees that Boehme's cosmology—unlike that of contemporary science—is complemented by an anthropology, which is to say that in his doctrine man is viewed as a veritable microcosm, in the full traditional sense of that term. And since the primary structure of the cosmos, as Boehme conceives of it, is given by the seven-part planetary system, this entails that a corresponding structure must be discernible in man as well. It is astonishing, therefore, that Boehme does not speak explicitly of the seven primary "spiritual centers" comprised within the integral human anatomy, which Hindu tradition knows as *padmas* or *chakras*. It should, however, be noted that these centers, together with their planetary correspondences, have been clearly indicated by Johann Gichtel, a "posthumous" Boehme disciple, in his *Theosophia Practica*, published in 1696. Could it be that Boehme, while choosing not to speak publicly of these matters, conveyed this knowledge nonetheless to his disciples? Be that as it may, it has been established that the phenomenology of the classical planets (as viewed from Earth) corresponds to the *chakra* anatomy, as described in the texts of Kundalini Yoga, *down to*

---

18. See my essay on "Bell's Theorem and the Perennial Ontology," in *The Wisdom of Ancient Cosmology*, op. cit., pp55–67.

the finest details, a fact which may be cited as compelling *scientific* evidence validating the traditional concept of microcosm.[19]

Like the cosmos at large, man himself is engaged in a cycle which in a way recapitulates the eternal Birth of God. In Boehme's doctrine, however, that "journey"—which begins in time and ends in eternity—assumes a distinctive form: an alchemical form, one can say. The successive stages, namely, are not "left behind," as they are in the case of an ordinary voyage, but accompany the *viator*; in fact, they become his *flesh*, the celestial body that will be his in eternity: they become the "wedding garment" to which Christ alludes.[20] It is we who produce that body in the course of our earthly life: we do so principally by our thought, which is invariably an *imagination*, and thus an "embodiment." The spiritual life, therefore, consists in this: *to conform our thought and will to the Will of God*. And that conformity, according to Boehme, is made possible through *grace*: the grace that comes to us in Christ. Here is a passage (from *De Incarnatione Verbi*) which expresses the very essence of the Christian Way, as Boehme conceives of it:

> Now it is apparent in what our new life stands: in nothing, namely, but the imagination, that we with our will enter into God's will, and conform and submit ourselves to him, which is called faith. It is a partaking of God's nature, a bringing of God's nature into the fire-nature of one's soul [*"sein Seelen-Feuer"*], appeasing one's hunger therewith, and thus putting on God's nature, not as a vestment, but as a body of the soul: the soul must have God's nature in its fire, she must eat of God's bread if she would be [his] child.[21]

---

19. I refer again to the remarkable treatise by O. M. Hinze, *Tantra Vidyā: Archaic Astronomy and Tantric Yoga* (New Delhi: Motilal Banarsidas, 2002), and to my review of Hinze's book in *Science and Myth*, op. cit. As I have noted in that essay, the empirical facts adduced by Hinze warrant a "design inference" in William Dembski's sense (as defined in *The Design Inference: Eliminating Chance Through Small Probabilities*, Cambridge University Press, 1998), to the detriment of contemporary scientific theories regarding planetary and human evolution.

20. Matt. 22:11–14.

21. *De Incarnatione Verbi* I.11.8.

It is evident that the "new life" of which Boehme speaks is already a "life in Christ"; and in fact, he refers to it as a *"Wiedergeburt,"* a "rebirth." But does this mean that our "second birth" has already taken place at that point? In a way it does: for when "we with our will enter into God's will," eternity enters into time, and we already live "in Christ." Yet, even so, "the birth of Christ in us" will be consummated precisely at the termination of the seven-part cycle: not when eternity enters into time, but when time enters into eternity. It is then—"in a moment, in the twinkling of an eye" as St. Paul declares[22]—that what we have brought forth over time in will and imagination shall be crystallized, *Deo volente*, into an angelic form, a body "made of Light."

We have referred to "the birth of Christ in us": but who is Christ? How exactly does Boehme conceive of him? Christ is the Incarnate God, the God who reveals himself: *the God who becomes Man.* This happens on two levels: it happens, first, on the plane of eternal nature, at the termination of the seven-part cycle; and it happens on the plane of human history, when the Blessed Virgin Mary conceives and gives birth to a Son. Who is it, then, that was born at Bethlehem? It was none other than the eternal Christ, the primordial Hero who first vanquished the Darkness and established the World of Light. The Christ of history does likewise: that is his mission, which he fulfills at Calvary upon the Cross. That historical Act, however, differs fundamentally from the primordial: it is not creative, but is indeed redemptive, as theology teaches. What stands at issue, for Boehme as for the Kabbalah, is a restitution of something primordial that was lost or destroyed. It needs to be understood that this loss or destruction took place twice, and on two different levels: first through the fault of Lucifer, and later (ontologically speaking) through the sin of Adam. The two are not the same; and whereas Lucifer became discarnate as a result of his Fall, Adam was left with a body such as our own. Suffice it to say that the

---

22. 1 Cor. 15:52.

Genesis tale, and with it the Christian Bible, begins where the saga of Lucifer leaves off; and that is why Christ is viewed as the "second Adam": the one who "atones" for the sin of the first and restores to us the Paradise from which Adam was expelled. But Christ does more: he "atones" for the sin of Lucifer as well, and opens to us the Sefirothic Paradise.[23]

We have said that God "became man" in Jesus of Nazareth; according to Boehme's doctrine, however, God becomes incarnate also in all who are truly "reborn in Christ." In a way, of course, theology maintains this too; yet Boehme's position, on this issue, differs sharply from the theological, to the point of heresy. Simply put, Boehme has in effect extended the concept of Incarnation to all who have truly realized the second birth; as Deghaye says plainly: "Every man born *from above* is the Christ."[24] One might add that, from a theosophical point of view, this tenet is not only unobjectionable, but necessary: if Christ is man "inhabited" by God, then every man thus inhabited is Christ. However, since God can be said to "inhabit" man in many ways, it is necessary to understand this "inhabitation" in precisely the sense dictated by Boehme's doctrine. In the words from *De Incarnatione Verbi* quoted above, God thus inhabits man when his soul has "put on God's nature, not as a vestment, but as a body." Therefore, if man consists of body and soul, and if it is the soul that inhabits the body, then a body inhabited by a soul which has itself "put on God's nature" is indeed "inhabited by God" in the strongest theosophically conceivable sense.

What happens "in eternity" is in a way re-enacted here below: both man and cosmos are "in process," as we have said; both are in a state of flux, a kind of *samsāra*, a perpetual "birth-and-death," or "death-and-birth" as Boehme might say. And what is it that is being born: what is the transcendent terminus of this process, its Eschaton? Given that the archetype of this *genesis* is the eternal Self-Revelation of God, that Eschaton can only be Christ and His Kingdom.

23. As noted in chapter 3, the Adam of Genesis, according to Lurianic Kabbalah, is situated, not in the Sefirothic world, but in a realm designated by the term *Asiyah*, which corresponds *roughly* to the intermediary realm of the Vedic *tribhuvāna*.

24. Op. cit., p59.

The God who is born is Christ, and the eternal creation, which is God's Masterpiece, is his Kingdom. Now, in Boehme's doctrine as in theology, Christ—as the God who is born—is indeed the Embodiment of the Son, whom Boehme conceives as a dynamic Centre in God, from which the divine Creation springs. But then, who is the Father? Boehme speaks of the Father on two levels, or from two points of view: as transcending the seven-part cycle, and as manifested therein. Viewed in the first perspective, the Father is "the eternal Will" that gives birth to the aforesaid Centre, which latter Boehme also designates by the virtually untranslatable term *Gemüt* (meaning "heart", "mind", or even "feeling"); and let us add that the Holy Ghost is then "the Spirit that emanates from the Will and the Heart"[25] and drives or powers the manifestation: that manifests, but is not itself manifested. On the other hand, Boehme does also conceive of the Father on the plane of the seven-part cycle: strange and indeed shocking as it seems, the Father is then none other than the Dark and Devouring Fire that engenders the Light. It is he that dominates the first three phases of the eternal cycle, even as the last three are dominated by the Son.

Having associated the Father with the first three degrees and the Son with the last, we need to remind ourselves that the cycle in question is not temporal, but eternal, and that "the seventh degree reunites the totality of the emanation." At this terminal stage all seven degrees "become" simultaneous. As is said of the *Sefiroth*: "their end is in their beginning, and their beginning is in their end"—to which the *Sefer Yetzirah* adds the significant words: "as the flame is bound to the coal." In the spirit of Boehme's doctrine, we can now interpret this Kabbalistic dictum: clearly, the "flame" is the Son and the "coal" is the Father. And this entails that the Father is in the Son even as the Son is in the Father, which is to say that in reality the two constitute one God. But then, where is the Holy Ghost? He is, as we have seen, "the Spirit that manifests, but is not itself manifested." Thus conceived, the Holy Ghost—though not yet "the love that moves the Sun and the other stars"—is the Spirit that gives birth to Christ, who *is* that Love. And in the Light of that personified Love,

25. *Mysterium Magnum* 1.2–4.

the Father himself is transformed; as Boehme writes: in that Light "the Father with the eternal Essences in his eternal and primordial Will becomes lovely, friendly, mild, pure, and gentle."[26] This is the Father, clearly, to whom we address our prayer in the words of the *Pater Noster*: he is *our* Father, who *is in Heaven*. We do not pray to a Devouring Fire: to the Fire that burns in Hell! Here, then, is another interpretation of the Christic logion "No man cometh to the Father, except by me,"[27] an exegesis which evidently carries Boehme's signature and differs profoundly from the theological: for as Boehme states explicitly: "and if the Father were no longer luminous in the Son, the Father would be a dark valley."[28] It is needful to understand, of course, that what is "lovely, mild, and gentle" was in a way comprised "from all eternity," as we say, in what Boehme terms the eternal Essences; the point, however, is that what was thus "contained" was not manifested: was yet, indeed, "a hidden treasure."

According to Boehme's doctrine, the Unknown God "enters" into the seven-part cycle, not primarily to reveal himself to others, but precisely to know himself: for Boehme, the imperative "Know thyself" applies first of all to God. As he explains in *Mysterium Magnum*:

> The unfathomable and divine Intellect (*Verstand*) enters into a terrifying Fire-will and Life, in order that his great Love and Joy, which are termed God, becomes manifest: because if all were only One, the One itself would not be revealed to him; but through the Manifestation (*Offenbarung*) the eternal Good is revealed and gives rise to a world of Joy (*ein Freudenreich*). If there had been no Fear, the Joy itself would not have been made manifest, and there would be only a single Will, which would ever do only one thing; but when it enters into Adversity (*Wiederwärtigkeit*) the Conflict turns into a Desire and a Love-play (*ein Liebe-Spiel*) that gives rise to and accomplishes the Delight of Joys, humanly speaking.[29]

26. *De Triplice Vita Hominis* I.54.
27. John 14:6.
28. *Aurora* 3.22.
29. *Mysterium Magnum* 3.22.

One may note that the "Love-play" spoken of here is Boehme's very own version of what the Vedanta terms *lilā*, the eternal "play" of *Mahāshakti*. Yet the conception of the German theosophist has an altogether different cast. For Boehme the world of Joy to which this "play" gives rise is undeniably real; and so, one might add, is the unspeakable Torment of the third stage, the Agony of the Death that needs first to be vanquished. For Boehme the primary locus of reality is precisely the realm of eternal manifestation; and in fact, to set one's sights beyond that realm is to take the path of Lucifer which ends in Hell. In this optic, to deny the eternal world is to deny what God himself *has become*: it is to *reject Christ*, the true God and Savior.

But if Boehme is not a Vedantist, neither is he an orthodox theologian; for whereas he speaks of a Trinity, it is not the Trinity of theology. To be precise, Boehme formulates in fact two very different conceptions of the Trinity, as we have seen, neither of which is orthodox. His "transcendent" conception of the Trinity, first of all, is theologically unacceptable, because neither the "Will," nor the "Heart," nor the "Spirit" qualifies as a Person in the sense of Trinitarian theology. His second Trinity, on the other hand, consisting of a Father giving birth to a Son in the course of a seven-part cycle driven by the Holy Ghost, is even less acceptable theologically: for in addition to the fact that it is not a Trinity of Persons, it confounds the Trinity with the Incarnation.

The problem stems from the fact that Boehme conceives of the transcendent God—the God who "precedes" the seven-part cycle— as bereft of self-knowledge: as "an Eye that does not see itself."[30] According to Boehme's doctrine, the "fullness of knowing" is attained only at the end of the seven-part cycle, and only in the Incarnate Son: "God is not a Person," he tells us, "except in Christ."[31] Now, this is clearly unacceptable from a theological point of view, first of all because, theologically speaking, there are *necessarily three* Persons, which is to say that each presupposes the other two. What is more, theology conceives of that Trinity of Persons "on the level of the Unknown God," who is therefore Unknown, not to

30. *Sex Puncta Theosophica* II.3.11.
31. *Mysterium Magnum* 7.5.

himself, but only to us, that is to say, to creatures. Theology insists that the Trinity "precedes" the Creation, be it the "aeviternal" realm of angels or the temporal world. It maintains, therefore, that God creates, both the world of angels and our world, not to know himself, but *to give himself*: simply put, creation is an act, not of Desire, but of Love. The God whom we conceive as Unknown—whom the Kabbalah refers to as *En-Sof* and Boehme calls *Ungrund*—already possesses in himself the fullness of Knowledge, Life, and Blessedness. For Boehme, on the other hand, that plenum is realized precisely in Christ, the *Incarnate* God, "in whom dwelleth all the fullness of the Godhead bodily."

According to Boehme's doctrine, the "blind" Will of the transcendent Father, together with "the Spirit that emanates from the Will and the Heart," seek nothing but this Incarnate God, to whom the seven-part cycle gives birth eternally. As Deghaye recapitulates:

> The dark Fire becomes the Flame that illumines. The Fire that devours was the Desire of greed that can only increase its own opacity. The Flame that illumines is Desire become *the gift of Self*. The Light is grace, it is Love. God resides in the Light: the true God is to be found only in the God of Love.[32]

Such is Boehme's interpretation of the Johannine "*Deus caritas est*."[33] The God of Love—the God who *is Love*—is the true God: *the only God*. And this God is Incarnate: he is the eternal Christ. For Boehme, Christ is in truth the only God; and this God is not Trinitarian in the theological sense.[34] As Deghaye points out: "Boehme adopts the notions of Father and Son to transpose them into his theory of emanation, yet the system he constructs is not properly speaking a Trinitarian theology."[35] It *cannot be*: it is, after all, a theosophy, a doctrine whose subject, finally, is the Incarnate God.

---

32. Op. cit., p83.
33. 1 John 4:8.
34. However, as I propose to show in the sequel, Boehme's doctrine is yet profoundly "Trinitarian" in another sense, which may be characterized as "indigenous" to his own perspective.
35. Op. cit., p42.

⊕

But perhaps we have drawn the contours of Boehme's teaching too sharply; for despite the fact that his doctrine is centered upon the eternal manifestation of God, he also refers—in his later writings—to a principle that "precedes" the seven-part cycle: to something, namely, which seems to stand between the *Ungrund* and the eternal world. In *Mysterium Magnum*, for instance, Boehme alludes to *"das Auge des Ungrundes"* ("the Eye of the *Ungrund*"), which he associates with Jehovah, and speaks of in terms reminiscent of an Upanishad:

> ... has neither beginning nor end, is unmeasured, no number can express his extent and magnitude, is deeper than thought can penetrate: he is nowhere far from anything, nor near to anything, he is beyond all and in all things; his Birth is everywhere, and without him nothing exists; he is Time and Eternity, *Grund* and *Ungrund*. . . .[36]

Elsewhere he speaks of an Eye within which "all beings are encompassed," which he likens to "a Mirror in which the Will beholds himself" and identifies as "the Eternal Wisdom of God,"[37] a concept, not yet mentioned in the *Aurora*, which proves to be pivotal in his later doctrine. It is here, in the transcendent and enigmatic personage of *Sophia*, that what may be called the "feminine aspect of God" begins to manifest. And let us note what this implies: it means that "the mystery of *Eros*," properly so called, precedes the creation, and in fact constitutes its principle.

One sees that the distinction between Eye and Mirror prefigures the Masculine/Feminine polarity, even as it prefigures what philosophy terms the subject/object dichotomy. It should likewise be noted that the Eye, thus conceived, constitutes an *active* principle, unlike the receptive organ commonly denoted by that term: it is the Mirror, and not the Eye, that is *receptive*. What, then, is Wisdom: is it Eye, or is it Mirror? According to the primary sense of the term, it is the

---

36. *Mysterium Magnum* 1.8.
37. *De Incarnatione Verbi* II.1.9.

former; and yet, since Eye and Mirror imply one another, and each, in its own way, "contains" what the other does, one may conceive of Wisdom in feminine terms as well. And as a matter of fact, language generally sides with the latter point of view: think of the words *sophia*, *sapientia*, *Weisheit*, or *sagesse*, all of which carry feminine gender. The Kabbalah, in any case, distinguishes Eye and Mirror as *Hokhmah* and *Binah*, the second and third *Sefirah*, respectively; and one might add that whereas *Hokhmah* is invariably taken to mean Wisdom, as indeed it should, one generally speaks of *Binah* as "Intelligence"—whatever that may be—presumably because the term "Wisdom" is already spoken for.

Boehme, as we have noted, conceives of Wisdom sometimes as Eye and sometimes as Mirror. Yet he tends to favor the masculine interpretation, which is to say that he typically refers to *Binah* as the Virgin, or more explicitly, as the Eternal Virgin. He does so, for example, when he tells us that "The Word is in Wisdom and the Eternal Virgin is also in Wisdom, and none can be without the other."[38] The Virgin, then, is "She who receives," and what is received is the Word; it is Wisdom, however, that "speaks the Word." Wisdom, clearly, is here conceived as the active or "masculine" principle. But then, wherein lies the "virginity" of that Virgin? It lies, first of all, in Her supernal Purity, together with the fact that She is also, in a way, "androgynous": for She is said to be "in Wisdom," and may consequently be identified as the feminine aspect of the primordial bi-unity. What confronts us here, clearly, is Boehme's version of the *Shiva-Shakti* polarity, which precedes all worlds or *lokas* as their transcendent Principle. According to the theosophic conception, when the *Verbum Domini* is "spoken into Her," the Virgin conceives and becomes the Supernal Mother of all Creation, beginning with the eternal world: "*die Jungfrau der Ewigkeit*"[39] conceives and gives birth to the Eternal Christ, even as, on a temporal plane, the Blessed Virgin Mary conceived and gave birth to Jesus, the Word "made flesh" that dwelt among us.[40]

38. *De Triplici Vita Hominis* 6.73.
39. Literally "the Virgin of eternity."
40. John 1:14.

It is Wisdom that "speaks" the *Verbum Domini*, and it is the Word that "takes flesh," be it in eternity or in time. What then *is* that Word? Boehme tells us that "the Word is in Wisdom," and that each cannot be without the other. Word and Wisdom, therefore, are not two separate things, and it is clear that in speaking the Word, Wisdom is in a way "speaking itself." As Deghaye has put it: "God inhabits Nature in his aspect as Wisdom," and "it is of Wisdom that Nature is the Body."[41] It is Wisdom—as *Verbum Domini*—that incarnates: it is the Word that "was made flesh," in literal compliance with the Johannine text. But that Word is not a Person: for Boehme, as we have seen, there *is* in fact no Person "prior to" the Eternal Christ.

We have said that the Virgin "receives" the Word; but is not that already a "manifestation," an *embodiment* of a kind? In a way it is: the very conception of Wisdom, Word and Virgin implies as much. The Kabbalah, moreover, stakes the same claim when it speaks of the supreme tri-unity as a Face of God. But that Face is the *arik anpin* or Great Face, which "precedes" the Small.

Where there is an Eye and a Mirror, there is already a "seeing"; and in this "seeing" that precedes the seven-part cycle—in which the Deity, as it were, "first beholds itself"—there is already a Joy. That Joy, however, is none other than the Virgin Herself; as Deghaye has beautifully said, in reference to the Eternal Virgin: "She is the Joy of a Divinity that takes possession of itself."[42] For Boehme, however, that Joy subsisting in Wisdom harbors a Will and a Desire, a Longing, one might say, for something as yet unborn. It is noteworthy that Boehme speaks, in this context, of "*Lust*," a word which connotes both *joy* and *longing*: the delight which accompanies a love that is fulfilled, and also the craving of an unfulfilled love, corresponding to the sense of the English word "lust." According to Boehme's doctrine, it is this "craving" within the Heart of Wisdom that both initiates and drives the seven-part cycle in its quest of the Eschaton, an ultimate Fulfillment variously described as the Wedding Feast, the Sabbath, or the New Jerusalem.

41. Op. cit., p31.
42. Op. cit., p243. As we read in Proverbs 8.30: "Then I was by him, as one brought up with him: and I was daily his delight, rejoicing always before him."

Even so, there is nothing in the Sefirothic world that did not "pre-exist" in Wisdom, that is to say, "pre-exist" in the Word: "As above, so below." It is Wisdom that incarnates, it is the Word that "is made flesh." And if Nature is Wisdom's Body, Wisdom is Nature's Soul. Like body and soul, Wisdom and Nature co-exist, but do not fuse; though co-existing, Wisdom yet pre-exists: though immanent, it remains ever transcendent.

In his conception of Wisdom, Boehme has discovered the Foundation of the eternal world, the *Grund* within the *Ungrund*. It is with reference to this Ground, this transcendent Foundation, that the seven-part cycle is to be understood. One sees, in the first place, that the Darkness too is a manifestation: that in fact it manifests the *Ungrund* itself, if one may put it so. Next one sees that the Light which emerges in the course of the seven-part cycle, and becomes, as it were, "crystallized" in the Precious Substance, must be derived, not from the antecedent Darkness, but from a Light that precedes the creation: and what can that be, but the Light of Wisdom![43] And that is the Light which shines within all created light: the Light "by which all things are lighted" as an Upanishad proclaims.

The immanence of Wisdom is apparent even in our "fallen" world: for it is by virtue of that "hidden presence" that the things of this world are intelligible to the extent that they are. All science, therefore, is rooted in Wisdom, which it "reflects" however distantly. What we know as harmony and proportion, for instance, or as the regularities and "laws" of Nature, is but an attenuated manifestation of that eternal Root. And is this not indeed what Albert Einstein was saying, in his own way, when he spoke of "the Old One"? The great physicist found it amazing that "science" is possible at all: "The most incomprehensible thing about the universe," he said, "is that it is comprehensible." The reason it is has however been given long ago; in the words of the Psalmist: "In Wisdom thou hast made them all."[44] To which one might add a verse from another Psalm: "For

43. This too is presumably what Scripture refers to as "the glory of God": "the glory I had with thee before the world was" as Christ declares (in John 17:5) in words addressed to his Father.

44. Psalm 104:24.

with thee is the fountain of life; in thy light shall we see light."[45] The "fountain of life," as we know, is *Hokhmah*, which is to say that "thy light"—the Light in which "we see light"—is indeed the Light of Wisdom. That Light, however, is needed not only to "light" the objective universe, but to "light" the eye of the beholder as well: it is "in thy light" that *we* "see light."

Getting back to the primary focus of Boehme's doctrine—which is Christ and his "birth in us"—let us ask once more: who, then, is Christ? For it happens that Boehme's final answer to this question hinges upon his sophiology. It is to be noted, in the first place, that Boehme distinguishes between Christ and Jesus: whereas Christ is "man inhabited by God," Jesus is "the God who inhabits the Christ-like man." Who, then, is that God? He is Wisdom, Boehme maintains: the very name "Jesus," which he associates with Jehovah and thus with the Tetragrammaton, identifies Wisdom (according to an admissible interpretation) as "the God in us."[46] Jesus, then, is "Wisdom inhabiting man." But Wisdom is also Love; and as Boehme avers in *Mysterium Magnum*, the name "Jesus" signifies "*die höchste Liebe der Gottheit*" ("the highest love of the Godhead").[47]

It was imprecise, therefore, to speak of "the birth of Christ in us": it is Jesus, rather, who is born in us when we "become Christ." This Christology differs fundamentally, of course, from that of theology. In Boehme's doctrine there can be no question of a Hypostatic Union, because, in this optic, the concept of Person refers to the plane of manifestation alone. It appears that Boehme conceives of "personhood," not in terms of person-to-person relation, but as Center to Periphery; and since the Center is unique, so is the Person. The Sefirothic Creation at large is therefore in truth the Body of Jesus. And this metaphysical fact, let us note, accounts for the miracles Jesus wrought when he walked upon this earth: when, for example, he "rebuked the wind, and said to the sea, Peace, be still," and the disciples wondered "What manner of man is this, that even

45. Psalm 36:9.
46. See Geneviève Javary, "A propos du thème de las Sekina: variations sur le nom de Dieu," in *Kabbalistes Chrétiens*, op. cit.
47. *Mysterium Magnum* 56.15.

the wind and the sea obey him?"[48] The wind and the sea obey Jesus by virtue of the fact that "Nature is Wisdom's Body": the Body of Jesus himself.

Having sketched the doctrine of Jacob Boehme—admittedly, in rather broad strokes—I propose, in conclusion, to ponder three questions: In what respect does Boehme's doctrine differ from the Kabbalah? Is it yet, *in a sense*, Trinitarian? And finally, is it *in a sense* nondualist? We begin with the first.

It is beyond doubt that Boehme's seven-part cycle corresponds to the Sefirothic septenary known as the *Sefiroth* of Construction: the two conceptions cover the same ground, which is the Self-Manifestation of God in the eternal world referred to in Kabbalah as the Kingdom. That Boehme conceives of this septenary in seemingly temporal terms as a "seven-part cycle" does not alter this fact: does not the Kabbalah itself conceive of that Kingdom in "dynamic" terms, for example, when it speaks of *Hokhmah* as "the mystical Eden," from which "a river went out to water the garden"? Yet there *is* a discrepancy, an apparent conflict between Boehme's doctrine and the Kabbalah, which in fact makes its appearance at the very outset: namely, where Boehme places (as the first phase of his seven-part cycle) a violent Contraction, a "constriction" which he perceives as a Darkness and a Death, the Kabbalah places *Hesed*, the first *Sefirah* of the septenary, which it conceives as the Love or Mercy of God. In Boehme's doctrine it is only at the fifth stage of the cycle that Love appears upon the scene, born of a Victory over Death: how can this vision be reconciled with the Kabbalistic teaching, which places Love at the very threshold of Creation as its first Sefirothic principle? On the face of it we have here an outright contradiction, an irreconcilable disparity.

I propose however to show that this discrepancy results from a difference in standpoint and *modus operandi*: that it pertains to perspective as opposed to "substance." Admittedly, both Boehme

---

48. Mark 4:39, 41.

and the Kabbalah are theosophical in their primary orientation; but within this generic category their standpoint and operative *modus* are by no means the same. What characterizes Boehme's perspective and distinguishes it from the Kabbalistic is the fact that he views the creative process from the side of creation: his is the standpoint of the human seer. The Kabbalah, on the other hand, views what it terms the *Maaseh Bereshith* or Work of Creation from the opposite direction: that is to say, from "the side of God" if one may so put it. Now, as seen "from below," the process does begin in Darkness and Death; yet the same commencement, viewed "from above," proves indeed to be an Act of Love: this is what I would like now to explain.

Following F. C. Oetinger, we will identify the Contraction, which Boehme places at the head of his cycle as its first phase, with the Kabbalistic *Tsimtsum* that initiates—or renders possible—the Work of Creation.[49] Thus perceived, the Contraction becomes a kenotic and indeed sacrificial act: the very Act—unique and eternal—by which God gives himself to be "shared," to be "dismembered" as the Vedas say. The Work of Creation begins thus in an *agape*, a Love which finds embodiment, according to the Kabbalah, in *Hesed*; and this is indeed the *amor* of which Dante sings: the love that literally "moves the Sun and the other stars" (namely, the *Sefiroth*!).

We have said that the Kabbalist views the creative process "from the side of God"; but how is that possible? Now, it is the *modus operandi* that defines the perspective or point of view, and it is the prerogative of the Kabbalah to operate *deductively*, by means of Notarikon, Gematria, and Themura, on the basis of "axioms" revealed by God in the form of the Tetragrammaton.[50] The way of Kabbalah constitutes thus a "top-down" approach: it is not a matter of "seeing God in the world"—of seeing God "in all creatures, even in weeds and grass" as Boehme declares—but rather of "seeing the world in God."

It appears, in light of these observations, that Boehme was not a Kabbalist: he may have spoken of Kabbalistic secrets "more openly

49. See Pierre Deghaye, "La philosophie sacrée d'Oetinger," in *Kabbalistes Chrétiens,* op. cit.

50. See pp106–108.

than the *Zohar*," but this in itself does not make him such. It is a question of *modus operandi*, as we have said; and the mere fact that Boehme was not conversant with Hebrew suffices to prove that he did not operate by Kabbalistic means. Certainly one has reason to suppose that he was "taught by God," and that he perceived the divine creation; but he did so apparently from a "creaturely" point of view, which in fact was distinctly his own. The "perspective" of the Kabbalah, on the other hand, is passed on from master to disciple by way of operative means definitive of that tradition, and cannot be accessed *effectively* "from the outside."

The two deepest questions, posed above, remain yet to be considered, and need to be dealt with in conjunction: for it turns out that Boehme's nondualism is in a sense Trinitarian. We begin where he himself begins: with what he refers to as the *Ungrund* or as "*das Nichts*," meaning "the Naught," a term which accords with the Kabbalistic "*ain*." As Boehme explains: "God is like a Naught to the creature, because he cannot be grasped by her."[51] Yet, strange as it may seem, the *unio mystica*, as he conceives of it, entails a certain union with that Naught. As in Buddhism, the emphasis in Boehme's system is placed upon the will: it is will or desire that determines "who" we are, and "with whom" we are united. By silencing the will—by way of what he terms *Gelassenheit*[52]—man can attain to the highest and most perfect union with God:

> Because what is void of will is one with the Naught, and is outside of all nature, in the *Ungrund* which is God himself.[53]

We need, however, to remind ourselves that Boehme is Christian to the core, and that what he propounds is neither Buddhism nor

51. *Mysterium Magnum* 24.27.
52. The word—a key term in Meister Eckhart's vocabulary as well—literally means "detachment" or "letting go." Boehme has written an entire treatise on the subject of "*Gelassenheit*."
53. *Theosophia* 2.20.

Vedanta, but indeed Christianity. And this means that the Knowledge of God—or *unio mystica*—is to be attained *in Christo*: "No man cometh unto the Father, but by me."[54] Our union is with the Incarnate Son of God, *and through him*, with God the Father. Now, in this union the creature does not disappear—does not, like the dewdrop, "slip into the shining sea"—but rather becomes assimilated to the Mystical Body of Christ. The Christian Eschaton—let it be clearly understood—is realized *in an incarnate state*. We know this from the words of the Savior himself (when he prayed for his disciples, and for all Christians yet unborn, on the eve of his Passion):

> And this is life eternal, that they might know thee, the only true God, and Jesus Christ whom thou hast sent.[55]

These words are crystal clear: for the Christian, life eternal is not a matter of knowing the Father, or the transcendent God, but of knowing *both* the Father *and* Jesus Christ, whom the Father "has sent." It is evidently not a question of two separate acts of knowing: what stands at issue is a single cognitive act encompassing both. It is *in* Jesus Christ that God the Father is to be known; and this knowing *is* life eternal. This means that, for the Christian, the nondual or advaitic state is realized in the Incarnate Son of God.

Boehme speaks of that state in the *Mysterium Magnum*, in a passage which holds the key to his doctrine:

> But when the creature directs its desire into God, that is, into the Naught, then the creature becomes a Something of the Naught, and the Naught flows and acts in the Something of the creature, and the creature does likewise in the Naught. In this action, clearly, no *Turba* can arise, since it is his own love-play, which loves itself, and stands in its Life at Nature's End.[56]

We need, first of all, to explain the word *Turba*, which admits of no translation: it belongs to Boehme's own vocabulary, and refers to a

---

54. John 14:6.
55. John 17:3.
56. *Mysterium Magnum* 24.27.

manifestation of the Dark Fire, from which all that exists in Nature springs. "In this action," Boehme tells us, that Dark Fire cannot manifest, because here we stand "at Nature's End," in the perfection of what the Kabbalah terms *Malkhuth*, the Kingdom of God. Boehme conceives of Life Eternal, here "at Nature's End," as a "love-play" between the Naught or *Ungrund* and a Something which has emerged therefrom, and stands on the side of manifestation, in the Great Sabbath wherein God "finds his rest." This "love-play" is reminiscent, once again, of what Hindu tradition knows as *lilā*, now conceived, however, in Christian terms. The notion proves actually to be Trinitarian: what the Father loves is the Son, and that Love itself is the Holy Spirit.

But if Boehme's view of the nondual state is indeed Trinitarian, his conception of the Trinity proves not to be theological. True to his theosophical point of view, Boehme perceives "the begetting of the Son," not in the absolute eternity of the Godhead, but precisely in the seven-part cycle of eternal Nature: it is here, theosophically speaking, that the Father "eternally" gives birth to his Son. Admittedly, Boehme speaks also at times of a Trinity "beyond Nature," which as we have seen, he conceives as "seeking manifestation." Yet what ultimately counts is not a hidden Trinity, but the one which "stands in its Life at Nature's End": for that is the Trinity wherein Life Eternal resides.

It is crucial to note that Boehme does not separate the transcendent God from his eternal embodiment: what is revealed or manifested "in the mirror of Eternal Nature" is God himself, the very God to whom he refers as the *Ungrund* or "the Naught." But if his doctrine is thus nondualist where eternal Nature is concerned, what is to be said of the world or worlds which came into being as the result of the Fall, first of Lucifer and then of Adam? It will be noted that the world of Lucifer (which theology knows as Hell) and "our" world both possess *Turba*, that is to say, entail a manifestation of Darkness. One may be tempted, therefore, to interpret this teaching from a jnanic point of view by assimilating that Darkness to the Vedantic conception of *avidyā*, or to *avidyā-shakti*, the inscrutable Power that deludes, and by its magic conjures up these worlds of *māyā*. To do so, however, would be to falsify Boehme's teaching, to miss its theosophic point. In Boehme's eyes, the Darkness is a primordial Power which as such is indestructible. One may think of it as a universal force of contraction that solidifies or "coagulates": the concept pertains in fact to the very *Naturphilosophie* which may have inspired Newton to formulate his theory of "universal gravitation."[57] The Darkness of which Boehme speaks is consequently no more "illusory" than is the gravitational force which holds the planets in their elliptic orbs and binds the universe. We must remember that, for Boehme, the real is the manifested, and thus the "perceivable," in the widest sense of that term. The two nether worlds, therefore, have each their own reality, and Boehme goes so far as to insist that Hell itself is eternal.[58]

Yet Boehme can nonetheless be seen as a nondualist: one must remember that there are different kinds of nondualism, and that even in Vedanta, the *advaita* of Shankara represents but one school, one "point of view" if you will. What is it, then, that defines Boehme's brand of nondualism: what is it that renders his doctrine "advaitic"? It is the fact that he conceives the *unio mystica* as the Supreme Identity: "Because what is void of will is one with the Naught . . . in the *Ungrund* which is God himself." This is the crucial point, the advaitic Truth as Boehme conceives of it. That nondualism, however, is placed "at Nature's End": for Boehme, *it is only at the termination of the seven-part cycle that duality comes to an end.* Boehme remains ever true to the theosophic premise upon which his doctrine is based: *the perceived is real, because the real is the perceivable*; even the lowest and most ephemeral thing in this world has therefore its reality. Boehme's nondualism proves thus to be *eschatological*: an *advaita* to be realized in the wake of a Victory which, for us, remains to be won.

---

57. See Jean Zaffiropulo and Catherine Monos, *Sensorium Dei dans l'hermetisme et la science* (Paris: Les Belles Lettres, 1976).

58. On this point both Oetinger and Franz von Baader (perhaps Boehme's two greatest disciples) parted company with the Master.

6

MEISTER ECKHART
ON CREATION

WE ACTUALLY KNOW rather little about the man to whom Ananda Coomaraswamy referred as "the greatest European ever born." Even the year of his birth, held to be 1260, is conjectural. We do know that he joined the Dominican Friars, and that he studied in Paris and later in Cologne, where he may have met Albert the Great. Thereupon Eckhart was engaged in various administrative functions, ranging from prior of Erfurt in Thuringia to vicar general of the Bohemian province. One knows that the academic years 1311–12 and 1312–13 saw him back in Paris in a professorial capacity, following which he returned to Germany, first to Strassburg, and later to Cologne. It was during this period that Eckhart rose to become the celebrated preacher, whose sermons, both in Latin and in the Middle High German of his day, have come down to us in numerous transcriptions. And here, in these incomparable homilies, we meet the Meister face to face: by the power of his speech he breaks through the barrier of time and stands before us as the consummate sage "from whom God hid nothing."

Given the "provocative" nature of Eckhart's sermons, it is little wonder that he eventually attracted the attention of Inquisitorial magistrates. Beginning at Cologne, he came under scrutiny; and it is from this point onward that a more detailed record of his presence survives in the archives of history. We know the charges that were brought against him—a long list of them—and we know the dates of the hearings, and the text of his defense. We know that the Inquisitors at Cologne ruled against him, that he appealed to the Pope, and was ordered to stand trial before the papal court at Avignon. We know that 26 propositions attributed to Eckhart were condemned in the Bull "*In agro dominico*," promulgated on March 27, 1329.[1] And we know that the beleaguered Master died before the publication of that decree, presumably at Avignon.[2]

Meanwhile, through the centuries, Eckhart continues to inspire, to challenge, and to intrigue. The resultant literature reveals a bewildering variety of perceptions, which however, for the most part, tell us more about "the eye of the beholder" than about the Meister himself. As Armand Maurer observes:

> He has been considered the father of German mysticism, the enemy of Christian orthodoxy, the persecuted champion of truths higher than Christianity, a spokesman for the Enlightenment, and even a forerunner of Luther and German idealism. At the same time it has been recognized that he has inspired, and was held in reverence by such thoroughly orthodox spiritual writers as Tauler, Ruysbroeck, Suso, and Nicholas of Cusa.[3]

What has moreover fascinated many, and has contributed to a "rediscovery" of the Meister in our day, is the fact that his teachings have at times a distinctly Vedantic ring. Early in the nineteenth century, already, the young Schopenhauer had been struck by the apparent similarities between Eckhart and Shankara, and a century later that theme was taken up again, first by Rudolf Otto, and thereafter by an array of prominent authors, ranging from the incomparable Ananda Coomaraswamy to literary figures such as Aldous Huxley and Thomas Merton.[4] In the wake of these publications, Eckhart has come to be seen by an educated public as the quintessential Christian "Vedantist." He ranks today as perhaps the leading "ecumenical figure" in the encounter between Christianity and Hinduism.

1. See E. Colledge and B. McGinn, *Meister Eckhart: The Essential Sermons, Commentaries, Treatises and Defense* (New York: Paulist Press, 1981), pp77–81. Henceforth referred to as EME.

2. The year of Meister Eckhart's death is held to be 1327.

3. Armand Maurer, *Meister Eckhart: Parisian Questions and Prologues* (Toronto: Pontifical Institute of Mediaeval Studies, 1974), p7.

4. On this subject, see Harry Oldmeadow, *Journeys East* (Bloomington, IN: World Wisdom, 2004) and *Mediations* (San Rafael, CA: Sophia Perennis, 2008).

But whereas such claims may perhaps be justified, it must not be forgotten that Eckhart was in fact a Scholastic: not only was he formed in the Scholasticism of his time, dominated by the towering figure of Aquinas, but one has reason to believe that he remained true to that legacy till the end of his life. One may surmise that Eckhart arrived at his doctrine, "mystical" and in certain respects "Vedantic" though it be, not by jettisoning the teaching of the Schools, but precisely by thinking it through to the very end, to the point where it opens upon a gnosis, in comparison to which the preceding levels appear to be "mere straw."

This is not to say that Meister Eckhart was necessarily in full accord with his peers on every issue; and in fact, we shall have occasion to consider a fundamental question on which he flatly contradicts the teaching of Aquinas. The point, however, is that he did so on the basis of Scholastic principles, or on Scholastic grounds, as one can say. As a rule, Eckhart does not simply state a truth: he *proves* it; and to be sure, he does so as a Master of the Schools. As he tells us himself in the Prologue to his *Commentary on John*: "My intention is the same in all my works—to explain what the holy Christian faith and the two Testaments maintain *through the help of the natural arguments of the philosophers*."[5]

The very arrangement of Eckhart's opus testifies to his Scholastic bent. It was apparently his intention to bequeath, as his masterpiece, a single work of gigantic proportions, the so-called *Opus Tripartitum*, consisting of an *Opus Propositionem*, an *Opus Questionem*, and an *Opus Expositionem*. In the first he intended to formulate, discuss and defend over a thousand propositions; the second was to be a comprehensive treatise organized around an ordered sequence of questions, in the manner of the *Summa Theologiae*; and the third was to consist of scriptural commentaries, plus an *Opus Sermonem* comprised of sermons. It is believed that Eckhart devoted himself to this project from about the year 1314 almost to the end of his life, but it is not known whether he ever completed it. Although only three Prologues remain as identifiable fragments of the *Opus Tripartitum*,

5. EME, p122.

it is presumed that the work was to include his extant scriptural commentaries and Disputed Questions.[6]

One sees that the vernacular sermons and works of spiritual counsel do not suffice: to grasp Meister Eckhart's doctrine accurately, and in its fullness, one has need as well of all that pertains to the *magnum opus* by means of which Eckhart himself wished to transmit his doctrine to posterity. We need, thus, to encounter not only Eckhart the preacher and spiritual guide, but the Scholastic as well: the Parisian Master who could discourse with consummate precision on whether "an angel's understanding as denoting an action is the same as his existence," or whether "motion without a terminus implies a contradiction."[7] Even discourse such as this is not to be waived aside as "pedantry" or "medieval hairsplitting": who can tell whether such Scholastic conundrums may yet have their use as "skillful means" in the service of enlightenment.

Getting back to the "Vedantic connection": to the extent that one probes beyond the German sermons, the visible similarity between Eckhart and Shankara dims. It is hard, in fact, to recognize a consistent doctrine in Eckhart's opus taken in its entirety; as Etienne Gilson points out: "The difficulty is not to find a good interpretation of Meister Eckhart, but rather to choose between so many consistent interpretations, based upon unimpeachable texts, which yet differ among themselves to the point of being contradictory."[8] But while this is no doubt true, one needs to realize that Eckhart does not speak always from one and the same point of view, and that, had he done so, his teaching could never have attained to the heights for which in fact it is renowned. Even ordinary visual perception, it turns out, requires movement, that is to say, multiple points of view.[9] The difference is that when it comes to intellectual perception, the kind

---

6. Of the latter, only a few, originating in Paris, are extant. See Armand Maurer, op. cit.

7. These are, respectively, the second and fourth Parisian Questions.

8. See Etienne Gilson's introduction to V. Lossky's doctoral dissertation, *Théologie Négative et Connaissance de Dieu chez Maître Eckhart* (Paris: I. Vrin, 1960), p 8.

9. See my article, "The Enigma of Visual Perception," *Sophia*, vol, 10, no. 1 (2004). Reprinted in *Science and Myth*, op. cit.

Eckhart wishes to convey, it is evidently not a question of continuous movement, as of an actual point of view, but of a radical discontinuity, a leap, ultimately, from the standpoint of the creature, to what, for lack of a better term, one might call the "standpoint" of God—which of course is not, strictly speaking, a standpoint at all, but an absolute knowing untouched by relativity, a knowing which therefore transcends all "points of view." What distinguishes Meister Eckhart—and accounts for his "Vedantic" visage—is the fact that he dared at times to assume that "divine standpoint," and in so doing, give utterance to a Truth that flies in the face of all creaturely wisdom. He does so, for example, when he says: "All creatures are one pure nothing. I do not say that they are a little something or anything, but that they are pure nothing."[10] To be sure, this proposition is humanly unacceptable: to speak thus is to be demented; and in fact, one needs to be quite literally "demented" to uphold that position in truth. It is no wonder the proposition was condemned (as Article 26) in the papal Bull.

How, then, can we—who are not thus "demented"—understand what Eckhart wishes to convey? How can *we*, for whom the "ten thousand things" of this world are most assuredly "real," grasp the notion that "all creatures are one pure nothing"? The key, once again, lies in the realization—as simple and obvious as it is basic— that the things we know, be it by way of sense perception or in thought, constitute the intentional object of that knowing. This is the universal "principle of relativity" that resolves, as we have seen, a host of conundrums: from the so-called "quantum enigma" all the way to Meister Eckhart's "shocking" statement.[11] What stands at issue, again, is the Upanishadic distinction between *para* and *aparavidyā*: supreme and non-supreme knowing. The former is absolute, unconditioned and divine, the latter relative, conditioned and creaturely. Consider, now, the non-supreme knowing, which happens to be ours; consider, if you will, a particular such act: say, the conceiving of an object X. Obviously, X is the intentional object

10. B. McGinn, *Meister Eckhart: Teacher and Preacher* (New York: Paulist Press, 1986), p250. Henceforth referred to as METP.

11. See chapter 2.

of that act. It can, of course, be "dissociated" from that act, but only by way of a second cognitive act: an act, namely, which dissociates it. One can thus proceed from X_1 to X_2, and so on; one can even define an X^* as the invariant of which each X_n in the resultant series is a particular representation; and yet we are left in the end with but another intentional object. The point is analogous to Wittgenstein's contention to the effect that "we never get out of language." What we know, and what we *can* know—every X, every "creature"—is the intentional object of that knowing, which *as such* has no place in the divine, the *paravidyā*. Whatever may become of X in the *paravidyā*, it ceases to be an object of *our* intentionality, which in Meister Eckhart's terminology is tantamount to saying that it ceases to be a "creature." And since the divine knowing is absolutely normative, this entails precisely what he affirms (speaking, as it were, from the supreme "point of view"): "All creatures are one pure nothing. I do not say that they are a little something or anything, but that they are *purus nihil*, pure nothing."

The question presents itself whether Eckhart, in his "controversial" utterances, has in fact repudiated the Scholastic teachings. On the face of it he obviously has; yet it is nonetheless conceivable that Scholasticism, deep down, aims precisely at its own demise in the realization of gnosis, the very enlightenment to which Eckhart has given a kind of doctrinal expression. Not that every member of the Scholastic community, let alone the Roman Church at large, could be expected to view the matter in that light. Yet it is hard to believe that St. Thomas Aquinas, for one, could have failed to recognize the drastic insufficiency of human knowing in the face of gnosis, no matter how "Scholastic" that human knowing may be; and indeed, in his very last didactic utterance—the "*mihi ut palea videtur*" ("to me appears as straw")—the Master himself attests to this fact.

We are not, however, obliged to accept a "straw versus enlightenment" dichotomy as the last word: there exists a third term or middle ground, I contend, that mediates between the two. I shall argue that the "straw"—which Eckhart and Aquinas both negate in the end—constitutes but the outer shell of Scholastic doctrine, the "exoteric" side of the coin. The integral doctrine, I maintain, encompasses in addition an inner kernel of truth, which may rightly be termed its "esoteric" aspect; and even though that too, strictly speaking, pertains to the *aparavidyā*, it yet exceeds immeasurably the corresponding exoteric sense, and constitutes a veritable "key of gnosis" on the plane of human knowing.

What is it, then, that defines the "esoteric" side of Scholastic doctrine: by what criterion are we enabled to distinguish its "esoteric" from its "exoteric" sense? It is the attendant *cosmology*, the implied or presupposed notion of the *created order*, I say. Strange as it may seem, the Scholastic doctrine, as commonly understood, is already "esoteric" in its strictly theological dogmas, which as we know, are founded upon Revelation; what proves to be "human, all too human," on the other hand, is the underlying cosmology. There are, basically, two conceptual possibilities: either the cosmos is something *real*—something, therefore, "made by God"—or it is not, in which case it exists simply "for us" as an object of intentionality, like the Vedantic "snake in the rope." I shall henceforth take the first stance—that of *creatio ex nihilo* theology—as definitive of what I will term the *exoteric* point of view, whereas the second shall define the *esoteric*. What distinguishes the exoteric from the esoteric position, thus, is precisely its recognition of an *aliud* or "other than God": it is this belief in "otherness"—in *duality*—that characterizes what I shall label "exoteric."

As thus defined, the two orientations are not only "worlds apart," but mutually exclusive. To the *creatio ex nihilo* theologian, the implications of esoterism—the implications of gnosis!—are heresy, pure and simple: it is "pantheism" and "blasphemy"; and that is why esoterism needs to be hidden, needs in fact to be concealed. On the other hand, it is also clear that there can be no absolute or pure esoterism here below, no esoterism unaccompanied by an exoterism, even as there can be no soul or spirit without a body. Esoterism, moreover, is not in fact an option, a personal choice, but a *call*; and most assuredly, it is not for everyone. We must not think of it as a competing system of thought; it is comparable, rather, to a mathematical limit. Think of an infinite series converging, say, to an irrational number, such as π: though that limit may indeed exceed each term and every partial sum, it is yet in a sense "given by" that series. My point is that despite their logical opposition, exoterism and

esoterism are not antithetical: in fact, the first finds its consummation in the second. One is reminded of the four *āśramas* or "stages
of life" in ancient India, in which the fourth, named *sannyās*, entails
the renunciation of all previous attachments and mundane goals.
Suffice it to say that no matter what the rank and file theologian
may think, esoterism has a role to play, in the total economy of
Christian life, precisely as the symbol or representation of gnosis on
the doctrinal plane. The esoteric, therefore, is something the
Church is obligated to admit on pain of divine censure: did not the
Savior himself direct one of his most stinging rebukes precisely to
the pharisaical exoterists of his day, when he said: "Woe onto you,
lawyers! for you have taken away the key of gnosis: ye entered not in
yourselves, and them that were entering in ye hindered."[12]

The question, of course, is whether Scholastic doctrine—say, in
its Thomistic formulation—does in fact admit, or carry, an esoteric
sense, as defined by the stipulated criterion. That the teaching,
according to its customary interpretation, is indeed exoteric is clear;
but what about the definitive texts, as given, for example, in the
Summa Theologiae: do these, perhaps, carry an esoteric sense? I
contend that they do, "hidden" though that sense may be. What distinguishes Eckhart, thus, is not that his teaching is esoteric where
that of Aquinas, say, is not, but the fact, rather, that he brought out
into the open what had hitherto been concealed. And let us note
that such an occurrence is by no means untypical at the termination
of an era. One must bear in mind that Eckhart stands at the end of a
"golden age": on the brink of the very "fall" which gave rise, in rapid
succession, to the Renaissance, the Enlightenment, and the modern
world. At such critical times it does happen that esoteric truths,
which in days gone by had been carefully concealed, are promulgated more or less openly: think of Proclus, for example, who at the
termination of antiquity "lifted the veil" to reveal, at least in some
measure, the arcana of the Platonist schools. Eckhart, I say, did likewise: so far from repudiating the Scholastic tradition, he gave voice
to its esoteric core—of which few, perhaps, had been effectively cognizant even in the best of times.

12. Luke 11:52.

One cannot, therefore, separate Meister Eckhart's teaching from the Scholastic: the flower or fruit from the tree upon which it grows. To do so—to interpret that teaching, say, in Vedantic terms—would be in a way to falsify his doctrine, to clothe it in a foreign garb. Like it or not, Eckhart *was* a Scholastic, and taught as one. The greater part of his Latin treatises is in fact devoted to what is demonstrably *exoteric* Scholastic doctrine, such as the standard exemplarism, which apparently he did not despise, but regarded important enough to explain and elaborate upon at great length. Such teachings serve as the springboard, if you will, from which Eckhart takes his leap into the esoteric domain. To be sure, *logically* the respective doctrines are indeed incompatible, or so, at least, it seems from the exoteric side; and this explains why "unimpeachable texts yet differ among themselves to the point of being contradictory." Yet, even so, in the organic unity of Eckhart's teaching, everything has its place.

For the most part, Eckhart speaks in a "creaturely" way, which of course is hardly surprising; what amazes us mortals, on the other hand, is that at times he does not. It is these occasional leaps, into what might be termed a doctrinal *samādhi*,[13] that mainly distinguish Eckhart from his peers. No wonder that this teaching has rarely been understood, especially in the West, where the idea of gnosis and its effective realization appears far more strange and suspect than it does in the East. Eckhart authorities, for their part, have labored to eliminate doctrinal incongruities, or bring them to light, to condone or to critique, depending upon their individual predilections; I know only of one who appears to have recognized, in full clarity, what actually stands at issue. I am referring to C.F. Kelley, a Benedictine, who has, very accurately, stated the crucial point in his book, *Meister Eckhart on Divine Knowledge*.[14]

So much by way of introduction. Having defined the notion of "esoterism"—from what amounts to a Kabbalistic point of view—I

13. The term refers to the state of perfect concentration, when our intellect or inner eye becomes "single." It refers thus to the realization of gnosis.

14. Although it is not clear whether Kelley had knowledge of René Guénon, it may interest some readers that there are passages in his treatise which sound, for all the world, like a page from the French metaphysician.

propose in this Chapter to delineate Meister Eckhart's doctrine, not in its entirety, but specifically as it pertains to the idea of "creation." I do so in order to display its esoteric nature—as enunciated in his occasional "moments of doctrinal *samādhi*"—in accordance with the stipulated criterion.

There is however a task that needs first to be accomplished: having made the claim that the standard Scholastic teaching—say, in its Thomistic formulation—"encompasses also an inner kernel of truth, which may rightly be termed its 'esoteric' aspect," it behooves me to justify this foundational contention. To this end we will now examine a few definitive texts regarding creation, taken from the *Summa Theolgiae.*

The subject is broached in Question 44 of Part I, dealing with "The Procession of Creatures from God, and of the First Cause of All Things," which initiates *The Treatise on Creation.* In the very first Article we read:

> All beings apart from God are not their own being, but are beings by participation.

What does this mean? From the exoteric point of view, it means that all things in creation derive their being from God. St. Thomas gives the example of iron, which "becomes ignited by fire": just as heat, which belongs to fire essentially, belongs to the red-hot iron "by participation," so too, he asserts, does being, which belongs to God essentially—since in God essence and being (*esse*) are one and the same—belongs to the creature "by participation." It is as if "being" were "given" or "lent out" to the creature by God. The created entity, thus, has being by virtue of the fact that God has bestowed being upon it: that is the exoteric view, the exoteric interpretation. What, then, is the esoteric? What does the statement mean—what *can* it mean—if one concurs with Meister Eckhart to the effect that "All creatures are one pure nothing"? It can only mean that creatures manifest a being which is not their own: God did *not*, in fact, "give" or "lend out" being to creatures. The esoteric sense, here, is precisely that of Exodus 3:14: God alone has being, God alone *is*. Creatures possess a mere "semblance" of being, which actually belongs to no one but God. Their status is thus indeed that of the Vedantic "snake in the rope": the rope does not actually bestow being upon the snake, for the simple reason that the snake *has no* being: in plain terms, there *is no snake*. Yet, non-existent though it is, it yet manifests in some way the being of the rope. From the esoteric point of view, the cosmos is *in reality* a self-manifestation of God, a *creatio ex Deo et in Deo* in precisely the Kabbalistic sense, seen however "as through a glass, darkly." What distinguishes the cosmos from the *creatio in Deo*, therefore, is not something positive, not something "created by God" as the theologian thinks, but something that has no reality at all: the "glass" to which St. Paul refers is indeed "nothing," and so are the things "seen darkly." Conceived as an *aliud*, as "other than God"—conceived as a *creatio ex nihilo* in the theological sense—the cosmos is in truth a *purus nihil*, as Meister Eckhart declares. The theological "Uncreated versus created" dichotomy proves ultimately to be spurious: in the final count, there is nothing on the hither side.

We turn now to a second key text, pertaining to Article 3 of Question 44, which, according to the customary exoteric interpretation, founds the Augustinian doctrine of exemplarism:

> In the divine wisdom are the types of all things, which types we have called ideas, i.e., exemplar forms existing in the divine mind. And these ideas, though multiplied by their relations to things, in reality are not separated from the divine essence, according as the likeness of that essence can be shared diversely by different things. In this manner, therefore, God himself is the first exemplar of all things.

Let us note, first of all, that Kabbalistically speaking, "the divine wisdom" is *Hokhmah*, the second *Sefirah*, and "the divine mind" is *Binah*, the third.[15] The "exemplar forms" of all things in creation derive thus from the supreme tri-unity: it is on this highest level that the first theophanic act takes place, which we may conceive as a

---

15. See chapter 3.

bi-polarization of *Kether-Elyon*, the "Supreme Crown," giving rise to *Hokhmah-Bina*, the biune pair from which are derived all being, all power, and all bliss.

What, then, are the "things" by which the "ideas" existing in *Hokhmah-Bina* are "multiplied"? Exoterically speaking, they are of course the "ten thousand things" which make up what we deem to be the world. By its substantial form or created essence, such a cosmic entity "exemplifies" an idea in the divine wisdom or mind. Now, in God there is no actual diversity of ideas (since all "are one" in the divine essence), whereas on the cosmic plane—the plane of exemplification—there is of course a multiplicity of forms. We may think of the ideas as comprising the center of a circle, and of their exemplifications as points on the circumference: as the center is "multiplied" by its relations to the peripheral points—or by the diversity of the radii—so the ideas in God are "multiplied by their relations to things." What confronts us here, clearly, is a Christian exemplarism tracing back at least to St. Augustine.

How, then, does the matter stand from the esoteric point of view? The answer turns out to be simple: nothing need be changed in our reading of the given text, except the meaning of the term "things," which now refers, not to the realm of cosmic entities—which in truth do not exist—but precisely to the Sefirothic world, the things *in Deo* which *do* in truth exist. We know from the Kabbalah that the deployment of what Leo Schaya calls "the infinite and indivisible aspects of the One," which takes place "supernally" in the supreme tri-unity *Kether-Hokhmah-Binah*, is "continued", so to speak, in the "Edenic flow" terminating in the *Shekhinah*, also known as *Malkhuth*, the Kingdom. Here, in that, for us, "supra-cosmic" realm, are to be found the multitude of creatures, "from the *Hayoth* and the *Serafim* to the lowest worm on earth"[16]: whatever is real, whatever has being, whatever actually exists, is *here*; and as an ancient text has it, "What is not here is nowhere" (is a *purus nihil*, as Eckhart says).

Such is the esoteric interpretation of the Thomistic text; and let us add—in light of what has been said in Chapter 2—that it is, in the

---

16. The *Hayoth* and the *Serafim* are angels belonging, respectively, to the highest and second-highest orders.

final count, *the only tenable reading*. Let me recall, as simply as I can, why this is so. Take a lump of salt. To our senses, it is something hard and white, which has a salty taste. To the physicist, on the other hand, it is an aggregate of sodium chloride molecules, which as such can be neither seen, touched, nor tasted. What, then, *is* that lump of salt? Is it the hard, white, salty thing we ordinarily take it to be, or is it an aggregate of sodium chloride molecules? It turns out that neither reductionism is tenable.[17] We are forced in the end to acknowledge that the so-called lump of salt is neither a corporeal nor a physical object, that in fact it is literally "not of this world": and that is, finally, all we know, all we presently *can* know. To proceed further, one needs the operative means of an integral esoterism: only thus can one break through to the actual "thing," which in fact pertains to the Sefirothic world: the creation *in Deo* as opposed to the theological *creatio ex nihilo*.

If now we go back, and read what St. Thomas has to say concerning "ideas" and their exemplification in "things," we find that it applies *verbatim* to that Sefirothic realm. However, it needs to be realized that there, *in Deo*, the notion of multiplicity can no longer be understood in the customary "exclusivist" sense. We are here in the realm of *advaita*, a nondualist world in which there is in truth no "other," no *aliud*. Even as the "ideas" in God, "though multiplied by their relations to things, are not separated from the divine essence," so also it can now be said that the "things" which diversely exemplify these "ideas" are yet profoundly *one*. It could not be otherwise, given that "the first exemplar of all things," as St. Thomas declares, is none other than God himself, the "One-without-a- second." One sees that the Thomistic text, thus interpreted from an esoteric point of view, turns into a sublime statement of *advaitic* truth.

We turn finally to Question 45, beginning with Article 1, where St. Thomas *defines* "creation" as "the emanation of all being from the universal cause, which is God." What is remarkable, first of all, is the choice of the word "emanation," which seems indeed to proclaim a *creatio ex Deo* in place of the theological *creatio ex nihilo*.

---

17. See *The Quantum Enigma* (San Rafael, CA: Angelico Press/Sophia Perennis, 2011), pp7–51.

One has the impression that St. Thomas labors, as it were, to render his definition inclusive of the esoteric sense, even at the risk of ecclesiastic censure. It appears, in fact, that the tables are now reversed: it is now the *esoteric* sense that predominates. That first impression, however, is soon dispelled: "As the generation of a man," St. Thomas goes on to say, "is from the non-being which is *not-man*, so creation, which is the emanation of all being, is from the *not-being* which is *nothing*." The overt meaning of this statement is clear: it specifies the exoteric *nihil* as a "nothingness" in the privative sense. Yet this too carries also an esoteric sense: for as we read in the *Zohar*, the "emanation of all being" is from the *ain* or "nothingness" of *En-Sof*, which in a way is the polar opposite of the exoteric *nihil*.

In Article 2, St. Thomas goes on to say: "Creation is not change, except according to the mode of understanding." Here again the exoteric sense predominates: creation is not change, because the created thing has no "prior state." The same can however be said of "creation" in the esoteric sense, but for a different reason: even on the *ad intra* level, "creation is not change," because now creation is but the manifesting of something that exists eternally in God. Again there is no "prior state," not however because the created thing did not previously exist, but rather because the created thing is not temporal, is not subject to time. The esoteric *creatio* is thus distinguished from the exoteric by the fact that it is eternal; and let us note that it was the Fourth Lateran Council, held in the year 1215, that, in a way, proclaims the *temporal* nature of the creation by the following words (which go beyond the Apostolic Creed): "who by his own omnipotent power at once *from the beginning of time* created each creature from nothing".[18] A decade before the birth of Saint Thomas, the esoteric doctrine had thus been, in effect, outlawed as "heretical": one must not forget this fact.[19] Is it any wonder that the Angelic Doctor treads cautiously?

18. H. Denzinger, *Enchiridion Symbolorum*, 428.
19. Since earliest times, the Church has been apprehensive of an "eternal world"; as S. Baldner and W. Carrol point out: "For the Church Fathers, to claim that the world is eternal is to claim that it is equal to God." Yet a certain latitude

Getting back to the statement from Article 2, one sees that the words "except according to the mode of understanding" apply to both the esoteric and the exoteric version: for in either case we are forced to conceive of "creation" in terms of "before" and "after." Even Jacob Boehme, we recall, was obliged to speak of the eternal creation in such terms: "I must indeed speak in a devilish manner," he tells us, "otherwise I cannot teach you, so that you will understand."

Enough has perhaps been said to make my point. The question remains, of course, whether St. Thomas himself was cognizant of what we have termed the esoteric sense of his dicta, and most importantly, whether he would in any case have accepted that interpretation as true. Nowhere, to be sure, does he assume an esoteric stance *explicitly*; yet this is hardly surprising, given that he was, after all, an official theologian of the Catholic Church, and subject, therefore, to its theological constraints. What *is* surprising, on the other hand, is the fact that he formulated the definitive texts relating to this question in such a way—with such meticulous care, one is tempted to say—as to carry, in addition to their exoteric meaning, an esoteric sense as well, "hidden" though it be. For my part, I cannot conceive that this could have happened "by accident," much less can I believe that one of the mightiest theologians ever born could have been permanently confined to an exoteric plane.

---

remained with regard to this question, and theologians as eminent as John Scotus Eriugena did occasionally espouse the "suspect" view. In fact, a debate relating to this question was intensively pursued during the twelfth century in the form of an "ecumenical" encounter involving such major non-Christian figures as Avicenna, Averroes, and Maimonides. However, as the debate expanded, so did opposition to the idea of an eternal creation on the part of the ecclesiastic authorities intensify. There is the case of Amaury of Béne, for instance, a follower of John Scotus, who was posthumously excommunicated for his "Eriugenist" views: a council of bishops, convened in Paris in the year 1210, ordered his body to be exhumed and re-buried in unconsecrated ground. Such in part is the historical background to the decree of 1215, which constitutes, as Baldner and Carrol inform us, "the first conciliar statement that the world had a temporal beginning." See *Aquinas on Creation* (Toronto: Pontifical Institute of Medieaval Studies, 1997), pp1–34. The important point, however, is that the Lateran IV declaration *need not be* thus interpreted, as I have shown in the Postscript.

We begin our inquiry into Meister Eckhart's "doctrine of creation" with the *Expositio Libri Genesis,* the first of his two commentaries on Genesis. It is to be noted that exoteric commentary prevails in both, whereas the esoteric occurs sparsely, and invariably in hidden form; as a rule, it is in his German sermons that Eckhart openly "crosses the line." Occasionally, however, one does encounter an "almost explicitly" esoteric passage even in one of his exegetical treatises; and such is the following text:

> The "beginning" in which "God created heaven and earth" is the first simple now of eternity. I say that it is the very same now in which God exists from eternity, in which also the emanation of the divine Persons eternally is, was and will be... When someone asked me why God had not created the world earlier, I answered that he could not because he did not exist. He did not exist before the world did. Furthermore, how could he have created earlier when he had already created the world in the very now in which he was God... In one and the same time in which he was God and in which he begot his coeternal Son as God equal to himself in all things, he also created the world. "God spoke once and for all." (Jb. 22:14) He speaks in begetting the Son because the Son is the Word; he speaks in creating creatures, "He spoke and they were made, he commanded and they were created." (Ps. 32:9) This is why it says in another Psalm, "God has spoken once and for all and I have heard two things." (Ps. 61:12) The "two things" are heaven and earth, or rather "these two", that is, the emanation of the Persons and the creation of the world, but "he speaks" them both "once and for all"; "he has spoken once and for all."[20]

To begin with, it is not without interest to note that the first two sentences were attacked at the Cologne trial, and that the following three were cited in the papal Bull of condemnation. Does this mean that these statements contradict the official teaching of the Church?

20. EME, pp 84–5.

Actually they do not. The problem, in this instance, is caused by Eckhart's manner of expression, which is evidently designed to shock, and in so doing, to "jar" the listener out of his inveterate complacency; it is in essence the way of the Zen *koan*, whose function is quite the same. Thus, when Eckhart responds to the question "why God had not created the world earlier" by saying "because he did not exist," this is not to be interpreted abstrusely as referring to a "God beyond God," but is simply a "koanic" way of saying that in eternity *there is no* "earlier," no "before." Everything Eckhart asserts in these first five "controversial" statements derives from his initial premise, namely, that God created the world "in the single moment of eternity," which is in essence no more than what St. Augustine had said centuries earlier. The likely first impression of absurdity, or indeed of blasphemy, is thus dispelled the instant we grasp the point (which apparently Eckhart's Inquisitorial critics never managed to do).

So far nothing "esoteric" has taken place; for that we need to read on. What is of prime significance, clearly, is the stipulation that, "in the single moment of eternity," two very different acts are said to take place: the begetting of the Son, namely, and the creation of the world. One needs thus to ask oneself how these apparently disparate acts can "coexist": how can God both *beget* and *create* in one and the same "now"? How, in other words, can he "do two things at once"? Eckhart answers that he does *not* in fact "do two things": that is the crux.

The basis, moreover, upon which Eckhart arrives at this conclusion is purely scriptural. There are three steps. The first consists in the recognition that the acts of *begetting* and of *creating* are related by the fact that both reduce to *speech*. The proof is succinct: "He speaks in begetting the Son because the Son is the Word; he speaks in creating creatures, 'He spoke and they were made, he commanded and they were created.'" The second step is to recognize that "God spoke once and for all" (as one reads in the Book of Job). And let us note that this truth—"God speaks but a single Word"—is central to Christianity: for indeed, what God speaks is none other than Christ, "the only-begotten Son of the Father."

At this point, however, so far from having resolved the problem, it seems that we have arrived at a flat contradiction: it now appears that the creation—this world in which we find ourselves—has become identified with Christ, which of course is absurd. A major stroke of insight, clearly, is needed to break this impasse; and that is precisely what Eckhart supplies in the third step: "This is why it says in another Psalm, 'God has spoken once and for all, *and I have heard two things*.'" It is *we* who have "heard two things": and what is it that we have heard? Eckhart's answer is itself twofold: on the one hand, "the two things" are said to be "heaven and earth," and on the other, they are "the emanation of the Persons" and "the creation of the world."

Let us reflect upon the first: "heaven and earth." This polarity can of course be understood in numerous ways: as "heaven and earth" in the literal sense, as form and matter, or as existence and essence, to cite but a few out of the many considered by Eckhart himself, in *Expositio Libri Genesis* and elsewhere. What is however most germane, in the present context, is simply the idea of *duality*, the notion of "two." It is *we* who perceive duality, it is "I" who "have heard two things." Yet, even though "I have heard two things," God has spoken "once and for all." Note that the scriptural text stops short of saying that God spoke "one thing": it says he spoke "once and for all." It is not a question of numerical oneness, of 1 as opposed to 2. It is a question, rather, of "not-two", of "nonduality": it is "I"—and not God—who hears "two things." To "hear two things" is to fall into duality, to succumb to the *dvandvas*, the "pairs of opposites."

However, to "hear two things" has also another sense: the "two things," Eckhart tells us, can be taken to mean "the emanation of the Persons" and "the creation of the world." It is *we* who "hear" these "two things": it is *we* who perceive the emanation of the Persons and the creation of the world as "two different things": that is the crucial point. It is we, if you will, who create the very problem we are now attempting to solve. There is no such problem for God—no such problem *in truth*—since "God speaks once and for all." In reality, "the emanation of the Persons" and "the creation of the world" are *not* "two things".

It is to be noted that Eckhart stops short of stating explicitly what in fact his argument implies. Advisedly so, seeing that the conclusion contradicts what could well be termed the fundamental premise of theology; for indeed, as A. N. Williams points out: "The most fundamental distinction in Christian theology, the distinction that lies at the root of both patristic and Thomistic thought, is the distinction between Uncreated and created."[21] What Eckhart does not say—but his argument permits us to conclude—is that this "most fundamental distinction" exists "for us," that is, from the human point of view, but *not* "from the divine": not in point of absolute truth.

The argument, we have said, proves that the begetting of the Son and the creation of the world are *not* in truth "two things." But what, precisely, does this mean? In the final count, it can only mean that the creation, or world, is none other than the "only-begotten Son," *seen however "as through a glass, darkly."* And this, clearly, is tantamount in essence to the Kabbalistic doctrine, the conception of the Sefirothic world. To be sure, Eckhart does not—and cannot— express himself in such terms. He continues, in fact, to employ the word "creation," be it as a noun or as a verb, in its exoteric sense, that is to say, as referring precisely to the *temporal* world, in keeping with the decree of 1215. Yet the idea of an "eternal creation," con- ceived in Trinitarian or Christological terms, implicit or "hidden" though it be, stands at the very heart of Eckhart's doctrine: the pas- sage from the *Expositio Libri Genesis*, quoted above, permits us to conclude as much.

A key passage in the Book of Wisdom which Eckhart loves to cite is the verse: "He created all things that they might be." We turn now to his commentary on this text, beginning with a passage from Article 19:

> The first point to be made is that becoming is from secondary causes, but the existence of everything, either natural or artifi- cial, in that it is what is first and perfect, is immediately from God alone. "God's works are perfect." (Deut. 32.4)[22]

21. *The Ground of Union* (Oxford: Oxford University Press, 1999), p88.
22. METP, p147.

It is evident, first of all, that Eckhart, once again, conceives of "creation" exoterically, that is to say, with reference to the temporal world: the very fact that he distinguishes between "natural" and "artificial" things leaves no doubt on that score. Yet, even so, the statement that "becoming is from secondary causes" has a distinctly esoteric ring, for it suggests that what God brings into being "directly"—without the mediation of "secondary causes"—is *not* in fact temporal. Admittedly, the notion that "becoming is from secondary causes" makes sense from an exoteric point of view, and can in fact be interpreted in standard Aristotelian terms. My point, however, is that it can also be understood esoterically, which appears, moreover, to be the interpretation Eckhart is driving at when he goes on to say that "the existence of everything . . . *in that it is first and perfect, is immediately from God alone.*" If what "is first and perfect" is "immediately from God alone," it follows that what is "first and perfect" is *not* "from secondary causes," which in turn implies— given that "becoming *is* from secondary causes"—that it is *not* a "becoming" or *genesis*, not *temporal*, but is in fact *eternal*, as the esoteric teaching affirms. It matters not whether we employ the word "creation" with reference to that supra-temporal realm; its existence is in any case assured.

At this point we appear to be left with two distinct realms: an eternal world, derived immediately from God, and a temporal universe, produced by secondary causes; the problem, now, is to grasp how the two are related. The single clue Eckhart gives resides in the phrase "in that it is what is first and perfect": what does this mean? How can something of this world be in some way "first and perfect"? How can something temporal be, in a way, eternal? Let us note that Eckhart is not here speaking exemplarism, at least not in the usual sense, since the "eternal things," which now stand in the place of exemplars, are themselves, in a sense, "produced" by God. So, too, he does not say, of a temporal thing, "in that it manifests" or "exemplifies" what is "first and perfect," but "in that it *is*" what is so. And since what is "first and perfect" is supra-temporal, as we have seen, it also must make sense to say, of a temporal thing, "in that it is eternal." We need now to ask ourselves what, precisely, this means.

The answer, quite clearly, is implied by our earlier considerations (e.g., the esoteric interpretation of the text "All beings apart from God are not their own being, but are beings by participation" from the *Summa Theologiae*): the recognition, namely, that there are not in fact "two realms." What is real—what actually exists—is the same in both: there *is in truth* no "temporal" as distinguished from a "supra-temporal" being. One can say that temporal things exist "insofar as" they are supra-temporal, even as Eckhart says "in that they are what is first and perfect." What differentiates the temporal from the eternal order, thus, is not a *kind* of being—temporal as opposed to eternal—but a certain indigence, a "lack of being," precisely. It is as if temporal things had not yet fully attained their being: as if they were yet striving "to be." And this is after all what the term "becoming" connotes: it is what distinguishes "to become" from "to be." It makes sense, moreover, to say, of a thing that becomes, "in that it *is*," since nothing can "become" unless in some way "it is." Paradoxical as it may sound, it can be affirmed, of temporal things, that they both "are" and "are not," or as has often been said, that they consist of both "being" and "non-being."

What, then, is the meaning of Wisdom 1:14: "He created all things that they might be"? Certainly the verse conforms to the teaching of Avicenna, who defines "creation" as the conferring of "being after non-being," a definition generally accepted by the Scholastics. Yet the critical question—whether "created things" are *temporal* or *eternal*—remains. Now, what tips the balance, in the passage cited above, is the fact that Eckhart adjoins the quote from Deuteronomy: "God's works are perfect"; for indeed, the temporal world is evidently *not* "perfect." The verse, therefore, must mean: God created all things that they might be *eternal*.

Oddly enough, however, the interpretation at which Eckhart arrives in the present Article is simply that "everything made is nothing without God who is the source of existence"—which is certainly true, but hardly captures the meaning of the verse. There is in that text a sense of *telos* Eckhart fails to convey, an implied idea of *perfection* which is manifestly lost in his rendering. One could charge, in fact, that Eckhart's commentary (as given in Article 19) misses the point.

Why this apparent obfuscation? Is it due simply to the constraint imposed by the decree of 1215? This is hardly credible, given that Eckhart does, at times, assume an esoteric stance, at least by implication. More to the point is the fact that Eckhart evinces a propensity to interpret every scriptural verse in all possible ways: to extract, so to speak, the fullness of meaning it contains. It is this predilection that renders his commentaries immune to summary, and accounts for the existence of "unimpeachable texts which yet differ among themselves to the point of being contradictory." It seems that Eckhart respects and values all possible ways of looking at any given subject, and takes delight in what to the reader may well appear as a bewildering conglomerate of exegetical options, most of which, moreover, prove to be incurably exoteric, a fact which does not seem to disturb the Meister in the least, nor to mitigate the care he takes in expounding even the humblest such rendering. From the vantage-point of gnosis one can enter into all the limited perspectives of which the human mind is capable and enjoy the "panorama" each affords, without being in any way deceived: from the top of a mountain one can look into the plains, in every direction, "as far as the eye can see."

By way of example, consider the following passage (comprising Article 21, still from Eckhart's commentary on Wisdom 1:14):

> Note that in its essential or original cause a thing has no existence, and the same is true of the art and intellect [of an artist]. The house in the mind is not a house; heat in the sun, in motion, or in light is not heat. House and heat receive their respective formal existences insofar as they are produced and extracted from a cause and through an efficient cause. All things are in God as in the First Cause in an intellectual way and in the mind of the Maker. Therefore, they do not have any of their formal existence until they are actually produced and extracted on the outside in order to exist. This is why it says here, God "created all things that they might be."

Now, this is standard Scholastic exemplarism, pure Aristotle, if you will. To create "that they might be" is to bestow "formal existence"— the kind defined by a substantial form—upon the things of this world. For the moment it has apparently been forgotten that the so-called things of this world are in a state of "becoming," a state of perpetual flux: forgotten that Plato asked: "How can that which is never the same *be* anything?" Above all, it has been roundly forgotten that "All creatures are one pure nothing"! For the moment all these "creatures"—from "heat" to "houses"—exist, all have a "formal existence" of their own.

One may, of course, ask how Eckhart can do otherwise than to assume an exoteric stance regarding creation, given that he has chosen to employ the word "*creatio*" in its exoteric sense: how, in other words, can one speak of an "eternal creation," if to "create" means to produce a *temporal* world? Yet, in the midst of his wide-ranging and predominantly exoteric commentary on Wisdom 1:14, Eckhart "slips in" an esoteric paragraph; to be precise, he breaks the aforesaid impasse—with a single master-stroke—by co-opting the term "generation," which now takes the place of "creation" in the esoteric sense. Here is what he writes (in Article 29):

> From all that has been said it is clearly evident that every agent of nature, morality, and art in general intends as the goal and repose of its whole action and "pilgrimage" that its effect exist and receive existence. He says, "He created them that they might be." Existence is through the substantial form and generation. Everything which precedes that is dissimilar—the agent always finds something not his own in it. This is why it hates it, and gets rid of it through the process of change, until it finds itself in the offspring through generation. This is the "Father's perfect image," having nothing dissimilar or foreign to the Father, and possessing everything which is his, if it is truly a "Son" and an image, as in the Godhead. "All the things that the Father has are mine" (John 16:15). Therefore, the Father is well pleased with the Son, because he finds everything that belongs to him there, and nothing dissimilar. "This is my beloved Son in whom I am well pleased" (Matt. 3:17).

All activity here below, be it "natural," "moral," or "art in general," is directed to a single goal, which is the production of "the Father's perfect image." All life on earth, all motion, in fact, is in essence a "pilgrimage"; all things in creation seek "repose."[23] Eckhart gives us to understand that the ultimate agent or First Cause of "motion," in all its modes, is indeed God the Father, and that the *telos* of all becoming is the Birth of his Son. Whatever is other than the Son—whatever is "dissimilar" to the Father—is to be eliminated "through a process of change." It is clear, moreover, that Eckhart does not here ascribe "existence" to the things that are "dissimilar": existence—or better said, *being*—is the goal, the end to be attained: "Existence is through the substantial form *and generation*" he tells us. The sense of the statement is evident from the context: it means that *substantial form alone does not bestow existence.* Form needs to be "perfected through generation"—purified of all that is "dissimilar"—before existence is realized. The things in creation attain authentic existence or being only in the Son, in a state of "repose" beyond the temporal order.

Let us note that this in a way inverts the theological exemplarism, which places generation first—in the Trinitarian order—and attributes existence to substantial form. In light of what Eckhart says in Article 29, the so-called creation has now become, in effect, a means to an end which evidently breaches the categorical divide between the Uncreated and the order of creation: the very dichotomy which, from the exoteric point of view, is axiomatic, and therefore binding upon theology. To put it plainly: the notion that something "in creation" can "become the Son" through "a process of change" which eliminates what is "dissimilar" is outright heresy. And as a matter of fact, the tenet appears in the papal Bull of condemnation in the form of Article 10, which reads:

23. It is of interest to note that not only classical mechanics, but indeed the fundamental laws of physics can in fact be understood as expressing a tendency, on the part of Nature, to "seek repose." I am referring above all to the various "principles of least action," from those of Euler, d'Alembert, and Lagrange, to the elegant version given by Hamilton, which reaches as far as quantum field theory. My point is that the physicist's "least action" cannot but correspond ultimately to "maximum repose" in the sense of Eckhart. The "final cause"—the *telos* that drives every process of Nature—can be none other than what Pico de la Mirandola likewise calls "complete repose," which shall be attained in what the Kabbalah knows as the Great Jubilee. Eckhart is in perfect accord on this issue with the Kabbalistic teaching.

We shall all be transformed totally into God and changed into him. In the same way, when in the sacrament bread is changed into Christ's Body, I am so changed into him that he makes me his one existence, and not just similar. By the living God it is true that there is no distinction there.[24]

Although this particular passage is taken from one of his German sermons (namely, Sermon 6), it is evidently tantamount to the position Eckhart assumes in Article 29 of his Commentary. One sees that the Inquisitors knew their theology: this *is* heresy.

However, as Jean Borella points out: "None of the articles condemned in the Bull of 1329 concern a single sacred dogma."[25] There is a crucial distinction to be made between dogmatic formulations which define the fundamental tenets of Christian belief—primarily of a Trinitarian and Christological nature—and their theological interpretations: it is the former that constitute the "sacred dogmas" which indeed neither Eckhart nor any other Christian "Master of gnosis" has ever denied. By the very fact, however, that these dogmas are truly sacrosanct, they exceed the level of human understanding, and consequently demand *interpretation*: and that is where theology, properly so called—and with it, a touch of the "human, all too human"—enters the picture. To be sure, the factor of divine inspiration may intervene here as well, *but in a different degree*: that is the point. As Borella has made clear, the distinction between "sacred dogma" and "theological dogma"—though often enough overlooked—proves to be critical when it comes to "*problèmes de gnose*." Getting back to Article 10 of the papal Bull: one sees, in light of the aforesaid distinction, that Eckhart's heresy is to be categorized as "theological but not dogmatic."

That "heretical" tenet, however, is not only *esoteric* in the previously specified sense, but is evidently allied to the teaching of Jacob Boehme. To be sure, Eckhart does not speak alchemy, any more than Boehme speaks the language of the Schools; yet it would be

24. EME, p78.
25. "Dogmatique Chrétienne et Gnose Schuonienne," in *Problèmes de Gnose* (Paris: L'Harmattan, 2008), p256.

hard to deny that their respective visions of "process" culminating in "generation"—in the Birth of God!—are inherently concordant. Both, finally, capture the esoteric sense of *telos* implicit in the biblical verse: "He created all things that they might be."

While the preceding commentary has evidently transgressed the limits of *creatio ex nihilo* theology, it does not take us to the very core of Eckhart's doctrine: for that we turn now to his Latin Sermon XLIX, one of the loci which does.

The Sermon is based upon the words "Whose are this image and inscription?" from Matthew 22:20. What apparently fascinates Eckhart, to the point of eliciting a discourse of unsurpassed profundity, is the notion of "image" itself, or more precisely, the fact that there are two kinds of "image": the "mundane" kind which is separated from its exemplar—even as the image on the Roman coin differs from Caesar—and the divine, where the two are one. The first or *formal* kind, Eckhart tells us, is not, properly speaking, an image at all: "the image transcends and is higher than any form." What distinguishes a *form* from an image is the fact that it is separated from its exemplar, whereas "image as such cannot be separated from that of which it is an image."

But while *image* and *form* are thus distinguished, Eckhart gives us to understand that image constitutes *the principle* of form: forms "derive" from image. It is evident from the start that in differentiating between "image" and "form," Eckhart is seeking to comprehend what it is that distinguishes "the two things" of Psalm 61:12: Trinity and creation, namely. Here is how he broaches the subject:

> Note that an image, properly speaking, is a simple formal emanation that transmits the whole pure naked essence. The metaphysician considers in abstraction from efficient and final causes according to which natural scientists investigate things. The image, then, is an emanation from the depth of silence, excluding everything that comes from without. It is a form of life, as if you were to imagine something swelling up from itself

and in itself and then inwardly boiling, without any "boiling over" yet understood.[26]

Clearly, Eckhart is speaking of the eternal birth of the Son, which he conceives as "a simple *formal* emanation": the emanation is "simple" because the Son "is one," even as the Father "is one"; and it is "formal" because what is emanated constitutes the principle of form: not in fact a plurality of forms, but "the whole pure naked essence." Having thus specified the Trinitarian notion of "image," Eckhart goes on to say that "the metaphysician considers in abstraction from efficient and final causes according to which natural scientists investigate things": why does he say that? To be sure, what Eckhart's "natural scientist" has his eye upon is the created order, which he analyses in terms of Aristotelian causality. The metaphysician, on the other hand—who "considers in abstraction from efficient and final causes"—is concerned with *form*, not as it manifests here below, but in its principle; and therefore, where the "natural scientist" perceives a temporal process, a "becoming," the metaphysician perceives "a simple formal emanation that transmits the whole pure naked essence." It is all about *knowing*: one kind perceives the created order, the other perceives the divine. The metaphysician proceeds by "abstraction"—by eliminating all that is outside "the pure naked essence"—whereas the (Aristotelian) scientist, while admitting "formal emanation" (which he conceives as the conferring of forms) admits "efficient and final causes" as well.[27]

"The image," Eckhart goes on to say, "is an emanation from the depths of silence, excluding everything that comes from without." It is however clear that nothing *can* "come from without"! What is

---

26. METP, p236.

27. It is to be noted that the contemporary scientist has in effect done away with both formal and final causation. Yet it turns out—to his consternation!—that the phenomenon of state vector collapse, as conceived in quantum theory, is in fact irreducible to efficient causality. What makes it so is that it presents itself as "instantaneous," and thus as a discontinuity which cannot be explained by way of differential equations. What distinguishes that so-called "collapse" from an ordinary physical process is that it constitutes a *substantive* change, that is to say, a conferral of form, which is "instantaneous" by virtue of the fact that it does not take place "in time." See *The Quantum Enigma*, op. cit., pp52–76.

actually "excluded," therefore, is in truth "nothing": the very "nothing" which constitutes the cosmos as conceived from the standpoint of "the natural scientist." The metaphysician, then, is he that concerns himself exclusively with "what is," as opposed to what the Goddess of Parmenides terms "the non-being that is not"; and clearly, Meister Eckhart, no less than Parmenides, understands full well that this very "non-being that is not" constitutes, in a way, what the "scientist" perceives.

Eckhart goes on to speak of that "simple formal emanation" as a "life," which he describes as a *bullitio* or "boiling." Most assuredly, this is pure Trinitarian doctrine, but stated in terms reminiscent of Jacob Boehme, and indeed of the Kabbalah. Even as the latter avails itself of a natural symbolism, based upon an esoteric reading of the Torah—think of the verse "a river flowed out of Eden to water the garden"[28] understood as referring to the *creatio in Deo*—so does Eckhart speak likewise in "naturalistic" terms. Having thus introduced *bullitio* as a metaphor for the Trinitarian emanation, he forthwith goes on to distinguish *bullitio* from *ebullitio*, or "boiling over," by which he evidently alludes to the formation of the created order. This is what he says, speaking of the "simple formal emanation": "It is a form of life, as if you were to imagine something swelling up from itself and in itself and then inwardly boiling, without any 'boiling over' yet understood." What does this mean? The key resides in the last two words: "yet understood." He does not say, of the Trinitarian "life," that it is "an inward boiling, without any boiling over," but says instead: "without any boiling over *yet understood*." The "boiling over"—the act of creation, exoterically conceived—is not something that actually takes place; it is rather something "understood." In reality—according to the Knowledge of God himself—there *is no* created order: that order is "not yet understood," because "as yet" there has been no Fall, no descent into duality, into "the knowledge of good and evil," as Genesis has it. There is as yet no *aparavidyā*, no "outside"; there is only the Trinitarian life.

It is to be noted that Eckhart speaks of that Trinitarian life or "emanation"—"uncreated" though it be—in the language of exem-

28. Gen. 2:10.

plarism, which however becomes radically altered: for as he goes on to say, in that emanation "the image and the exemplar are not numbered as separate substances, but the one is in the other. 'I am in the Father, and the Father is in me.'" We are here in the domain of *advaita*: a Trinitarian *advaita*, in fact, whose contours are beginning to emerge. Not only is there the nonduality of "image and exemplar," but Eckhart goes on to conclude that "it is consequently necessary that the image be found in the intellectual nature where the same reality returns to itself in a *reditio completa* or 'perfect return.'" The Trinitarian life, thus, is literally "intellectual": it is indeed a "knowing"; as Eckhart says elsewhere: "God is pure intellect, whose whole being is knowing."[29] And that divine knowing does not proceed *beyond* the image—no "boiling over is yet understood"—nor does it terminate in the image, but rather "returns to itself in a *reditio completa.*" The Trinitarian knowing is "circular": it is a *perichoresis* or circumincession, as the theologians say. And that is precisely why that knowing is a life: an *eternal* life, to be sure; or better said, "life eternal," singular: for indeed, *there is no other.*

In truth, there is nothing apart from that life: nothing "outside" the Trinitarian order, nothing that "departs" and nothing that "enters" there; truly, God dwells in *phos aprositon*, in "unapproachable light."[30] On the other hand, from the standpoint of the creature, there is of course an entire cosmos "outside" of God, and therefore "outside" the divine Intellect. To be "outside the divine Intellect" is in fact definitive of creaturely existence; as Eckhart says elsewhere: "Every kind of existence outside or beyond intellect is a creature; it is creatable, other than God, and is not God."[31] It behooves us to ponder these words carefully: what is the nature of that creaturely kind of existence "outside or beyond intellect"? Or to put it another way: what kind of a thing *is* a "creature"? Clearly, it can be none other than what we have all along referred to as the "intentional object" of creaturely knowing, which is indeed "outside

---

29. *Meister Eckhart: Die lateinischen Werke*, vol. I (Stuttgart: W. Kohlhammer, 1936), p314.

30. 1 Tim. 6:16.

31. Sermon XXIX, METP, p226.

or beyond intellect" virtually by definition. Take a mountain or a tree, for example: it pertains to the very conception of a mountain, or of a tree, to be "out there": beyond the confines of mind. Now, it is this, precisely, Eckhart maintains, that defines the created order: "Every kind of existence *outside or beyond intellect* is a creature."

We are beginning to see that the conception of "image" plays a central role in Eckhart's doctrine; yet to grasp in full what stands at issue one requires further clarifications. To this end we turn now to one of his German sermons (Sermon 69), which speaks of "image" with unsurpassed precision and lucidity. It is here, in fact, in this Sermon—addressed apparently to women religious and laity—that Eckhart gives us the master-key to his doctrine.

The Sermon takes a portion of John 16:16 as its text: "A little while, and ye shall not see me; and again, a little while, and ye shall see me." Unlike everyone else, however, Eckhart interprets the Vulgate "*modicum,*" not in a temporal sense—as "a little while"—but as signifying simply "a little bit" or small something, whatever it might be. The text, which now reads "A little bit, and ye shall not see me; and again, a little bit, and ye shall see me," prompts Eckhart to begin his Sermon with the words: "However small a thing it is which sticks to the soul, we shall not see God."

Again, it is all about knowing: about *how* and *what* we see. And this is what Eckhart proceeds to investigate by means of the mirror/image metaphor: "The eye and the soul are such a mirror," he tells us, in which everything appears as an "image." The crucial point, however—the point upon which everything hinges!—is that this image is known "*without a medium and without an image.*" A stone, for example, is known by means of something that is not a stone; one can in fact define an entire sequence of intermediary causes, or *media,* by which the stone is perceived. There must, however, be something—on pain of infinite regress—that is seen directly, without a medium: and that is the image, precisely. As Eckhart puts it, image itself is "without image."

The great question, now, is this: what *is* this "image without image" that is seen "without a medium"? Eckhart answers that it is none other than the eternal Word: "The eternal Word is the medium and the image itself that is without medium and without image." The image, thus, is literally "not of this world." It is not a created thing; and yet, strangely enough, it is that which we know— know truly, without a medium—when we know a created thing. This is the startling fact—incalculable in its implications—which Eckhart has now brought to light.

Think of it: when we see a created thing, say a stone, the image by which we see that thing is none other than the eternal Word! And why? Because that image is precisely what is seen "without a medium." In this recognition the secret of the mystical life—the secret of *yoga*—is in truth comprehended. What *is* yoga, in the broadest sense? It is the removal of that *modicum*, that "little bit" which stands in the way of gnosis, in the way of "seeing me," the eternal Word: for indeed, what we do see—what we see *without a medium*—is the eternal Word. It sounds tautological: all that is needed is to see what in fact we do see, what in fact stands before the eye of our soul without a medium. And yet, strange to say, this is not what we normally perceive. We are like those of whom it is said that "seeing they see not"[32]; in us the imprecation of the Lord, "see ye, indeed, but perceive not"[33] has in fact been realized. And let us note what is the cause of that inability to perceive: "make the heart of this people fat," the text goes on to say. What is it, then, that "makes the heart fat"? Clearly, it is the *modicum*, that "little bit" which interposes itself, as it were, between the seer and the eternal Word. This is what Patanjali, in the Yoga Sutras, identifies as *chittavṛitti*, "modifications of mind," and what the disciplines of yoga are intended to eradicate: the very first aphorism defines yoga to be *chittavṛittinirodha*, the "uprooting" of the "modifications."

This brings us to the question of "means." Eckhart replies that the "eradication of the *modicum*" is to be effected by "a power in the soul, namely, the intellect." This is what, elsewhere, he speaks of as the *vünkelîn*, the "little spark," which he affirms to be *increatus et*

32. Matt. 13:13.
33. Isa. 6:9.

increabile: "uncreated and uncreatable." Eckhart contends that this "little spark"—and this alone—has power to "burn up" all that stands in the way of gnosis: all created things, namely, in so far as they *are* created. That *vünkelîn*, too, is "a little thing"; and as Eckhart proceeds to explain, it is in fact the very *modicum* to which the Savior alludes in the second half of John 16.16, when he says: "*et iterum modicum et videbitis me.*" According to Eckhart's remarkable interpretation of this verse, it is the second *modicum* that destroys the first. One is reminded of the "staff of Moses" which turned into the serpent that swallowed up the serpents of Pharaoh, a concordance which proves to be of considerable interest, and relates in fact to the symbolism of Kundalini Yoga.

Having thus introduced the second *modicum* as a "power," Eckhart proceeds to enumerate its characteristics or "properties," of which there are five: the first is that the power "separates from here and now"; the second is that "it is like nothing"; the third is that "it is pure and unmixed"; and the fourth is that "it is operating or seeking within itself." So far, clearly, Eckhart is indeed speaking of a power, properly so called; and let us note that the first of these gnostic powers—the one that "separates from here and now"—is precisely what enables the Christian yogin to transcend the bounds of space and time, and in so doing, to know "in abstraction from efficient and final causes," as behooves the metaphysician. The fifth and last so-called power, on the other hand, is not, strictly speaking, a power, but something else: "it is an image," we are told. What Eckhart is listing as "the fifth property" is in fact the *source* of the power: in the metaphoric terms of Exodus, it is the "rod" that turns into the "serpent." Thus, in answer to the question "whence comes the power," Eckhart replies that it derives from "the image," that is to say, from the eternal Word; as Christ told the disciples: "without me ye can do nothing." In the final count, the *vünkelîn* is the eternal Word, the "Christ in us." This is what Eckhart himself asserts near the end of his Sermon, where he speaks of the "image in the soul":

> The fifth, that it is an image. Ah, now pay close attention and remember this well. In this you have grasped the whole sermon at once. Image and image are so completely one and joined

together that one cannot comprehend any distinction between them.[34]

The *vünkelîn*—the "little spark"—and the eternal Word are "joined together" so perfectly that "one cannot comprehend any distinction between them." We have here the Christian equivalent of "*tat tvam asi*", the Trinitarian understanding of "that thou art".[35]

In the preceding discourse (Sermon 69), Eckhart distinguishes, by implication, between two mutually exclusive modes of knowing: the *supreme* and the *non-supreme*, one can say; it behooves us now to reflect further upon this—itself supreme!—distinction. What is it that characterizes the two kinds of knowing? It is the absence or presence of a *medium*: to know "without medium" is to know as God himself knows; to know "with medium," on the other hand, is to know in a creaturely manner, what St. Paul refers to as knowing "through a glass, darkly." What is it, then, that is known in these respective modes? What is perceived "without medium" is none other than the eternal Word, the Image of the Father; and what is perceived "with medium"—or "through a glass darkly"—pertains to the "ten thousand things" of this world.

Yet even in our "creaturely" knowing, there is—there must be!—something that is known without medium ("on pain of infinite regress" as we have said). Let us suppose, now, that we know an object X by way of something, call it A, which plays the role of a "first medium," one not itself mediated. We need not, at the moment, consider what kind of a thing this A proves to be: whether it is a "form" in the sense of Aristotle, or an "idea" in the sense of Plato, for example, or whether it be indeed "the eternal Word" as Eckhart declares. Our immediate concern is purely logical: A is that which, in the act of knowing X, is known "without medium"; that is

---

34. METP, p314.
35. One of the Vedantic *mahāvākyas* or "great dicta."

all. Two conceptual possibilities now present themselves: either A and X are the same, or they are not the same. If A and X are the same, then X is known without medium, contrary to what we have assumed; therefore A and X are not the same. It follows that, in knowing X, we know in a sense *two* things: namely, X *and* A.

It appears that Eckhart's discourse has brought to light what may prove to be the deepest reading of the "two things I have heard": in the final count, they are X, the created thing, and A, the eternal Word.[36] And let us note that this accords with Eckhart's interpretation of "the two things" in *Expositio Libri Genesis*, when he differentiates between "the emanation of the Persons" and "the creation of the world." However, his approach is now epistemological: the ontological issue—the distinction between "emanation" and "creation"—is thereby reduced to a question of *knowing*: to the distinction, namely, between *para* and *aparavidyā*, the divine and the creaturely knowing. The former, Eckhart explains, does not proceed "beyond the image"—does not go "outside or beyond intellect" as he says—but in fact "returns to itself in a *reditio completa*," whereas the creaturely knowing transgresses the image—transgresses intellect—and having thus "overshot the mark," finds itself unable to return. It is to be noted, finally, that this "transgression of intellect" is precisely the *ebullitio* or "boiling over" to which Eckhart refers in Sermon XLIX: the *ebullitio* is thus none other than that fateful transition from A to X. It is this transgression—in both senses of that ambivalent term—that gives rise to the world or worlds consisting of the resultant objects X.[37]

What, then, are the "media" which falsify our knowing: the *modica* that cause us to "hear two things"? Eckhart distinguishes two kinds: "sensible images" in the case of perception, and "concepts" in the case of rational knowledge or thought. These are the "modifications of mind" that giver rise to "duality" or "otherness," and prevent us from "seeing true." Here is what he says:

36. It may be noted that the "*omnia duplicia*" ("all things are double") of Ecclesiasticus 42:25 can likewise be seen as referring to the (X, A) duplicity.

37. A and X correspond respectively to the "rope" and the "snake" in the Vedantic metaphor.

The soul has something in it, a spark of intelligence, which never goes out, and in this spark, as the highest part of the mind, one places the image of the soul [which is identical with the eternal Word]. There also exists in our souls a capacity for knowing external things. This is a knowing through the senses and through reason, that is, a knowing through sensible images and through concepts. Such knowing conceals this other knowing.

The "spark of intelligence," the *vünkelîn*, is in a way both "power" and "image." From one point of view, the "power" derives from the "image" ("Without me ye can do nothing"), and from another (more fundamental still), the "image" derives from the "power" ("This day have I begotten thee"). We must bear in mind that we are here in the Trinitarian domain: the "image of the soul" cannot be separated from the eternal Image "begotten of the Father." The "spark of intelligence," thus, conceived as "proceeding from the Father," is inseparably related to the "image," which in a way it "contains": that is why Eckhart places "the image of the soul" *in* "the spark of intellect." To know by that "spark" is to know as God himself knows. However, "there also exists in our souls a capacity for knowing external things": a knowing, namely, "through sensible images and through concepts." Eckhart, however, is not presently concerned with the distinction between "sensible images" and "concepts"; he lumps the two modes together as "such knowing," which he forthwith opposes to the divine: "Such knowing," he declares, "conceals this other knowing." We are back to the "*ajñānena avritam jñānam*" of the Bhagavad Gita: "Knowledge is veiled by ignorance; thereby mortals are deluded."[38]

Eckhart's epistemology is of course exceedingly strange. What strikes us, however, as *more* than strange—as in fact paradoxical—is the claim that different things in creation are seen by way of the same "first principle": in perceiving X and Y, let us say, what is seen "without medium," in either case, is none other than the eternal

38. V.15.

Word, the unique Image of the Father.[39] Yet the familiar exemplarism, which goes back to St. Augustine, entails precisely the same "paradox," for it maintains that the exemplars, though "many" in their participations, are one "in the divine essence": here, too, "one" turns into "many." The problem resides ultimately in our conception of "one" or "oneness," which is too "numerical," too radically opposed to diversity: "In God," says Nicholas of Cusa, "identity *is* diversity."[40] The point is made with exceptional cogency by Clement of Alexandria, when he declares that "the Son is neither simply one thing, nor many things as parts, but one thing as all things, whence also he is all things."[41] It needs to be understood that Christian metaphysics, like the Vedantic, is not a monism, but a nondualism, an *advaita*—which is hard to grasp, for the simple reason that *there is no advaita* here below, in the order of creation: the fact that the latter is "outside or beyond intellect" precludes that possibility.

What we take to be "the world"—along with all the "worlds" or *lokas* referred to in the traditional cosmologies—derives from *media*: from a *modicum* or "little something" that obstructs our view. One sees, once again, that these "worlds"—and all they contain—exist "for us" as intentional objects of an *aparavidyā*, caused by *media* or "mental modifications," which in fact have no existence apart from the cognitive act within which they "mediate." In a word, Eckhart's cosmology constitutes an "anthropic realism," as indeed it must.[42]

It appears that Eckhart's doctrine is based upon "the primacy of knowing": *to know* is in a way more basic than *to be*. "Knowledge," Eckhart declares, "is a solid bedrock and foundation for all being."[43]

39. Here is yet another interpretation of the dictum "I have heard two things": all "duality" is a matter of "hearing two things" where God "speaks but one Word."

40. *De Docta Ignorantia*, II.9.

41. *Stromata* IV.25. We have touched upon this question in chapter 1.

42. As I have argued in Chapter 2: *every* cosmology "*conceived in the face of gnosis*" must conform to "the principle of relativity" by which anthropic realism is defined.

43. Sermon 71, METP, p324.

The principle applies, in the first place, to the supreme knowing, and such, apparently, is the overt sense of the given statement; but it applies also, *de jure*, to the non-supreme. In the first case, what it signifies or implies is a Trinitarian metaphysics, a pure Trinitarian *advaita*; and in the second, it is the tenet of anthropic realism, as we have come to see. And that, I submit, is Eckhart's final word on the subject of "creation."

This is not to say that Eckhart, always and everywhere, maintains that "primacy of knowing," even with reference to the *paravidyā*. As we have seen, it pleases him to speak at sundry times from different points of view, even the most exoteric, to the displeasure of exegetes desirous of extracting a consistent doctrine. There are major loci, moreover, where Eckhart appears to maintain a "primacy of being" in opposition to the "primacy of knowing," a fact which has caused some scholars to speak of "stages" in the unfolding of his doctrine.[44] For my part, I take the view that nowhere, in the final count, does Eckhart deny the primacy of knowing, nor propound a doctrine which contradicts that principle. I would argue that the idea of cognitive primacy winds through the discourse of Meister Eckhart like a thread through a string of pearls, and like the drone in Hindu music, is always present, even when it is not heard. But these are questions that take us beyond the scope of the present study.

What I propose to consider in conclusion is something else: there is in Eckhart's extant opus a treatise in which he not only affirms the primacy of knowing, but *proves* it; let us now examine that proof. The document to which I refer is the first *questio disputata* of the *Parisian Questions*, which is this: "*Are Being and Knowing the Same in God?*"

A point of terminology needs first of all to be addressed. Armand Maurer, whose translation of the given text[45] I shall follow in the main, renders "*esse*" as "existence," a step which in principle opens

---

44. The first of the "Parisian Questions" and the General Prologue to the *Opus Tripartitum*, in particular, seem to take opposite sides on the issue. It appears, however, that most scholars regard the conflict as more apparent than real; see, for instance, Vladimir Lossky, op. cit., pp 207–220.

45. *Meister Eckhart: Parisian Questions and Prologues*, op. cit.

the door to utter confusion.[46] After all, the word "existence" derives evidently from "*ex*" plus "*sistere*," and therefore means literally "to stand out." To say that something "exists" is thus to affirm that it "stands outside its cause," a predication which is in fact definitive of the created order. By the same token, on the other hand, to attribute "existence" to God constitutes an absurdity; as Eckhart observes: "They speak of God as if he were a cow!" Certainly the word "existence" can be understood in other ways as well; yet I submit that the danger of "bovine" interpretation is too great to be worth the risk.[47] The term "being," meanwhile, is by no means unacceptable: certainly it need not be interpreted in the strict sense of "existence," which is to say that one can reasonably speak of "being" with reference to the divine or "uncreated" order, a usage which in fact has a venerable history, tracing back to the Patristic era. On similar grounds, I shall prefer the word "*know*" to Maurer's "*understand*": for whereas the former is cognate to the Greek *gnosis*, which (like the Sanskrit *jñāna*) refers traditionally to the supreme knowing, it obviously makes no sense whatever to speak of God's knowing as a "standing under."

Eckhart begins "innocuously" enough: "I reply that they [i.e., *being* and *knowing* in God] are the same in reality, and perhaps both in reality and in thought." And he goes on to offer proofs: five based on the *Summa Contra Gentiles*, and one on the *Summa Theologiae*. He then proceeds to establish the same conclusion "by a method I employed elsewhere" (a reference no one, apparently, has been able to trace). So far Eckhart's deviation from Aquinas is slight: it resides

---

46. Admittedly, in following the translations in EME and METP, we too have been guilty of this practice.

47. Some have argued in favor of rendering "*esse*" by the term "isness." Here is what C. F. Kelley has to say on the question: "'Isness' (Eckhart's '*istigkeit*') is by far the best English term available to convey the meaning of the Latin *esse* ('to be' as noun), thus running less danger of confusing it with *ens* (being) which designates 'existence-essence,' or that which derives from *esse* as from its principle. Only since the sixteenth century has the term 'existence' been commonly used for *esse*, and this unfortunate usage has led to much confusion by actually distorting and restricting the metaphysical significance of *esse*." (*Meister Eckhart on Divine Knowledge*, op. cit., p251, fn. 25)

in the word "perhaps." Where Aquinas admitted a difference "in thought" between God's "being" and God's "knowing," Eckhart maintains that even that may be too much: to do so, he suggests, is "perhaps" to miss the very conception of God.

Having established that *being* and *knowing* are thus "convertible" *in divinis*, Eckhart proceeds, abruptly, to take the definitive step:

> I declare that it is not my present opinion that God knows because he *is*, but rather that he *is* because he knows. God is an intellect and a knowing, and his knowing itself is the ground of his being [or *isness*, as one can very well say in this instance].

Here is an unequivocal affirmation of cognitive primacy. What is primary, to be precise, is not a *being*, but an *act*: not "intellect," conceived as something that *is*, but a "knowing," precisely. The "act" comes first: there is an analogy, here, with the doctrine of Jacob Boehme, where also "act" in the form of a "process"—a "seven-part cycle," to be exact—comes first.[48] Eckhart, to be sure, is not a theosophist, but a metaphysician in the purest sense; and so too, Scholastic that he is, no sooner has he stated his thesis, than he proceeds to its *proof*:

> It is said in John 1: "In the beginning was the Word, and the Word was with God, and the Word was God." The Evangelist did not say: "In the beginning was being, and God was being." A word is completely related to the intellect, where it is either the speaker or what is spoken, and not being nor a composite thing. Our Savior also says in John 14, "I am the Truth." Truth has reference to an intellect, implying or containing a relation; and a relation owes its whole existence to a mind, and as such it is a real category. . . . So truth, like a word, clearly has reference to an intellect.

What Eckhart means, presumably, when he refers to a word as "the speaker," is what in Scholastic parlance was termed "the word of

---

48. One is reminded of the Faustian *"Am Anfang war die Tat"* ("In the beginning was the deed"), which, like so many of Goethe's aphorisms, carries a surprisingly profound significance.

the heart" as opposed to "the word of the voice": the "exemplar" as opposed to the "image." His point is that a word, whether as "speaker" or as "spoken," pertains in either case to intellect: like "truth," it "clearly has reference to an intellect"—to "intellect," namely, conceived *as act*, that is, as a "knowing" or gnosis.

He then goes on to consider the text "all things were made through him" which follows "*In principio erat verbum*," taking in effect "all things" to signify "being, life, and intelligence," the Scholastic triad which represents what may be termed the principal "degrees of manifestation":

> Some say that being, life, and intelligence can be viewed in two ways: in themselves, and then being is first, life second, and intelligence third; and in relation to that which participates in them, and then intelligence is first, life second, and being third.

Here "in themselves," first of all, means *in divinis*, while "in relation to that which participates" refers of course to the order of creation (where in fact "being" does become "existence," as Armand's translation has it). It is to be noted that the authorities who affirm the above-stated position include Dionysius, St. Augustine, and St. Thomas Aquinas,[49] with whom Eckhart now disagrees: "But I believe the exact opposite to be true," he goes on to say! "For 'In the beginning was the Word,' which is entirely related to an intellect. Consequently, among perfections intelligence comes first and then being." Taking Eckhart at his word, we have here an open "break" with the three most venerated authorities of Christendom. And strangely enough, our ordinary human wisdom sides squarely with the Meister on this point: for indeed, here below, in the order of creation, existence does evidently precede life, even as life precedes intelligence. What is far from obvious, of course, is that, *in divinis*, this order is reversed; as Eckhart puts it, "here the imagination fails":

49. Armand Maurer (op. cit., p47, fn. 12) lists the following loci in support of that claim: Dionysius, *De Divinis Nominibus*, V.5; St. Augustine, *De Libero Arbitrio*, II.3, n. 7; and *Summa Theologiae* I–II. 2,5.

For our knowing is different from God's. His knowing is the cause of things, whereas our knowing is caused by them. Consequently, because our knowing is dependent upon the being by which it is caused, with equal reason being itself is dependent upon God's knowing. Hence everything in God transcends being and is totally a knowing.

We need, first of all, to ask what are the "things" of which God's knowing is the cause: are they "created" in the theological sense, or "generated" in the Trinitarian: that is the crucial question. Exegetes are prone, of course, to interpret the passage according to the former sense; and yet, if one examines the matter with sufficient care, one sees that this option has been ruled out. For inasmuch as the "things" in question are caused by "God's knowing," they cannot be "outside or beyond intellect," and cannot therefore be "creature," according to the criterion given explicitly in Sermon XLIX. The things "caused by God's knowing," therefore, are *not* "created *ex nihilo*," but are "*generated*" in a Trinitarian sense. To put it in Kabbalistic terms: they are "begotten" as the progeny of a "sacred union" *in divinis*, which is indeed a "knowing" of the highest kind. From this point of view one can readily understand that, *in divinis*, "intellect" comes first, since it is realized in *Hokhmah*; "life" comes second, since it is realized in the "Edenic flow"; and "being" comes last, since it is realized in *Malkhuth*. One sees, likewise, that what is thus "caused" by "God's knowing" is something perfect and eternal, in keeping with the scriptural text "God's works are perfect." And these are the things, precisely, upon which "*our* knowing is dependent," as Eckhart says. We need, however, to realize, once again, that the eternal or Sefirothic world is not a multiplicity of finite beings, but an advaitic realm in which "each is all": it is in fact the eternal Word, the "only-begotten Son of the Father," to put it in Trinitarian terms. How, then, does *our* knowing "depend" upon that Word? This question has already been answered: in terms of our preceding analysis, the "Image that is Christ" is indeed the "cause" of human knowing, precisely as the "A" which is perceived as "X."

It appears that the traditional dichotomy God/world, or Uncreated/created, has now been replaced by the distinction between "*supreme*" and "*non-supreme*" knowing: where *knowing* assumes primacy over *being*, the epistemological dichotomy takes precedence over the ontological. As Eckhart himself declares: "Knowledge is a solid bedrock and foundation for *all being*." Now, there are two ways of interpreting this: if we take "knowledge" in the sense of "*supreme knowing*," then what that "knowing" founds is evidently "being" of the "uncreated" kind; and if this be "all being," as Eckhart maintains, it follows that "created being" is indeed the *purus nihil* he declares it to be (when speaking, as it were, from the "supreme" point of view). On the other hand, if we take "knowledge" to signify *non-supreme knowing*, then what is founded is "created" or "cosmic" being, the kind investigated, not by "the metaphysician" who considers things "in abstraction from efficient and final causes," but by "natural scientists." Eckhart's declaration, therefore, taken in its twofold sense, reduces the ontological dichotomy—the one that underlies all Patristic and Thomistic theology—to the epistemological: the distinction, namely, between *para* and *aparavidyā*. And this means that Eckhart's doctrine differs radically from its Scholastic antecedent, which yet, in a way, it "contains," somewhat as quantum theory, let us say, "contains" classical mechanics. Eckhart's metaphysics occupies thus a superior rank: a rank, in fact, which perhaps may not unjustly be termed "supreme."

7

ECKHART'S
TRINITARIAN
NONDUALISM

"WERE God not primal Knowledge," Meister Eckhart declares, "there would be no Trinity."[1] We are given to understand that the Trinitarian life of God springs from his Knowing. It is not enough to acknowledge that the Father knows himself in the Son; one needs also to realize that both the Father and the Son are inseparable from that Knowing. As Eckhart says elsewhere: "God *is* because he knows." The Father knows himself in the Son, and it is in that Knowing that he begets the Son; this is what Eckhart likens to a *bullitio* or "boiling": it is as if God were to "expand" and go out of himself. That outgoing or "expansive" phase of knowing is however complemented by a *reditio* or Recession which, as it were, completes the circle: and that Recession *is* the Holy Spirit. It is the function of the Holy Spirit to bring the Son—the divine Manifestation— back into the unity of the Principle, into the One; as Eckhart expresses it: "All possibility is in the Father, likeness is in the Son, and nonduality is in the Holy Spirit."[2] What confronts us in the

---

1. *Meister Eckhart: Deutsche Werke* (Stuttgart: W. Kohlhammer, 1936–), vol. III, p379. I have followed the translation of C.F. Kelley, who renders "*enwaere an gote niht verstantnisse*" as "were God not primal Knowledge," which though not literally accurate, seems to capture Eckhart's sense (better, for example, than Frank Tobin's "if God had no intellect"). *Deutsche Werke* will henceforth be referred to as DW.

2. DW, Vol. I, p50. Again I follow the translation of C.F. Kelley in rendering "*mügenheit*" as "possibility" (in preference to that of Edmund Colledge, who renders it as "power").

Trinity is none other than the mystery of divine Knowing, the secret of principial gnosis; and clearly, this differs from the theological conception of the triune God, which is ontological, and hinges finally upon the distinction between "substance" and "relation." An inversion has taken place: instead of viewing the Trinity "within being," Eckhart views "being" within the Trinity, now conceived as "an eternal and immutable going out and coming in: out of Godhead into being, and from being into Godhead."[3] It needs however to be understood that the being "into which" the "going out" is directed does not precede that "going out," but is—logically speaking—subsequent thereto. In the final count, there is nothing "outside" the Trinity; or to put it another way: what is outside the Trinity is *ipso facto* "pure nothing," *purus nihil.* We must bear in mind that when it comes to the apex of his doctrine—its "crucial point"—Eckhart takes his stand, as it were, *within* the principial Knowing: it is this that defines his orientation and distinguishes his teaching fundamentally from that of dogmatic theology; as he tells us himself: "The eye wherein I see God is the same eye wherein God sees me; my eye and God's eye are one eye, one vision, one knowing, one love."[4]

It should be emphasized that the "going out" to which Eckhart refers is not to be construed as an "exodus from God": it is not "creation" in the exoteric sense, which is to say that the Eckhartian "going out" entails no duality, gives rise to no *aliud* or "otherness," except in a purely formal sense. It is in fact the function of the Holy Spirit to forestall "otherness": to preserve or "restore" nonduality through what Eckhart terms "the negation of negations"; as he tells us in one of his sermons: "Thus it is for us to expire all duality as the Holy Spirit expires it eternally."[5] In consequence of this "eternal

3. DW, Vol. II, p11.

4. *Meister Eckhart: Teacher and Preacher*, Ed. Bernard McGinn (New York: Paulist Press, 1986), p270. We shall again refer to this anthology as METP.

5. *Meister Eckhart*, Ed. Franz Pfeiffer, 1857, Vol. II, p253. Again I follow C.F. Kelley in rendering "*geisten*" (a verbal form of "*geist*," meaning "spirit") as "expire," for which there seems to be little "linguistic" justification. I am persuaded, nonetheless, that Kelley's rendering hits the mark.

expiration," there *is no* "otherness," no duality *in divinis*: "All that exists in God *is* God" as a Scholastic dictum has it. One might say that, *in divinis,* "negations" are held in potency: like the "Dark Fire" of which Jacob Boehme speaks, they have been eternally conquered, eternally subdued by the Light of Christ, which is the Holy Spirit. Moreover, given that "being" subsists "within the Trinity," it clearly cannot be temporal or contingent, but answers perforce to the Kabbalistic conception of an eternal creation, a veritable *creatio ex Deo et in Deo.* Indeed, from the "standpoint" of principial Knowing—as we have had ample occasion to note—*there is no contingent being*: no *creatio ex nihilo* in the sense of dogmatic theology. In truth, there is nothing "outside" of God, nothing outside the Trinity: to "enter" there is truly to *know* all and to *be* all.

Before proceeding further, it may be well to remind ourselves that the idea of the Trinity—a conception unprecedented in human history—derives from the Christic Revelation: it was the Incarnate Son himself who disclosed to mankind the secret of God "hidden since the foundation of the world."[6] This is not to say, of course, that doctrine alone suffices to reveal the secret in question: more, surely, is required for this "disclosure" than simply a dogmatic definition of God conceived as "Father, Son, and Holy Spirit." What is ultimately needed is in fact the very presence and "intervention" of that Son and of that Holy Spirit; and that is why St. John begins his First Epistle with the ardent declaration: "That which was from the beginning, which we have heard, which we have seen with our eyes, and our hands have handled, of the Word of life . . . these things write we unto you that your joy may be full."[7] The "Word of life" is revealed to us, not primarily in theological conceptions, but precisely in the Incarnate Son of God, whom the disciples have seen with their eyes and touched with their hands, and whose presence is conveyed to the faithful by a twofold transmission: doctrinal, namely, *and* sacramental. The two go together: they function "hand in hand." The Christian life begins, as we know, with baptism, which is the first of

6. Matt. 13:35.
7. 1 John 1:1–4.

seven sacraments, and constitutes indeed an initiation.[8] But it also begins in *faith*, the first of the so-called theological virtues, which in a way constitutes the doctrinal counterpart of baptism. So too *hope* corresponds to confirmation, and *caritas*, the third theological virtue, is akin to the Eucharist, the third and final initiatic sacrament. If the theological virtues constitute "degrees" in the reception of the Christic teaching, the Eucharist constitutes the sacramental "fulfillment" of the entire doctrinal transmission; as St. Irenaeus has expressed it: "Our doctrine is in agreement with the Eucharist, and the Eucharist confirms our doctrine."[9]

The Unknown God—the God of the philosophers—is revealed in the Incarnate Son; as St. Paul said to the Athenians: "Whom therefore ye ignorantly worship, him declare I unto you."[10] The Unknown God is made present in Jesus Christ; and shocking as it may be to the philosophers of this world, the plenary Revelation of that God took place precisely upon the Cross. The event was in fact rendered visible—for all the world to see—when the centurion opened the breast of the Crucified with a lance: as every Christian knows by his faith, the sacred blood which poured forth from that wound was in truth the Blood of God. And that is the Blood the faithful receive—whether they realize it or not—when they partake of the Eucharist. This is how "That which was from the beginning, which we have heard, which we have seen with our eyes, and our hands have handled, of the Word of life" is transmitted within the Church down through the ages. What Christ offers through his Church—by way of a twofold transmission—is finally nothing less than his own being: not just a philosophical theory or a theology, but in fact the very "Word of life."

The object of the present chapter is to expound Meister Eckhart's vision of that Word. We proceed in two parts: the first pertains to the Trinity, conceived, as it were, "from within," and the second

---

8. The initiatory character of the sacrament has been established beyond doubt (against the objections raised by René Guénon) in Jean Borella, *Guénonian Esoterism and Christian Mystery* (San Rafael, CA: Sophia Perennis, 2004).

9. *Adversus Haereses* 4.18.3.

10. Acts 17:23.

concerns what appears to be a somewhat different subject: namely, "the birth of the Word in the soul." But whereas that "birth" presents itself as "other than" the eternal birth of the only-begotten Son—as something "additional"—we shall see in the end that this "otherness" is deceptive, that it pertains to the bounds of the *aparavidyā*; and this is the recognition, precisely, that takes us into the very heart of Meister Eckhart's doctrine.

I. THE TRINITY

We begin with the distinction between Godhead and Trinity. There are "unimpeachable texts" which *seem* to place the Trinity "outside" the Godhead—as if the "true God" were somehow "behind" the Trinity—a notion Bernard McGinn refers to as the "God beyond God" hypothesis. McGinn himself, let us note, is no friend of that theological position—which is basically modalist or Sabellian[11]— and advocates an alternative reading of the Eckhartian texts.[12] Yet many do accept an interpretation of the aforesaid kind, based upon what is at least the "surface meaning" of the loci in question. Moreover, when it comes to what might, broadly speaking, be termed "Vedantically oriented" exegetes, an inherently Sabellian interpretation of Eckhart's Trinitarian doctrine tends to impose itself, almost irresistibly, as the informed and authentically "esoteric" position, answering supposedly to a "jnanic" as opposed to a "bhaktic" perspective. Yet such a reading, I say, is not only unjustified, but misses the point: failing to grasp that Eckhart's doctrine is both advaitic *and* Trinitarian—that its very nondualism *is* in fact Trinitarian—one forces the doctrine into a Vedantic mold which simply does not fit. One forgets that Eckhart's teaching, esoteric and indeed advaitic

11. *Modalism* (also known as *monarchianism* and *Patripassionism*) is a heresy— a *dogmatic* heresy: one that not only contradicts theological interpretation but primary dogmatic definitions of the Church—which views the divine Persons as *three modes of Being*, or of the divine Principle. The teaching was refined in the third century by Sabellius, who conceived of the Persons as transitory modalities: God is Father, Son, or Holy Spirit according to his mode of action.

12. "The God beyond God: Theology and Mysticism in the Thought of Meister Eckhart," *Journal of Religion*, Vol. 61 (1981), pp1–19.

though it be, is yet profoundly *Christian*, and that, as such, it transcends in a way the doctrinal formulations of the non-Christian traditions: for it happens that the idea of a non-modalist or non-Sabellian Trinity is inseparable from the Revelation bestowed upon mankind by the Incarnate Son of God.

Let us, then, consider some of the major Eckhartian loci which seem, at least, to support a "God beyond God" hypothesis. As one might expect, it is mainly in the German sermons that texts of that kind are to be found; and the first of these—which happens to be one of the most challenging—occurs in Sermon 2. The homily is based upon Luke 10:38, which Eckhart renders (somewhat loosely) in the words: "Our Lord Jesus Christ went up into a little town, and was received by a virgin who was a wife." It is apparent from the start that the "little town" represents "the ground of the soul," and that what Eckhart wishes to speak about is in fact "the Birth of the Word in us." This is clearly why he "doctors" the text a bit, in the vernacular rendering, by interposing the words "a virgin who was a wife" where the Latin has simply "*mulier quaedam, Martha nomine*" ("a certain woman, named Martha"). Moreover, he evidently plays upon the double meaning of the German word replacing "*excepit*" ("received")—the verb "*empfangen*," namely, which means both to "receive" and to "*conceive*"—so as to suggest that in receiving the Word, the "virgin" becomes indeed a "wife."

We will not consider the Sermon—which deals at length with two "powers" said to reside in the soul—in its entirety; what concerns us is a passage near the end of the homily,[13] which reads as follows:

> And now see and pay heed! This little town, about which I am talking and which I have in mind, is in the soul so one and so simple, far above whatever can be described, that this noble power about which I have spoken is not worthy even once for an instant to look into this little town; and the other power too of which I spoke, in which God is gleaming and burning with

---

13. *Meister Eckhart: The Essential Sermons, Commentaries, Treatises and Defense*, Eds. E. Colledge and B. McGinn (New York: Paulist Press, 1981), pp177–188. This anthology will henceforth be referred to again as EME.

all his riches and with all his joy, it also does not ever dare to look into it. This little town is so truly one and simple, and this simple one is so exalted above every manner and every power, that no power, no manner, not God himself may look at it. It is as true that this is true and that I speak truly as that God is alive! God himself never for an instant looks into it, never yet did he look on it, so far as he possesses himself in the manner and according to the properties of his Persons. It is well to observe this, because this simple one is without manner and without properties. And therefore, if God were ever to look upon it, that must cost him all his divine names and the properties of his Persons; that he must wholly forsake, if he is ever to look into it. But as he is simply one, without any manner and properties, he is not Father or Son or Holy Spirit, and yet he is something that is neither this nor that.[14]

It is evident, first of all, in light of Eckhart's Latin treatises, that "the little town" is finally none other than what Eckhart refers to as *deitas*, what in English may best be termed Godhead. The text differentiates this Godhead—in the sharpest way—from the Trinitarian

14. An almost exactly parallel passage occurs in Sermon 48, which however adds a few enlightening touches of its own. Of particular interest is the fact that Eckhart refers to a "spark in the soul" as the sole power able to penetrate into what he terms "the simple ground": "This spark rejects all created things, and wants nothing but its naked God, as he is in himself" he declares. What, then, does it mean to "reject all created things"? This can of course be understood in a "moral" sense, as referring to an act of renunciation. The intended meaning is however more profound: clearly, to "reject all created things" is to realize that "all creatures are one pure nothing." Eckhart is putting us on notice that what he is about to enunciate is indeed "esoteric" in precisely the sense we have conferred upon this term (in the preceding chapter). So too he goes on to declare: "I speak in all truth, that is eternal and enduring," as if to say: "I speak from within the Godhead, from the standpoint of supreme gnosis." What he means, finally, when he goes on to maintain that the aforesaid spark "is not content with the simple divine essence in its repose," is that this power rejects the theological or "creaturely" view of the Trinity—the view "from the outside"—which does in fact conceive of the Persons within "the simple divine essence in repose" (as "relations," namely). In a word, Eckhart is making the point that in rejecting "all creatures," this "spark in the soul" rejects, in the same stroke, the Trinity *as conceived in creatio ex nihilo theology.*

God, conceived as consisting of the Father, the Son, and the Holy Spirit. Whereas the Persons are perforce defined in terms of their respective "manner and power," the Godhead "is exalted above every manner and every power." One has the impression that if one can still, under these auspices, speak of the Trinity as God, it must in any case be "a lesser God," a God somehow "reduced" by the very "godlike" characteristics in terms of which he is defined. The fact that the triune God is unable, even for an instant, to "look into" the Godhead, into this "little town," as Eckhart goes on to say, only serves to confirm this impression and "diminish" the triune God all the more. The argument for a "God beyond God" interpretation of this text seems thus to be conclusive.

The faithful Christian, meanwhile, may draw comfort from the biblical verse upon which the Sermon is based: "Our Lord Jesus Christ went up into a little town, and was received by a virgin who was a wife." The fact that "our Lord Jesus Christ" could "go up into the little town" and be there "received by a virgin who was a wife" seems to suggest that Godhead and Trinity are not, after all, quite as "distinct" as Eckhart's text might lead us to believe. Yet, how to interpret that text? What comes to mind—and what I propose now to reflect upon—is the well-known *hadith* which begins with the words: "I was a hidden treasure, I desired to be known." It is this "desire"—what some scholars prefer to render by the term "love"—that aspires to reveal or make known the "treasure" hidden in the Godhead. It is crucial, first of all, not to conceive of this "treasure" as an *aliud,* as something "other than" the Godhead itself: for indeed, as the *hadith* tells us, it is "I"—the Godhead!—who "was" that treasure. To be sure, this "was" is obviously not to be taken in a temporal sense. The Godhead, most assuredly, is not subject to the condition of time: in him there is no "before" nor "after," no "shadow of alteration" as the Epistle of St. James has it. What stands at issue, clearly, is the primal theophany; but whereas this divine "self-manifestation" is certainly not to be conceived as a temporal event, the limitations of human language force us to speak of that theophany as if it were indeed a movement or transformation from an initial to a final state. With this understanding, then, let us now ask: how *does* the "hidden treasure" become "known"?

Now, the Christian answer, clearly, is that the "hidden treasure" becomes known precisely *in the Son*, "in whom resides all the fullness of the Godhead bodily."[15]

This very fact, however, precludes the notion of a "lesser God." If it be true—and the claim is of course staggering—that the Son "contains" within himself, or "embodies," what St. Paul refers to as "all the fullness of the Godhead," there can certainly be no question of a "diminution," let alone of a "descent into *māyā*" as a doctrinal Vedantist might think. In a formal or purely logical sense, there is of course a "God beyond God," that is to say, a Godhead "prior to" the Trinity, just as, from a theological point of view, there is an Essence "prior to" the Persons. Yet it is in fact definitive of Christianity to transcend that "God beyond God" conception: to reject the idea of a *Sabellian* Trinity. Recall the words of Christ himself: "He that sees me sees the Father,"[16] which permit us to conclude that *the Father is the Godhead seen in the Son*. The Godhead—the "hidden treasure"—is revealed or "known" in the Son, in relation to whom he "becomes" the Father (again we speak "in a devilish manner").

However, this recognition—as simple as it is basic—not only resolves the "God beyond God" enigma, but enables us to understand the disputed text. When Eckhart affirms that "God himself never for an instant looks into it"—into that Godhead—he is saying, in effect, that the Unknown God "looked into" ceases to be the Unknown God, even as a hidden treasure "revealed" ceases to be a hidden treasure: that is all. The text means thus the very opposite of what the "God beyond God" proponents take it to mean. Likewise, to say that if God were, even for an instant, to look into the Godhead, "that would cost him all his divine names and the properties of his Persons," is simply another "koanic" way of saying the very same thing: for if the Son is indeed the theophany of the Godhead, it follows that to "look into the Godhead" is to look in the wrong direction: it is to gaze, as it were, into a darkness in which nothing whatever can be seen. And if God himself were to do so, it would surely "cost him all his divine names and the properties of his

15. Col. 2:9.
16. John 14:9.

Persons." Let us remember that Eckhart the preacher loves to shock his congregations—and especially, it seems, his hard-headed German compatriots—by means of seemingly preposterous or near-blasphemous assertions. In telling us what "God himself cannot do," and what "would happen to him if he did," Eckhart is simply proclaiming—in the most provocative terms—the distinction between Godhead as "hidden treasure" and the triune God wherein the Godhead stands revealed.

That distinction, however, does not entail "otherness." Not only is there no "otherness" between the Father, the Son, and the Holy Spirit—despite a difference in what Eckhart refers to as "manner and power"—but there is likewise no "otherness" between the Trinity as such and the Godhead: for the Trinity, as we have said, is precisely "the self-revelation" of the Godhead. The instant one steps beyond the temporal world or so-called creation—the instant one "annihilates all creatures" as Eckhart likes to say—one enters into the advaitic realm, the *alma de-yihuda* or "world of union," wherein there is indeed distinction but no duality, no *aliud*. And this is actually what Eckhart himself appears to be telling us—in his "koanic" way—at the very end of the quoted passage, when he declares, regarding the Godhead, that "he is not Father or Son or Holy Spirit, *and yet he is something which is neither this nor that.*" For indeed, "something which is neither this nor that" stands perforce above duality, above all "otherness," and cannot, therefore, be "other than" the Father, or the Son, or the Holy Spirit.

In Sermon 10, and especially in Sermon 21, Eckhart takes us into what might be termed the logic or "dialectic" of Trinitarian nondualism. To begin with the former text: here he speaks of "a power in the soul which in its first outpouring does not take God as he is good and does not take him as he is truth."[17] Now, "the true" and "the good" count among the so-called transcendentals: conceptions, namely, applicable to "being as being," which consequently

17. METP, p 265.

apply to all being regardless of its modes. There are said to be, basically, three transcendentals: the true, the good, and the one. The "power in the soul" of which Eckhart speaks, insofar as it transcends "the true" and "the good," must therefore transcend being itself: it penetrates, so to speak, beyond every relativity, beyond everything which in any way is "touched by *māyā*" as the Vedantist might say. The point, however, is that it does not transcend "the one," which therefore constitutes the only transcendental that transcends being itself; in a word, "the one" constitutes the sole designation or "name" of the Godhead as such. Now, this "oneness" is precisely what that certain "power in the soul" seeks, what in a way it craves; as Eckhart goes on to explain:

> It seeks the ground [of God], continuing to search, and takes God in his oneness and in his solitary wilderness, in his vast wasteland, and in his own ground.

There is an implied distinction between "seeking" and "taking": the soul, in this power, remains unsatisfied with any knowledge of God tinged by relativity or *māyā*; even the "lesser transcendentals"—the goodness and truth of God!—are discarded: the soul continues to seek. What "it takes" at the termination of its quest is indeed none other than the Godhead, what Eckhart terms "his solitary wilderness" or "vast wasteland," which is "his own ground." The burning question, now, is this: how does the Trinity stand in relation to that Ground? Is the triune God also to be discarded, like "the true" and "the good"? Is he, in other words, to be situated "outside" the Godhead, as it were? The answer to this question is given by Eckhart himself; having referred to the "power in the soul" that "seeks the ground" and "takes God in his oneness," he goes on to say:

> The difference comes from the oneness, that is the difference in the Trinity. The oneness is the difference and the difference is the oneness. The greater the difference, the greater the unity, because this is difference beyond difference.

It is to be noted, again, that the "oneness" of which Eckhart speaks is situated on the level of the Godhead; for it is the oneness in which the highest power of the soul "takes God in his solitary wilderness, in his vast wasteland, and in his own ground." But whereas the Godhead is thus characterized by oneness, the Trinity is character- ized by difference: by the "manners and powers," namely, which define and thereby differentiate the Persons, one from the other. What, then, does it mean when Eckhart declares that "the oneness is the difference, and the difference is the oneness"? What *can* this mean? It can only mean that *the Godhead is the Trinity and the Trinity is the Godhead.* Lo and behold: with this apodictic contention Eckhart has negated the "God beyond God" hypothesis!

However, the resolution comes at a price: to say that "the oneness is the difference and the difference is the oneness" flies in the face of human logic—a question to which we will return at the end. Mean- while it needs to be recognized that Eckhart's "identification" of Godhead and Trinity, *though dogmatically orthodox,* is theologically unacceptable: it is affirmed, after all, "from the standpoint of gno- sis," which negates "creation" as understood in *creatio ex nihilo* the- ology. The Trinity comes thus to be situated "beyond being," and hence also beyond the categories of "substance" and "relation," in terms of which Trinitarian doctrine is normally framed in Scholas- tic theology. In affirming the identity—or "non-otherness"—of Trinity and Godhead, Eckhart is in effect proclaiming the ultimate domain, the Christian *alma de-yihuda* or "world of union," *outside of which nothing exists.* What Meister Eckhart propounds—when he declares (in effect) that "to take God in his oneness" is to take him "in his difference"—is a Christian nondualism, that is to say, a Trin- itarian *advaita.*[18]

Although the logic—or better said, the dialectic—of Eckhart's *advaita* has now come into view, we have yet to consider what I take to be his last word on the subject. To this end let us now approach the distinction between Godhead and Trinity from a "dynamic" point of view, that is to say, in terms of "the Birth of the Son." As Eckhart explains elsewhere, this Birth entails "an eternal and immu- table going out and coming in: out of Godhead into being and from

18. One sees that the "Vedantic" exegete need not in fact turn Sabellian: *advaita* as such—in the name of which he feels obliged and justified to take this step—does not demand it.

being into Godhead."[19] Now, it is precisely this "going out and coming in" that defines the Trinity and distinguishes it from the Godhead. It can thus be said—speaking, once again, "in a devilish
manner"—that the "going out" gives rise to the Son, and therefore
to the Father as well (since there can be no Son without a Father).
At this point the Son is situated, as it were, "outside" the Godhead,
inasmuch as he is conceived as the term of a "going out." One needs,
however, to take account of "the coming in" as well: of the *reditio*,
namely, which proceeds "from being into the Godhead." It is the
reditio which—again, in a manner of speaking—defines the third
Person, the Holy Spirit, who "abrogates" that externality, and in so
doing, completes the Trinity. One might say that in the Holy Spirit
the Trinity transcends its own distinction and realizes its advaitic
identity with the Godhead in "an eternal and immutable going out
and coming in." It seems that, what a "static" logic is unable to
grasp, can be in a way expressed in "dynamic" terms; for whereas
the concepts of "oneness" and "difference" are logically incompatible, the "coming in" and "going out" are not. By introducing, if you
will, the fiction of "time"—which renders the "coming in" and
"going out" sequential—the contradiction has been resolved.[20]

Getting back to Sermon 10: Eckhart gives us to understand that
"identity with the Godhead" is attainable through a "transcending

19. DW, Vol. II, p11. This text sheds light upon two scriptural verses, and reveals
their sublime (and generally unsurmised) Trinitarian sense. The first is verse 8 from
Psalm 120: "The Lord shall preserve thy going out and thy coming in from this time
forth, and even for evermore." This evidently refers, according to its deepest meaning, to those who have "entered" according to the words of Christ: "I am the door:
by me if any man enters in, he shall be saved, *and shall go in and out, and find pasture.*" (John 10.9) One sees at the same time that Eckhart's doctrine is scriptural to
the core: although he does not refer explicitly to these two verses, we may be certain
that, in a way, they were resonating in his soul when he preached the "eternal and
immutable going out and coming in."

20. Jacob Boehme was right: the dimension of "time"—though fictitious—
needs to be introduced, "otherwise I cannot teach you, so that you will understand"
(*Aurora* 23.18).

of distinction." But what renders that "union" conceivable is pre-cisely Eckhart's claim that the primary transcendental (namely, "the one") *transcends being*. That seemingly innocuous contention proves to be a master-stroke: for if the Godhead is truly "the One," this entails that the attainment of "oneness"—i.e., the abrogation of "otherness"—suffices to establish *identity with the Godhead*.

It remains, however, to define what precisely it means to "abro-gate otherness"; and that is the question Eckhart resolves, in Ser-mon 21, with a second master-stroke: the "abrogation of otherness," he gives us to understand, is effected through what he terms "nega-tion of negation," as conceived in the following text:

> The One is a negation of negation. All creatures have a nega-tion in themselves; one creature denies that it is another. One angel denies that it is some other angel. But God has a nega-tion of negations; he is the One who negates every *other* that is anything except himself.[21]

If the One—the Godhead, namely—is indeed "a negation of negation," then it is by means of the *negatio negationis*—and only thus—that "access to the Godhead" can be achieved, if such an expression be allowed. The *reditio* or "coming in" phase of what Eckhart terms an "eternal and immutable going out and coming in"—the Recession realized in the Holy Spirit—comes thus to be conceived as "negation of negation." There is no other way to "pen-etrate" into that "silent desert" or "empty wilderness": no other way to attain gnosis! As Meister Eckhart states explicitly: "Thus it is for us to expire all diversity as the Holy Spirit expires it eternally."[22] However, "to expire all diversity" is not *our* doing, but that of the Holy Spirit: our task, if you will, is simply to "step out of the way" and let the Spirit do his work. Now, this "stepping out of the way" and letting the Spirit "expire all diversity" is tantamount to what

21. METP, p281. I have modified the translation (beginning with the words "he is the One") so as to conform to R.B. Blakneys' rendering, which in my view expresses Eckhart's point with greater clarity. See *Meister Eckhart: A Modern Trans-lation* (New York: Harper, 1941), p247.

22. See footnote 5.

Eckhart terms "the birth of the Son (or the Word) in us"; as St. John the Baptist declares: "He must increase, and I must decrease."[23] It is thus *in the Trinity* that gnosis is to be attained, in conformity with the teaching of Christ: "No man hath seen God at any time; the only-begotten Son, which is in the bosom of the Father, he hath declared him."[24] And again: "Not that any man hath seen the Father, save he which is of God, he hath seen the Father."[25] It is clear that "he which is of God" is indeed "the only-begotten Son." Strange— and indeed blasphemous—as it may sound: *to know the Father one must "become the Son."* That knowing—that supreme gnosis—is moreover to be achieved in the power of the Holy Spirit "sent" by Christ, "who shall lead you into all truth."[26] The term "all truth" can of course be interpreted on various levels; yet the highest of these, clearly, refers to gnosis, and thus, according to Eckhart, to the *negatio negationis,* which is indeed the work of the Spirit. It is, finally, by "negation of negation" that "all truth" is attained.

At the risk of a slight digression, I would like to comment once more on the "Vedantic" interpretation of Christian themes, by noting that the Eschaton promised by Christ[27] is not a question of knowing "a lesser God," a so-called *saguna Brahman*: what the Savior offers his disciples is not a *samprajñāta* as opposed to *nirvikalpa samādhi*,[28] as some tend to think.

To elaborate a bit: the Vedanta distinguishes between *nirguna Brahman,* the "one true God" or Godhead, and *saguna Brahman,* literally "Brahman with attributes," also known as *Ishvara,* the God

23. John 3:30.
24. John 1:18.
25. John 6:46.
26. John 16:13.
27. The promise, of course, is made to those who accept him as "the Way," in accordance with his declaration: "I am the way, the truth, and the life." (John 14:6)
28. The former falls short of supreme gnosis: one might say that it constitutes the *samādhi* or "mystic vision" of the accomplished saint, as opposed to a Master of gnosis. In Tantric terms, it corresponds to the *ājñā chakra*.

who is framed or defined by the highest conceptions to which the human mind can attain. Who, then, is *Ishvara*? Simply stated, he is the God worshiped and prayed to, the Blessed One manifesting himself to man in countless ways—as Father, Mother, Friend or Beloved, for example—the God who accepts every act of worship, from the humblest to the most sublime, and bestows his blessings upon all who call upon him sincerely, or seek to approach him in love. Such, then, is the "two-fold" conception of God proclaimed by the saints and sages of India; and the question before us is this: how does the Christian Trinity fit into this picture, this "sacred logic"? On which side of the *nirguna/saguna* dichotomy is the Trinity to be situated? Now, there are those who suppose that it stands on the side of *saguna Brahman*, and who thereby reduce the triune God to a Christian version of *Ishvara*, in keeping with the "God beyond God" hypothesis. Thus they demote the dogmatically orthodox understanding of the Trinity to the status of an exoteric teaching, while elevating the modalist or Sabellian heresy to the rank of an esoteric truth. To which one might add that those who perceive the teachings of Christianity in this optic are prone to regard Meister Eckhart as an ally: as a fellow-Vedantist, one might say.

My point—which I wish to make emphatically—is that these positions are fundamentally flawed, and that in fact the very opposite holds true. The Christ-given conception of the Holy Trinity, first of all, does *not* refer to "a lesser God"—call it *saguna Brahman* or what you will—nor is it in any sense "exoteric." What *is* "exoteric" are the various "human, all too human" ways of interpreting that teaching, which moreover includes the conception of those who advocate a "*saguna Brahman*" view of the Christian Trinity. As concerns Meister Eckhart, so far from concurring with the latter position, his doctrine actually proves the reverse: the fact, namely, that the Word or Image is to be apprehended "without medium"[29] implies that it is beyond human conception, literally "beyond mind." If, therefore, *Ishvara* is indeed "the Face of God turned towards man," then the Word, clearly, is infinitely more. I need not

29. See chapter 6, pp177–180.

belabor the point: to situate the triune God on the level of *Ishvara*—
as has become customary in some quarters—is to misrepresent the
Christian doctrine, to falsify it utterly.

Getting back to the *negatio negationis*, it is to be noted, finally, that
the "negation of negation" constitutes the supreme affirmation,
which might well be termed the Doctrine of God himself. By that
very token, however, what stands at issue is not a human doctrine,
not one we mortals can actually conceive. For what, to us, is conceivable is perforce *propositional*, and therefore "carries a negation
in itself."[30] To put it in logical terms: every proposition p admits a
negation p*, and is itself a negation, by virtue of the fact that p =
(p*)*. The negation of negation is thus *ipso facto* the negation of all
propositional truth, and consequently, of all truth that is humanly
conceivable.[31] To the extent, therefore, that what we have termed
"the supreme affirmation" can be expressed in human speech at all,
it will inevitably harbor an antinomy, a contradiction,[32] which
however may assume different forms: for example, that of speaking
in temporal terms of what is actually above time. It is therefore
astonishing that we are nonetheless able—as if by a miracle—to
contemplate or "grasp" that "more-than-human" affirmation: how
does one "conceive the inconceivable"? The answer can only be this:
we are able to do so because *we are, in truth, "more than" rational*,
more in fact than finite and mortal creatures. Now, that "more"
derives from the Intellect, properly so called, what Eckhart refers
to as the *vünkelin*, the "divine spark" in us, which is said to be
increatus et increabile. The very fact, moreover, that we are able, in a
way, to grasp the *negatio negationis*—able to comprehend Eckhart's

30. We see, once again, that Eckhart's Trinitarian nondualism stands "incurably" above the level of theology, properly so called.

31. One is reminded of the Vedantic "*neti, neti*": could this double "not so" be
indeed expressive of the *negatio negationis*?

32. Is this, perhaps, the "metaphysical" sense of the "*symeion antilegomenon*"
(sometimes rendered as "sign of contradiction") foretold in the prophesy of Sim-
eon (given in Luke 2:34)?

Trinitarian nondualism!—*proves* the existence "in us" of such a "spark." Furthermore, and by the same token, one sees that "negation of negation," as doctrinal truth, functions as a "skillful means" in the quest of enlightenment: by the very fact that it is rationally inconceivable, the thesis of *negatio negationis* "forces" the Intellect, "awakens" it as if by a blow; in the words of Jacob Boehme, it acts as "the hammer that strikes my bell."

II. THE BIRTH OF THE WORD IN THE SOUL

"Eckhart's genius," it has been said, "lay in his being imbued with but one single truth, one central idea from which all others of the Meister are derived and towards which all are orientated": and this "one single truth" is "the generation or birth of the Divine Word, or Son, in the soul."[33] So claims Karl Kertz, a noted Jesuit Eckhart exegete, and there is much to be said in support of that view. Nonetheless, I would contend that Eckhart's "one central idea, from which all others are derived" is in fact his Trinitarian nondualism: for it is precisely this Eckhartian *advaita* that renders the stipulated "birth of the Son in the soul" intelligible and validates the resultant claim. Construed on any other basis, I say, that supposedly "central idea" forfeits its sense and turns forthwith into some other notion, which most likely proves in the end to be absurd. With sufficient ingenuity, it may at best be rendered "Thomistic," which is in fact what Kertz has proposed: to refute the long-standing charge of heresy, he argues that the Meister's perhaps occasionally excessive statements have been misconstrued, that rightly understood, they accord with Scholastic notions and do indeed pass muster. But whereas Eckhart has, no doubt, been often enough misinterpreted, I maintain that an "orthodox" reading of his "central idea" misses perforce the point of his doctrine. A Thomistic interpretation would moreover imply that the Meister did not, after all, contribute anything substantially new: that all the notoriety and fuss was over nothing more significant than misleading or bombastic figures of speech, turning

33. Karl G. Kertz, "Meister Eckhart's Teaching on the Birth of the Divine Word in the Soul," *Traditio*, vol. 15 (1959), p328.

the Eckhart phenomenon into perhaps the ultimate example of "much ado about nothing."

It is true that Eckhart's "central idea" stands in need of "defense" inasmuch as it does, most assuredly, strike the theological mind as something odious if not indeed heretical; and as a matter of fact, 8 of the 26 propositions characterized as "evil seed" and "thorns of error" alleged to thrive "*in agro dominico*" ("in the Lord's field"), as charged in the Bull of that name, refer to the aforesaid doctrine. Consider, for example, Article 10:

> We shall all be transformed totally into God and changed into him. In the same way, when in the sacrament bread is changed into Christ's Body. I am so changed into him that he makes me his one existence, and not just similar. By the living God it is true that there is no distinction there.

Or Article 21:

> The noble man is that Only-Begotten Son of God.

And most flagrant of all, Article 13:

> Whatever is proper to the divine nature, all that is proper to the just and divine man. Because of that, this man performs whatever God performs, and he created heaven and earth together with God, and he is the begetter of the Eternal Word, and God would not know how to do anything without such a man.

No wonder charges were brought against "someone by the name of Eckhart from Germany" who "wished to know more than he should, and not in accordance with the sobriety and the measure of faith, because he turned his ear from the truth and followed fables"! One can hardly do otherwise than sympathize with the guardians of the faith who felt obligated to destroy such "evil seed" and uproot these "thorns of error" to protect "the good crop of Catholic truth," as the document states.

Admittedly, the impression of egregious heresy conveyed by statements of the kind cited above is due in part to Eckhart's propensity for "koanic" modes of expression, as is especially obvious in the case of Article 13. Yet more, clearly, stands at issue: given that the Meister speaks indeed "from within the heart of God," it is hardly surprising that he should be seen as someone who has "turned his ear from the truth and followed fables." My point is that the offending statements regarding "the Birth" are indeed "evil seed" and "thorns of error"—so long as they are understood in a "creaturely" way, that is to say, from the standpoint of *creatio ex nihilo* theology.

Getting back to Karl Kertz, it will prove instructive to consider the thrust of his "defense" with due care. He begins by reflecting on one of the Meister's most explicit statements regarding "the Birth," taken from his famous sermon on the text "*Justi vivent in aeternum*," now designated Sermon 6:

> The Father begets his Son like himself in eternity. "The Word was with God and God was the Word." It was the same in the same nature. I will say more: he has begotten him in my soul. Not only is it [my soul] with him and he with it alike, but he is in it. *The Father begets his Son in the soul in the same way as he begets him in eternity, and not otherwise.*[34]

As Kertz points out, Eckhart defended the italicized statement (on the 26th of September 1326, before a tribunal at Cologne) in the following words:

> Wherever God is, there likewise the unbegotten Father is begetting. And wherever God is, there likewise the Son is begotten. Whenever, therefore, God is in me, God the Father assuredly begets in me the Son, and in me [likewise] the same Son is begotten. One and undivided, since in the Divinity there is no other Son save one, and He [is] God.

Certainly Kertz is right when he notes that "this is perfectly sound Catholic doctrine." The real problem, however, resides in what Eckhart goes on to say:

> And I will say more: *he [the Father] begets me as his son and the same son.* I will say more: not only does he beget me as his son,

---

34. EME, p187. I have quoted the passage as rendered in Kertz's article.

but he begets me as himself, and himself as me, and me as his Being and his Nature. In the innermost spring I well forth in the Spirit. There is one life and one being and one activity there. *All that God works is one; therefore he begets me as his son without any distinction.*[35]

What confronts us here constitutes possibly one of the most enlightening enunciations of Trinitarian nondualism ever articulated: by this very token, however, the text proves to be irremediably esoteric, and thus incomprehensible from a theological point of view. And as a matter of fact, the two italicized sentences have found their way into the papal Bull in the form of Article 22, condemned as "evil-sounding, temerarious, and suspect of heresy." Now, in response to these charges, Kertz contends that the suspect statements are in fact orthodox, inasmuch as they refer to what he terms the soul's "eternal eidetic pre-existence in God" as opposed to "the temporal regeneration of man through Grace and his identification with the only-begotten Son of God." Let us reflect upon this claim.

It is clear, first of all, that what Kertz proposes as a theologically orthodox interpretation of Article 22 is indeed nothing more than standard Scholastic teaching: the traditional exemplarism, namely, which maintains that the Exemplar or Idea of all things in creation—in this instance, the human soul—exists eternally in God. Thus, when Kertz speaks of the soul's "eternal eidetic pre-existence," he is simply referring to its archetype. But what entitles us to assume that "the birth of the Son in the soul," as Eckhart conceives of it, reduces to the generation of the soul's archetype? If the archetype is in any sense generated or "born" at all, how can this "birth" take place "in the soul": does this actually make sense? Obviously the archetype must precede the soul, not temporally, to be sure, but ontologically. Moreover, if indeed the supposed "generation of the Divine Word, or Son, in the soul" constitutes Eckhart's "central

35. The words "without distinction" need to be read as meaning "without duality": what Eckhart propounds is not a "monism," but a "nondualism," which is something else entirely.

idea, from which all others of the Meister are derived and towards which all are orientated," then surely what stands at issue must be something *more* than the exemplarist assertion to the effect that the soul has an archetype.

The problem, however, resides in the fact that theology offers only two conceivable interpretations of Eckhart's "central idea": what comes to birth in the soul and partakes of eternity is either the "creature" in its final state of beatitude—when through Grace it has entered upon "life eternal"—or it must be the archetype, as in fact Kertz takes it to be. Yet neither alternative is felicitous. If we opt for the first, Article 22 becomes indefensible: to say that "*the temporal regeneration of man through Grace*" leads to "*his identification with the only-begotten Son of God*" is outright heresy.[36] On the other hand, to opt for the second alternative—to read Eckhart's thesis as referring simply to the archetype of the soul—is to trivialize his doctrine: what has been identified as the mark of Eckhart's "genius"—the "one central idea from which all others are derived and towards which all are orientated"—is thereby reduced to a notion comprehensible to first-year seminarians.

But the problem, as we have said, is that theology offers no third option, no "middle ground" between the archetype, properly so called, and the mortal creature. To "defend" Eckhart without emasculating his doctrine—to *understand* him, that is—one requires a notion that breaks the archetype/creature dichotomy: and this is something *creatio ex nihilo* theology cannot supply. For that one needs to look elsewhere: to the Kabbalah, evidently, and to the teachings of Jacob Boehme, which are in fact fixated precisely upon such a "middle term." What stands at issue is the conception of an

---

36. It is heresy not only in the sense of theology, but from an esoteric point of view as well: it is "intrinsic heresy," one might say. To put it plainly, the idea that a man, as we conceive of him, will be "transformed" into God by way of a temporal process—"grace-filled" though it be—is untenable by any count. On the other hand, Eckhart's "central idea," *correctly understood*, constitutes "theological" but not "intrinsic" heresy. To be precise, it constitutes theological heresy by virtue of the fact that it contradicts the tenets of *creatio ex nihilo* theology: such, according to our analysis, is the price of esoterism. At the same time, however, Eckhart's teaching does not contradict any truly theological dogma, as we have noted before.

"eternal creation," a veritable *creatio ex Deo et in Deo*, which does in a way "stand between" God and "creation" as conceived in theology. One might go so far as to contend that the Kabbalistic option constitutes, in essence, the only conceivable "middle ground" between what theology knows as archetype and creation: indeed, what else could it be?

Let us consider what such an interpretation entails; we do so on the basis of Boehme's formulation, which has, for us, the advantage of being expressed in explicitly Christian terms. The first thing to be noted is that Boehme, too, speaks of a "birth of the Word in the soul," a concept which evidently plays a central role in his teaching as well. Both Masters maintain that the spiritual life—human existence, in fact—has no other end, no other *telos*, than this "birth." Both, moreover, perceive that "birth" as the attainment of a perfect union with Christ, the eternal Son of the Father; it is only that Boehme, for his part, gives a far more explicit account of what this entails, an account which makes it perfectly clear that the "birth" in question is by no means a "return to the archetype." In fact, it is the very opposite: a matter of *manifestation*, of "embodiment" no less, which however is not *temporal*—not cosmic, not "other than God"—but eternal and indeed *divine*. That "birth," therefore, is something sharply differentiated, on the one hand, from a "return to the archetype," and on the other, from the kind of manifestation or embodiment theology knows as "creation." Clearly, what Boehme offers is indeed a "middle term," a conception which, most assuredly, breaks the archetype/creature impasse.

We need now to ask ourselves whether there are grounds for supposing that Eckhart's doctrine is susceptible to interpretation along such lines. We wish to know whether Eckhart, too, has conceived of a "middle ground": a divine mode of existence answering to the notion of a *creatio ex Deo et in Deo*, in which the true identity of man is to be found. It is from the start to be expected, moreover, that the answer to this question will prove to be affirmative: for as we have come to see, Eckhart's "central idea" *demands* such a "middle ground." The fact is this: having once grasped the conception of a *creatio ex Deo et in Deo*, one recognizes that idea in countless passages pertaining to "the birth of the Word in the soul." A case in point is the very text from Sermon 6, quoted above, in which Eckhart declares:

> In the innermost spring I went forth in the Holy Spirit. There is one life and one being and one activity there.

These words have a distinctly Kabbalistic ring, and it would be hard, if not impossible, to interpret them in other than Kabbalistic terms. Think of "the innermost spring": what could that be, if not the Edenic "fountain from which all bliss and blessings flow"! And let us note, in reference to Kertz's "defense," that to speak of a "going forth," of a "life," and a "being" or "nature"—the original text has the word "*wesen*," the very word used by Boehme to designate the term of his "seven-part cycle"—is hardly to speak of an archetype, or of the soul's "eternal eidetic pre-existence in God." Eidetic archetypes, clearly, do not have "life" or "activity," to say the least. Yet it is also evident that the "life" and "activity" to which Eckhart refers is not temporal—not the "life" and "activity" we know here below, in what theology conceives as the order of creation—because Eckhart speaks of that "life" and "activity" as "one." It is this "oneness" or "nonduality"—this "negation of negations"—that identifies the realm to which Eckhart refers as *divine*: as in fact *Trinitarian*.

Let us attempt to understand, as clearly as we can—based on Eckhart's own words—what his "central idea" actually affirms. We begin with a key text from Sermon 16b, a homily dealing ostensibly with "the divine image in the soul." The premise, upon which everything rests, is that "an image takes its being exclusively and without a medium from that whose image it is and it has one being with it and is the same being."[37] Eckhart's objective is to apply this basic principle to what he terms "the simple divine image which is pressed onto the soul in its innermost nature." Think of it: we carry within ourselves, in "the innermost nature" of our soul, a divine image which "takes its being exclusively and without a medium

37. METP, p277.

from that whose image it is and has one being with it and is the same being." Clearly, "that whose image it is" can be none other than God the Father; and so, too, the "image" itself must be the Son. We have evidently before us the metaphysical tenets upon which Eckhart's doctrine concerning "the birth of God in the soul" is—and must be—based. These same tenets, moreover, determine the conditions which permit or enable that "birth" to take place, and thus define what Eckhart terms "the just man"; as the Master goes on to explain:

> I say in truth, as long as something takes form in you that is not the eternal Word and does not derive from the eternal Word, no matter how good it might be, that is really not right. Hence only he is a just man who has annihilated all created things and stands without distraction looking toward the eternal Word directly and who is formed therein and is reformed in justice. Such a person takes where the Son takes and is the Son himself.

We are informed, once again, that to attain oneness or identity with "the Son" it is needful "to annihilate all created things"; at the same time, however, we are instructed that this is to be accomplished by what is clearly a yogic means: to stand still, namely, and gaze "without distraction" toward the eternal Word. This is the identical teaching given in Sermon XLIX, based on the "*modicum*" text from John 16.16, upon which we have already commented at length in the preceding chapter. As has been noted, it is a question of *chittavrittinirodha*, of "uprooting the modifications of mind." The objective of this yoga, in light of Eckhart's doctrine, is to prevent "the arrow of intentionality" from overshooting its rightful mark—which is the Word—and thus give rise to an object of intentionality "outside of intellect," that is to say, to a "creature"; for as Eckhart declares: "Every kind of existence outside or beyond intellect is a creature; it is creatable, other than God, and is not God."[38] The price of gnosis—the price of *jñāna*—is nothing less than that "annihilation";

---

38. Sermon XXIX; see METP, p 226.

and lo, he who has accomplished this Herculean feat is indeed "the Son himself": that is how Christ is "born in the soul."

The question presents itself how Eckhart conceives of the human soul as such: what in fact *is* that "soul" upon which "the simple divine image is pressed," and in which "the birth of the Son" is said to take place? It is evident by now that this "soul" is to be sharply distinguished from the *psyche* or *anima* of conventional anthropology, that indeed it cannot be conceived as pertaining to what theology knows as the order of creation. How then does Eckhart conceive of it? The answer to this question is implicit in the following key passage from Sermon 24:

> God generally made all things according to an image of all things that he has in himself, but not according to himself... But the soul he made not just according to an image, nor according to something coming forth from him, as one describes him. Rather, he made it according to himself, in short, according to all that he is in his nature, his being, his activity which flows forth yet remains within, and according to the ground where he remains within himself, where he eternally gives birth to his only-begotten Son, from where the Holy Spirit blossoms forth. God created the soul in accordance with this outflowing, inward-remaining work.[39]

How are we to understand this obviously difficult and perhaps somewhat elliptic text? It is to be noted, first of all, that it confirms what we have already pointed out: namely, that the soul is not to be counted among what we take to be "created things." However, Eckhart goes further: for in saying that God made the human soul "according to all that he is in his nature, his being, his activity which flows forth yet remains within, and according to the ground where he remains in himself," he has elevated the soul above all that exists, not only in the so-called order of creation, but also in the eternal world, *with the exception of "the only-begotten Son" himself.* To put it in Kabbalistic terms, Eckhart has placed the human soul above even the Sefirothic order of creation: it does not pertain to *Malkhuth,*

39. METP, p 284.

conceived as Kingdom or "Edifice," but like "the only-begotten Son," constitutes the "indweller": the King who lives and reigns in that Kingdom.[40]

However, the soul can itself be viewed on two levels: "begotten" and "unbegotten," or "before" and "after" the "simple divine image was pressed upon it," as one might say. Eckhart distinguishes, in other words, between soul as "the Image or Word in us," and what he sometimes terms "the ground of the soul," which is situated, as it were, on the level of the "still desert," within the Godhead itself. He does so in Sermon 24 when he goes on to speak of "something in the soul in which God is bare," and declares that "in the ground of divine being, where the three Persons are one being, the soul is one according to the ground." The soul, therefore, is not only "uncreated" (exoterically speaking), but is in a sense "ungenerated" as well. And this is another truth which generally comes across as "evil-sounding, temerarious, and suspect of heresy," for the temptation is great to interpret such references to "the ground of the soul" from a "God beyond God" perspective, a reading which not only *is* "evil-sounding" to Christian ears, but also misses the point of Eckhart's doctrine, as we have explained in the first part of this chapter.

Having "staked out" his conception of the soul in the aforesaid terms, Eckhart proceeds to view "the birth of the Word in the soul" from a Christological standpoint:

> Therefore God assumed human nature and united it with his Person. At this point human nature became God because he took on human nature and not a human being. Therefore, if you want to be this same Christ and God, abandon all that which the eternal Word did not assume. The eternal Word did not assume *a* man. Therefore leave whatever is *a* man in you and whatever you are, and take yourself purely according to human nature. Then you are the same in the eternal Word as human nature is in him; for your human nature and his are

40. Although this is indeed reminiscent of the Vedantic *Purusha*, Eckhart's conception of the human soul does not reduce to the latter. A comparative study on this topic might be of considerable interest.

without difference. For it is one, and whatever it is in Christ, that it is also in you.

It may be well to express this thought in Kabbalistic terms: human nature, clearly, is none other than the Adamic. This is the nature "assumed" by the Word, and this eternal "embodiment" or "incarnation" is what constitutes the Sefirothic realm. It is what Boehme conceives dynamically in terms of a seven-part cycle: in that perspective, to "assume" means to produce or generate by a "process," the kind "replicated" on certain levels in authentic alchemy. So, too, the "nature" to be assumed becomes in effect "the precious substance"—the substance "made of" the Taboric light—of which the bodies of angels, and the body of Christ himself, are formed. One may think of the angelic or Sefirothic world abstractly as a Circle, the Center of which is Christ. The Sefirothic world becomes thus the Mystical Body of Christ; and by the same token, the "indweller"—whom the Kabbalah knows as Adam Kadmon or Sefirothic Man—becomes the eternal and primary Incarnation, of which the historical—realized in Jesus born of Mary—constitutes the temporal manifestation.[41]

The question arises now at which point "human nature became God because he took on human nature and not a human being": does this refer to the eternal Incarnation, or to the temporal? Although in a way it refers to both, the primary reference is to the former Incarnation: it is "at this point" that human nature "became God." And let us note that "at this point" *there is as yet no* "human being" to take on: as Genesis teaches, the human race is descended from Adam by way of a Fall. Salvation, therefore, is Restitution, as the Kabbalah declares: it constitutes thus a return to that original Adamic nature, which has remained intact within the depth of the

---

41. Jesus himself confirms this in the famous logion: "Before Adam was, I am." Note that this can itself be interpreted in two ways. Taking "Adam" to mean *Adam Kadmon*—who is himself eternal—it means that Jesus is speaking of himself as the eternal Word or Wisdom of God, of which *Adam Kadmon* constitutes the primary Incarnation. Or, alternatively, taking "Adam" in the theological sense, that is to say, as the quasi-historical progenitor of the human race, it means that Jesus antedates the human race: "Before Adam was, I am."

soul. Here we touch once again upon the mystery of that eternal and uncreated Presence in the human soul, to which Eckhart refers as Word or Image; and again the message is the same: discard everything that is not this eternal and uncreated Word—annihilate all created things—and in so doing, realize your everlasting oneness with God.

It is apparent that Eckhart, like Jacob Boehme, has his eye upon what may be termed the primary or Sefirothic Incarnation; and as a matter of fact, he confirms this, at the conclusion of his discourse,[42] by his commentary on the text "In the fullness of time, the Son was sent":

> "Fullness of time" is of two kinds. A thing is full when it has reached its end, as the day is full at evening. Thus, when all time drops away from you, time is full. The second: When time comes to its end, that is eternity, because then all time has an end since "before" or "after" is no longer. There, whatever is, is all present and new, and you have present to your view whatever ever happened or ever shall happen. There, there is neither before nor after; it is all present there. And in this ever present view I hold all things in my possession. There is "fullness of time," and thus I am as I should be. And thus I am truly the only Son and Christ.[43]

There is much to be said, clearly, concerning this remarkable passage; the point I wish to make, however, is simply this: in contrast to the accepted theological interpretation of "the fullness of time"—which could be characterized as "historical"—Eckhart understands the phrase as referring precisely to *the transcendence of time itself*. It is "beyond time," or "in eternity," that the "Son is sent"; the Incarnation of which Eckhart speaks is consequently not temporal—not historical—but "eternal." Kabbalistically speaking, the Incarnation or "embodiment" is realized in the Sefirothic world, in which there is indeed "neither before nor after," where "whatever ever happened" is in truth "present," and where truly "I am as I should be."

42. We are still pondering Sermon 24.
43. Ga. 4:4.

We have been told[44] that it is needful "to leave whatever is *a* man in you and whatever you are, and take yourself purely according to human nature"; but how does one accomplish that? The answer to this question is given implicitly in Sermon 46, in a passage which it now behooves us to reflect upon:

That you are *not* a certain person, it is the *not* that differentiates you from this person. If you want to be without distinction, rid yourself of *not.* There is a power in the soul which is separated from nothing since it has nothing in common with any things. Nothing is in this power but God alone. He shines naked into this power.[45]

To be "*a* man" is *not* to be another. But what differentiates one person from another, Eckhart tells us, is "the not." What, then, *is* that "not"? Earlier (in Sermon 46) we have been told that "man is an accident of nature": namely, *this* man or *that* man is an accident (in the Aristotelian sense) of human nature. However, in itself an accident is "nothing": and this is the "nothing" of which we need to "rid ourselves." How, then, is that possible? It is possible precisely by way of a "power in the soul" which is said to be "separated from nothing." Note the double sense: it is separated from "the nothing," and it is *not* separated from anything. One might put it this way: the power in question is separated from "the nothing" by virtue of its transcendence, and is *not* separated from anything by virtue of its immanence.[46] That transcendence, however, and that immanence, are the prerogatives of God: "Nothing is in this power but God alone." It is, then, by virtue of this *divine* power that we are enabled to "abandon all which the eternal Word did not assume"—abandon "this-man-so-and-so"—and having rid ourselves of the "*not*," to attain oneness with the only-begotten Son.

44. In the "Christological" passage from Sermon 24.
45. METP, p305.
46. God's transcendence and immanence go together: they constitute two complementary aspects of the same divine prerogative. God can be "within all things" precisely because he transcends each and every thing. One can understand this by analogy with the soul, which likewise can be "within" every cell or member of the living organism precisely because it transcends every cell and every member.

It is finally to be noted that "to rid yourself of *not*" is indeed "to negate negation." The crucial "act," therefore, by which we "become the only-begotten Son" is precisely the *negatio negationis*: the very act, proper to the Holy Spirit, which realizes the *reditio*, and in so doing, establishes the Trinity. It could not be otherwise; for there is in truth only one "birth": namely, that of "the only-begotten Son." We tend to think that if the Son comes to birth in a thousand souls, he must be born a thousand times—but in this we are mistaken. The Son is born "only once," in an eternal birth which admits of no repetition, a birth which is absolutely unique; and if a myriad souls attain to Salvation in Christ, it is all one birth, one "activity which flows forth yet remains within," one "outflowing yet inward-remaining work." The very *negatio* which "rids of *not*" rids of multiplicity—of "otherness"—as well.

We have spoken at length of things our eyes do not see and our mind can barely conceive; but what about the things our eyes do see and our mind does conceive: *purus nihil* though they may ultimately be, must not "the real" be present in these as well? According to the doctrine we have attempted to expound, the intentional objects of human knowing derive in truth from the Sefirothic world, which in a way they manifest; they do so, however, primarily by means of the so-called "qualities." It is in these—from the taste of a fruit to the rarefied apprehensions of a mystic—that the Sefirothic light of God breaks through into our world: all that, here below, is joyous, sweet or blissful, in particular, constitutes a direct manifestation of the divine. The intentional objects of human knowing, be they perceptual or conceptual, are "less real," in fact, than the taste of a peach, for example, which is something no scientist and no philosopher is able to comprehend. While it is well and proper, thus, to speak of God in apophatic terms, one may speak of him in concrete and even sensuous terms as well, which is in fact what Eckhart loves to do. How often does he not refer to the delight God is said to experience in his Trinitarian life: "It is just as enjoyable to him," Eckhart tells us in Sermon 12, "as when someone lets a horse loose on a meadow":

Such is the horse's nature that it pours itself out with all its might in jumping about the meadow.... So too does God find delight and satisfaction where he finds sameness [that is, nonduality, *advaita*]. He finds it a joy to pour his nature and his being completely into the sameness, for he is this sameness himself.[47]

It is hardly surprising, then, that Eckhart speaks of the Christian *jñāni*—the man in whom the "birth of the Word" has been realized—in similarly concrete terms, as if he were actually someone living among us here below. "Look!" he tells us in Sermon 46:

The person who is thus one Son has movement, activity, and everything that he has as his very own.[48]

This is a far cry, obviously, from the way we are prone to envision the so-called Supreme Identity, or the Buddhist *nirvāna*, which literally means "extinguished" or "blown out," like the flame of a candle. There is a striking similarity, on the other hand, between the way Eckhart depicts the man "who stands in God's knowing and in God's love and becomes nothing other than what God is himself" and the description of the so-called *jivanmukta* or person "liberated in life" to be found in Vedantic texts. There is nothing in Eckhart's doctrine, moreover, to rule out the possibility of a Christian *jivanmukta*: the notion that someone "who stands in God's knowing"—a true Gnostic, namely—can live "here below," that is to say, can so manifest himself, or appear so to live, from *our* point of view. What is more, that possibility is in fact implied by the central premise of what might be termed Eckhart's "ethics": the claim, namely, that the "just man" has actually—here and now—become one with Christ. In principle, therefore, that "just man" is able to do all that Christ can do, which evidently includes "to descend upon the earth."[49]

47. METP, p269.
48. Sermon 46; see METP, p305.
49. In the words of the Gospel, the "just man" is able "*to go in and out, and find pasture*," a logion which admits a Trinitarian interpretation. (John 10.9) See footnote 19.

Much of what Eckhart has to say—especially in the German sermons—is in fact to be understood as referring precisely to the "just man"; take, for example, the following passage (again from Sermon 12, the one in which he likens God's joy to that of "a horse let loose to run in a meadow"):

> A person who is so established in the will of God wants nothing else but what is God and what is God's will. If he were sick, he would not want to be healthy. All pain is joy to him, all multiplicity is simplicity and unity, if he is really steadfast in the will of God. Even if the pain of hell were connected to it, it would be joy and happiness for him. He is free and has left himself, and he must be free of everything that he is to receive. . . .

Let us note, first of all, that the phrase "all multiplicity is simplicity and unity" identifies the advaitic or nondual state, the state of perfect gnosis. It is significant, too, that Eckhart concludes with the assertion (spoken in the first person):

> The eye in which I see God is the same eye in which God sees me. My eye and God's eye are one eye and one seeing, one knowing and one loving.

Not only, therefore, is the passage to be seen as a description of the "just man," but what is more: it implies—if we take the Meister at his word—that Eckhart himself speaks from that exalted state. Ananda Coomaraswamy may be right: perhaps Eckhart was indeed "the greatest European ever born."

It will be of interest, finally, to consider in this connection what Eckhart has to say concerning Saint Paul in his commentary on Romans 9.3, where the Apostle declares: "I would be willing to be eternally separated from God," a claim which has rightly puzzled exegetes. Eckhart points out that "the masters pose the question whether St. Paul was on the way to perfection or whether he was in the state of full perfection," and proceeds immediately to answer that question himself: "I claim he was in the state of full perfection" he avers. The argument runs as follows:

The noblest and most ultimate thing that a person can forsake is that he forsakes God for God's sake. Now, St. Paul forsook God for God's sake; he left everything that he was able to take from God and left everything that God was able to give him and everything that he was able to receive from God. And when he had left all this, he left God for God's sake, and there remained for him God as God exists in himself... It is a oneness and a pure union. In this state a person is a true human being, and such a man experiences no suffering, just as the divine being cannot experience it.[50]

Here again we have the unmistakable depiction of the Christian *jivanmukta*, the living master of gnosis, who has realized "oneness and a pure union" with "God as he exists in himself." For such a one there is no more "taking from God," or receiving "what God was able to give": to speak in such terms is to speak from a creaturely perspective. The point then—as the Apostle himself implies—is that Saint Paul had in fact "eternally separated himself from God" in that sense.

One has every reason to believe, moreover, that this "separation" occurred when Saint Paul—at that time, Saul of Tarsus—first "encountered Christ" on the road to Damascus: "and suddenly there shined round about him a light from heaven: and he fell to the earth...."[51] It was, presumably, at that moment that "enlightenment struck"; and it is most significant that when "his eyes were opened, he saw no man": for indeed, when one's "eyes" are truly opened, one sees God alone. It is universally recognized, moreover, that when the Apostle tells us[52] that he knew a man in Christ "who was caught up into the third heaven," this refers to his own realization; it is however to be noted that the term "third heaven" admits of a Kabbalistic interpretation, and may in fact be taken to refer to the supreme state or *alma de-yihuda*, the "world of *advaita*" if you will. And this explains why the Apostle states parenthetically

---

50. This passage, significantly enough, is again taken from Sermon 12. See METP, p268.

51. Acts 9:3, 4.

52. 2 Cor. 12:2.

"whether in the body or out of the body, I cannot tell: God knoweth"; for indeed, in that state—in which "God knoweth"!— there is no absolute distinction between "in the body" and "*not* in the body": remember, "the *not*" has now been transcended once and for all. We are now in the "world of union" where "oneness is distinction and distinction is oneness" as Eckhart says.

It is crucial to realize that this state, once attained, can never be lost, which is to say that he who "returns" does so in perfect freedom and without loss. Eckhart makes this abundantly clear when he declares—once again in Sermon 12, his "*jivanmukta* Sermon" if you will—that "whoever were to forsake himself for an instant would be given everything. And if a person had forsaken himself for twenty years and then took himself back for an instant, he had never really forsaken himself at all."[53] With these words he distinguishes what he terms the "just" or "noble" man categorically from what the Church conceives to be a "saint," and in so doing gives completion to his doctrine of Christian gnosis.

53. METP, p270.

POSTSCRIPT

WITH the preceding reflections on "Trinitarian nondualism" we have brought to a close our summary exposition of doctrinal gnosis pertaining to the Judeo-Christian tradition. Yet given the complexity of the trajectory "from St. Paul to Meister Eckhart" which we have traced, it behooves us now, by way of conclusion, to bring into sharper focus what it is, exactly, that differentiates the teachings in question from standard orthodox Christian doctrine to render them expressive of *gnosis*: of *Christian* gnosis no less.

As we have come to see, what distinguishes doctrinal gnosis as such from theology, properly so called, is its rejection of the *creatio ex nihilo* as commonly understood, a concept which for theology is axiomatic. To quote A.N. Williams again: "The most fundamental distinction in Christian theology, the distinction that lies at the root of both patristic and Thomistic thought, is the distinction between the Uncreated and the created"[1]—where of course "created" signifies *ex nihilo*. Doctrinal gnosis, on the other hand, can indeed be characterized by its rejection of that *creatio ex nihilo*, that is to say, its replacement by the metaphysical notion of a *creatio ex deo et in deo*. But whereas, on the face of it, the opposition between doctrinal gnosis and theology appears thus to be absolute, I will argue that the respective doctrines, so far from being contradictory, actually constitute *complementary* teachings expressive of one and the same truth, which however, in its own right, surpasses human comprehension. It is moreover evident that the two doctrines are not situated on the same intellectual plane, and in fact they appear to stand to each other, biblically speaking, as "*meat*" to "*milk*," or as "esoteric" to "exoteric" if you will.

It needs, first of all, to be clearly understood that doctrinal gnosis

---

1. *The Ground of Union* (Oxford: Oxford University Press, 1999), p. 88.

and theology differ, not in what they assert concerning the mysteries of God—i.e., the Trinitarian and Christological teachings which constitute the primary dogmas of the Church—but simply in regard to the cosmos, its metaphysical status namely. Whereas theology takes the universe essentially as it appears to our senses, doctrinal gnosis recognizes the categorical imperfection of human knowing by distinguishing ontologically between *appearance* and *reality*. To be precise, its stand on this issue reduces epistemologically to the recognition that *"what we take to be the universe exists 'for us' as an object of intentionality,"* a tenet we have termed *anthropic realism*;[2] and though one may very well question whether this seeming truism tells us anything of substance at all, it is evidently not—by any stretch of the imagination!—"heretical."

In fact, it proves to be inherently *biblical*, the point being that the "expulsion from Eden," so far from constituting a "geographic" relocation as the literal sense affirms, refers actually to a discontinuity in human apprehension, accompanied by a corresponding break in the ambient world—in keeping, one might add, with the Eckhartian *primacy of knowing*.[3] So far from constituting in truth an extra-Edenic region or world, the new ambience proves thus to be the effect of a diminished cognizance definitive of the *psychikos anthropos* "who knoweth not the things of God" as St. Paul apprises us. That resultant ambience, moreover, can evidently be none other than *our* world, the universe to which we too are presently confined *insofar as we ourselves are subject to the same cognitive bounds*. We find ourselves thus in a world that came to be, not directly by the *fiat* of God, but in consequence of Adam's Fall. Yet strictly speaking—and this is precisely the crucial point!—that world did *not* in fact "come to be," for in truth it *has no being*: no *real* or authentic being, that is. As every true philosopher has realized, the things of this world are in a state of "becoming," a state of perpetual flux in keeping with their subjection to the condition of time; and indeed, as St. Gregory of Nyssa states explicitly: *"None of the things which are comprehended*

2. See pp. 36–39.
3. See pp. 183–189.

by the senses or contemplated by the mind[4] *really subsist; nothing except the transcendent essence and cause of all.*"[5]

Clearly, this is no longer *creatio ex nihilo* theology, but an echo, rather, of a metaphysical wisdom comprising the very essence of doctrinal gnosis. What confronts us in this affirmation—so far from constituting heresy—is actually the very opposite: what in Hindu tradition would be reverentially termed a *mahāvākya* or "great saying." There *is* in truth no conflict, no actual contradiction between theology as such and doctrinal gnosis: what stands at issue is not truth versus error, but simply different modes and degrees of knowing.[6] One needs however to distinguish quite sharply between theology *per se* and a theology explicated to the point of closure: between the theology of the saints and of the "professionals" if you will; and needless to say, it is the latter kind that does in fact militate against doctrinal gnosis. What confronts us in that case is a theological academism which—like every academism!—lays claim to a perfection it does not possess and brooks no didactic input even "from above." There is reason to believe, moreover, that a didactic influence emanating from saintly advocates of doctrinal gnosis did in fact play a vital role within the Church more or less till the time of the Renaissance, when it began, quite visibly, to wane: the *mahāvākya* of St. Gregory itself testifies that such was the case in his day. But for about the last eight hundred years or so this has apparently not been the case, and I would suggest that it is the effective loss of such a sapiential presence that has rendered theologians increasingly susceptible to the "professionalism" of which I speak.

4. Mind, that is, as distinguished from Intellect, or *psyche* from *pneuma*. I refer to *Theistic Evolution: The Teilhardian Heresy,* op. cit., pp. 38–48, for an explication of these terms.

5. To which one might add the words of Christ Himself to St. Catherine of Siena: "I am He who *is,* you are she who is not."

6. I should point out that doctrinal gnosis itself comprises a number of different modes. As we have noted, the teachings of the Kabbalah and of Jacob Boehme are intrinsically *theosophical,* whereas the gnosis of Meister Eckhart is to be classified as *scholastic.* Thus, to pass from one to the other of these genres requires a kind of translation, an exegesis one might say; and here too hasty judgments fall short of the mark. Above all it needs to be said: whosoever approaches these ultimate domains without due reverence is sure to be misled.

The objection is bound to be raised that notwithstanding the human limitations of its theologians, the Catholic Church has infallibly declared that *"by His own omnipotent power at once from the beginning of time"* the one true God *"created each creature from nothing…"* But whereas this *de fide* text, promulgated at the Fourth Lateran Council, has been generally understood as a definitive affirmation of *creatio ex nihilo* theology, it need not be, but can be interpreted equally well from the standpoint of doctrinal gnosis. For it happens that a *creatio ex deo et in deo* is also in its own way a *creatio ex nihilo*, and conforms moreover to the remaining stipulations of the Lateran text as well. Surprising as it may be, that seeming mainstay of the theological *creatio ex nihilo* harbors at the same time an esoteric sense far above the naïve realism native to the *psychikos anthropos*. What then does *ex nihilo* mean on the level of doctrinal gnosis? It means exactly "from nothing"—literally "from no thing"! —and thus signifies a negation: the denial that creation is a "making" of one thing from another. It is to be noted, moreover, that the *ex nihilo* stipulation in the Lateran text merely amplifies what is already implied by the words *"at once"* (*simul*), which likewise affirm that creation is not a change, not an alteration, but constitutes indeed a supra-temporal act. The same applies, moreover, to the words *"from the beginning of time"*: they too affirm the supra-temporal nature of the creative act; for it needs to be understood that time *has no* temporal beginning, no "first moment," that in fact it comprises no "moments" at all: as St. Thomas declares with superlative brevity, "time has *before* and *after*."[7] It follows—presumably to the consternation of many—that the text does not after all mandate a theological *creatio ex nihilo*, but is permissive of doctrinal gnosis as well: of the ontological distinction, namely, between the creation as such and *our* world of "space, time, and matter."

What doctrinal gnosis affirms is a world transcending time and

---

7. *Summa Theologiae* I.10.4. It is to be noted that St. Thomas can be read on various levels; and whereas his ontological teachings can very well be understood on the plane of *creatio ex nihilo* theology, they are by no means limited to that point of view, but open in principle to the plane of doctrinal gnosis, where in fact they unfold their full significance.

duality, which yet contains all created beings: from the highest angel to the lowliest insect on Earth. And it avers that it is this supra-temporal and indeed *advaitic* realm—this supernal *"world without end"*—that confronts us here and now: it is what we *would* in fact behold if, even for an instant, we could let our *"eye be single"* as Christ enjoins.[8] Obviously that claim contradicts our ordinary Weltanschauung and is bound to scandalize all but a discerning few; yet the fact remains that doctrinal gnosis does not negate a single infallibly revealed dogma of the Catholic Church. On the contrary, it accepts as true all that has been thus revealed; the point, however, is that it views these truths on a level transcending *creatio ex nihilo* theology.

What we need above all to understand is that the universe, so far from being simply an existing entity, constitutes an object of human intentionality by the very fact of being thus perceived: for it happens that this seemingly innocuous discernment suffices to take us—instantly!—across the threshold of doctrinal gnosis, and enables us to gain at least a first impression of what that world-transcending gnosis entails. Strange as it may appear, the bare recognition that the act of human knowing conditions what is known—the realization that "objective" and "subjective" are actually correlative terms—constitutes in truth an opening to transcendence. One is reminded of the Socratic paradox: that to know that we do not know is actually to possess a wisdom rare among mortals. In like manner, by acknowledging its "anthropic" limitation, the aforesaid realism opens in principle to a gnosis transcending our present state—even as a sinner, if you will, overcomes his sinfulness by confessing his sin. My point is that anthropic realism, seriously entertained by a spiritually-oriented seeker of truth, opens quite naturally—yet in a marvelous way!—to a metaphysical wisdom normally hidden from human sight.

Let us now take note of two facts: first, that this realism refers, by its very definition—not to some metaphysical realm beyond nor-

---

8. Matt. 6:22. Judging by biblical commentaries, it appears that this logion has rarely been understood in depth. And no wonder, seeing that it pertains actually to doctrinal gnosis! I would argue that it constitutes in fact a key text in support of nondualism, of Christian *advaita*.

mal human reach—but indeed to what we take to be the universe; and that what this "anthropic" realism affirms is moreover *biblical*, as our previous reflections on the Fall of Adam have made clear. Given both of these facts, I say, it is hardly surprising that the tenet of anthropic realism proves to be enlightening first of all in reference to *this* world: the one we perceive with our senses and investigate by scientific means. The recognition that the cosmos as such is neither the objective reality we naively suppose it to be, nor on the other hand a subjective apparition answering to the postulates of idealist philosophy, but constitutes precisely *an intentional object of human knowing*: no more, and no less—this fact, I say, has consequences bearing upon the scientific quest. To be precise, it disqualifies at one stroke the ontological claims of contemporary science, and enables moreover a radical reinterpretation of physical science in particular by bringing the human observer into play.[9] To which we should add that once physics has been thus shorn of its ontological pretensions, the scientistic Weltanschauung, in its multitudinous facets, collapses case by case in the face of rigorous inquiry, as I have shown in a series of monographs.[10]

Let us not fail to note, however, that these facts do not bode well for *creatio ex nihilo* theology inasmuch as its commitment to a realism not thus "anthropic" leaves it vulnerable to scientistic influence. His own simplistic cosmology, in other words, renders the theologian incapable of refuting the reputedly scientific cosmology presently inundating the Church like a tidal wave; and it is *here*, I maintain, that heresy is indeed to be found: that scientistic myth, compounded with humanist ideology, has in fact wreaked havoc upon contemporary theology.[11] Theologians might thus be well

9. See *The Quantum Enigma*, op. cit., where such a reinterpretation has been carried out.

10. I would refer the interested reader especially to *Ancient Wisdom and Modern Misconceptions*, and also to *Science and Myth*, op. cit.

11. The prime heresiarch, I would add—the veritable Arius of our time—is unquestionably none other than Teilhard de Chardin, the renowned Jesuit who dazzled the theological intelligentsia with his science-fiction theology. I have dealt with this issue at length in *Theistic Evolution: The Teilhardian Heresy* (Angelico Press / Sophia Perennis: Tacoma, WA, 2012).

advised to reconsider their stand: so far from excommunicating doctrinal gnosis, it may actually be in their best interest to pay respectful heed to what that hitherto controverted teaching entails. And if that doctrine be indeed "esoteric," this simply means that the Church has in fact need of an esoterism; it could even be argued, in light of recent history, that her very survival in these days of "diabolical disorientation" demands ultimately nothing less.

Not only, however, is there no real conflict or contradiction between theology *per se* and doctrinal gnosis, but in fact *there cannot be*. For as we have had occasion to recognize in the preceding chapters, the latter—in its scholastic no less than its theosophical formulations—is not actually reducible to a logically consistent set of propositions: what it affirms simply cannot be thus specified. Whether it be the doctrine of the *Sephiroth* in what Gershom Scholem refers to as "the yet unbroken reality of mystical experience," or Jacob Boehme's *temporal* depiction of an inherently *atemporal* cycle, not to speak of Eckhart's *negatio negationis*,[12] the fact is that doctrinal gnosis cannot be fully explicated in the form of a logically coherent affirmation. Purists may call it "poetry" if they wish; the fact remains that logic and syllogisms simply do not carry us all the way, the reason being that these means hinge upon a scission, a post-Edenic "cutting asunder"—in short, a *dualism*—which must ultimately cease. "*God has spoken once and for all, and I have heard two things*" laments the Psalmist; and Nicholas of Cusa points out that the wall separating us from the Kingdom of God is composed of "opposites," in keeping with the Genesis account which characterizes the effect of the "*forbidden fruit*" upon the human race as a "*knowledge of good and evil*": a knowledge, thus, of what Hindus call the *dvandvas* or "pairs of opposites." It follows that doctrinal gnosis, if it is indeed to penetrate the aforesaid barrier, must perforce assume the form of a nondualism, an *advaita* of some kind. Whereas theology, in keeping with its exoteric function, entails a concession to human incapacity in the form of a simplistic cosmology, doctrinal gnosis takes the ultimate step: "*doctrinally*" to be sure. For what remains can only be what Eckhart terms "the breaking

12. See p. 206.

through," which is none other than *gnosis* itself: "*Ye shall know the truth, and the truth shall make you free.*"

One sees in light of these reflections that theology and doctrinal gnosis pertain in reality to the same human trajectory—to one and the same *itinerarium mentis in Deum*—but not necessarily to the same *viator*: for whereas theology speaks to the itinerant as such, whosoever he may be, doctrinal gnosis demands a level of understanding appropriate to the final stage of ascent. So far, therefore, from contradicting the tenets of theology, doctrinal gnosis actually "fulfills" them, if one may put it so. Let there be no more bias, then, against doctrines of that kind, no more ill-informed outcries brandishing terms like "pantheism" or "Gnosticism," or slurs against the Kabbalah, as if it pertained to some nefarious cult![13] Well-meaning and at times even venerable as these accusers may be, it is high time to expose their pious condemnations for the misconceptions they are. Let it be henceforth understood that so far from being subversive or insidious, doctrinal gnosis actually elucidates, confirms, and ultimately completes the orthodox teaching of the Church. Consider, for instance, that marvelous theological conception known as the Mystical Body: it is doctrinal gnosis, with its advaitic and indeed Trinitarian metaphysics, which takes us to the very heart of this incurably mystical teaching.[14] Even the most childlike belief or devotion, moreover, pertaining to Catholic tradition, receives thus its ratification: what ultimately elucidates and justifies all proves to be indeed none other than a Trinitarian *advaita* indigenous to doc-

13. To name at least one such publication, let me cite *Fumus Satanae* by Atila Sinke Guimarães (an English translation of which has been published by Tradition in Action, Los Angeles, 2015), which pertains to a remarkable 11-volume collection entitled *Eli, Eli, Lamma Sabacthani?* Whereas this exceedingly erudite author has much to offer by way of deconstructing progressivist theologies, such as that of Hans Urs von Balthasar for example, he clearly misses the mark when it comes to doctrinal gnosis properly so called. Here again we need to remind ourselves that no matter how brilliant we may be, or how well-read, doctrines of that order will remain hermetically closed to us—unless we approach them "with folded hands."

14. The problem of "celestial corporeality," in particular, proves ultimately to be insoluble from the standpoint of dualist theology. For a nondualist interpretation of that quintessentially Christian conception I refer to chapter 4 in *Ancient Wisdom and Modern Misconceptions*, op. cit.

trinal gnosis. It can be said with certainty that neither a monism nor a dualism can comprehend the Christian Way, which transcends both these conceptions—what to speak then of its Eschaton!

I will mention, in passing, that a "touch" at least of esoterism may likewise be needed to enter the belief-systems of non-Christian religious or sapiential traditions with a modicum of understanding. It is finally a certain transcendence of what may be termed "the letter" that enables us to partake of truths enshrined in these—to us foreign—teachings without being destabilized or disoriented thereby. I concur that the "dialogue" with other religions, so highly extolled by proponents of Vatican II, may indeed be profitable—but only for those, I would add, who have some access, however modest, to doctrinal gnosis: an initial glimpse, at least, of vistas formally beyond the range of theology *per se*. In the absence of that qualification, our choice as Catholic Christians is between a simplistic intolerance on the one hand, and on the other a facile and ideology-driven ecumenism which betrays the authentic teaching of the Church.

It needs finally to be pointed out that whereas doctrinal gnosis speaks to the few, Christ Himself speaks to all—even to the least among us. And that teaching proves in fact to be *more than doctrine*: for the words the Savior speaks "*are spirit and life.*"[15] Let no one, therefore, conceive of Scripture as simply a Greek or Latin text: for in a manner above human comprehension that sacred text *is* in truth "*spirit and life.*" And from this supernal Source as from a celestial spring, Christians throughout the centuries— from the simplest believer to the Masters of gnosis!—have drawn "*the living waters*" that sustain and ever deepen their spiritual life. There exists also, of course, a secondary literature, which serves to clear the way to that Christic Spring; and as Meister Eckhart himself informs us, all his writings serve in fact no other end than "to explain what the holy Christian faith and the two Testaments maintain."

I believe there are in our day seekers who will find the teachings of doctrinal gnosis profoundly relevant to their spiritual quest; for some it may in fact provide the only effective access to an authentically Catholic life. This seems to hold true especially of those who,

15. John 6:63.

in some way, have had contact with the wisdom of the East, enough perhaps to give them a faint premonition of what gnosis entails. My point is that such persons require more than a catechism, more presumably than what the present-day theologians of the Church are prepared to dispense. Could it be that what is finally needed by such aspirants in quest of ultimate truth is in fact the "*key of gnosis*"[16] to which the Savior alludes: the very "*key*" which the "*lawyers*," who "*entered not in themselves*," have "*taken away*"? It suffices to note that by its nature—its very definition if you will—doctrinal gnosis is oriented towards gnosis as to its authentic end. And this implies, on pain of invalidity, that this teaching must itself provide the requisite conceptual means: that in the final count *the doctrine itself proves to be the Key.*[17]

16. Luke 11:52.

17. I should perhaps note that this answers the objection to doctrinal gnosis based upon the fact that it does not reduce to a logically consistent affirmation, the point being that if it did thus reduce, it would *ipso facto* forfeit its use as a Key: for it is manifestly the function of a key—not to offer something of value in its own right—but precisely to facilitate passage into a space as yet unoccupied, a region as yet unknown. One might go so far as to suggest that doctrinal gnosis not only facilitates but actually *forces* such a passage by the very fact that it finally offers no "mental" support to the *psychikos anthropos*, no mental picture which he can put in place of the *Eschaton* as he is wont to do. It literally forces him "out of his mind" if you will—that is to say, in Platonist terms: forces him to ascend from *psyche* to *pneuma*.

INDEX

Printed in April 2022
by Rotomail Italia S.p.A., Vignate (MI) - Italy